The
REASONABLE
Person

Due Process of
Law, Logic, and Faith

Steven R. Sedberry, Esq.

THE REASONABLE PERSON

Copyright © 2012 Steven R. Sedberry

ISBN: 1477640622
ISBN 13: 9781477640623

Library of Congress Control Number: 2012935591

Createspace, North Charleston, SC

For the girls:
Beth, Lauren, and Meredith

About The Author

Steve Sedberry is a corporate attorney whose career path included a few detours before he reached his final destination of law practice. A business executive for almost twenty years, he left the corporate world, started over, and followed his lifelong dream of law school. In 2002, he earned his law degree from Vanderbilt University Law School. In *The Reasonable Person: Due Process of Law, Logic, and Faith*, Sedberry uses many of the analytical tools that he uses in law practice to evaluate the claims of Christianity.

Sedberry's spiritual path included a few detours as well. He first became a Christian as a young boy in Houston, Texas. At the age of thirty-seven, after many ups and downs, he started over, and fully committed his life to God. His experiences provide a unique perspective on the common misconceptions about Christian faith.

Today, he is the vice president of legal services for an international apparel corporation. He is licensed to practice law in Texas and Tennessee and is admitted to the United States District Court, Eastern District in Texas, and the Western District in Tennessee. He is a member of the American Bar Association and the Association of Corporate Counsel. Sedberry is also the author of the legal education book entitled, *Law School Labyrinth: The Guide to Making the Most of Your Legal Education* (Kaplan Publishing, 1st Ed. March 31, 2009; 2nd Ed. May 3, 2011).

Foreword

Two thousand years ago, a man named Jesus lived in Galilee, a small nondescript area in the nation of Israel. Jesus left his home and traveled by foot throughout the region. It was a three year trip. His travels were limited to a few hundred miles of his birthplace. He didn't write any books. He didn't have an organized following, or any organization at all. Instead, he had a simple message from God.

People began to follow him. They were mostly from the wrong side of the tracks and outcasts. Some were working-class fishermen and tax collectors. Others had more questionable occupations. Many were poor and hungry; sick and hurting. All of them knew that they needed more than what the religion of that day offered.

The religious elite didn't like Jesus or what he had to say. At first, they wrote him off as a backwoods and uneducated troublemaker. Then they tried to discredit him. They tried to get him to incriminate himself. When that failed, they had him executed. He died the death of a criminal; capital punishment in the form of a horrific crucifixion. Although he didn't deserve it, he was ridiculed, beaten, whipped, and nailed to a wooden cross. He hung on it until he died.

They believed that his humiliating death would be the end of it. People would see Jesus for who he was; an uneducated Galilean troublemaker. With him out of the picture, his followers would go away quietly. It would be a lesson to all of them.

Things would return to business as usual; the business of their laws and their religion.

It didn't work out. It wasn't business as usual. Rather than going away quietly, Jesus' followers told anyone who would listen about the lesson of his life, death and incredibly, his resurrection. They shouted it from the rooftops. Some of his followers committed his story to writing. The book remains the bestselling book in the world. You've probably seen it. Maybe you've even read some of it.

It was a story so incredible, so fantastic, that it had to be either the biggest lie in history, or the truth of all truths. Jesus' followers believed it as Truth and were willing to die, rather than renounce it.

Jesus didn't go away, either. We're still talking about him today. His teachings became the basis for what was to become the world's largest spiritual belief system, with over two billion adherents. Despite the efforts of the religious elite, this uneducated Galilean had a greater impact on history than any other person who has ever lived.

The Reasonable Person- Due Process of Law, Logic and Faith was written for people who have that spiritual itch — the feeling deep in your hearts that there must be something more. You know that there is a God, somewhere. You observe the world around you and know that it can't all be explained by random biological processes. Nonetheless, you see the trappings of organized religion and the religious elite of today. You know that you do not fit into that mold. *"If that's what Christianity is about,"* you think, *"I don't want anything to do with it."* You want to know who God is. You don't care about the infrastructure that today's religion has created for Him.

Perhaps you think that you aren't good enough for God. People who grew up going to church every Sunday seem so different from you. You're from the wrong side of the spiritual tracks. Your life's road has been paved with all kinds of potholes, and you've wrecked the car a number of times.

Not only are you good enough, God has been waiting patiently all these years for you to realize it. That was Jesus' message. God loves you.

He proved it two thousand years ago.

Table of Contents

Introduction

You are browsing through this book at your local bookstore or perhaps online at your favorite Internet retailer. You scan the cover. You quickly read my biography.

"*Hmm, a Christian lawyer,*" you think. "*That has to be the oxymoron to end all oxymorons. Aren't lawyers and Christians at opposite ends of the spectrum? Christians are sweet and simple and happy — with a big emphasis on <u>simple</u>.*"

You chuckle at your own double entendre.

"*Lawyers, on the other hand, are anything but sweet.*" Several lawyer jokes come to mind. You think of a recently well-publicized criminal trial with an obviously guilty defendant. The defense lawyer came up with all kinds of reasons why his client couldn't have done it, and alternatively, why the client shouldn't be held responsible. You ask yourself: "*How can anyone defend someone who is so obviously guilty?*"

Even Christians may take offense at the idea of a Christian lawyer. After all, lawyers are from the wrong side of the spiritual tracks. That's why we became lawyers. It's a job requisite. For that matter, everyone knows that logic and faith are incompatible. Logic is intellectual and faith is emotional. Logic is for scientists; faith is for backwoods simpletons. Lawyers use shrewd logic to argue what the meaning of the word "is" is. Christians say, "Well, you know he has a point, God bless him."

"*Christian lawyer — yeah, right.*"

Hold on. Before you toss this book back onto the shelf (or close your e-reader) consider the possibility that you might be missing the point. In America, lawyers defend guilty people because they aren't guilty until a jury decides that they are. Our legal system requires it. Lawyers are trained to see both sides. It's not good or bad. It's just what we do. We do not check our souls at the door when we receive our license to practice law.

Here's another point. Logic and faith are entirely compatible. You climb into your car and have faith that the brakes will work. Scientists launch rocket ships to the moon based upon their faith that the moon will continue to orbit the earth.

Everyone has faith in something. It's because nothing is certain. Faith enables us to proceed in the face of that uncertainty.

Their logic is grounded in their faith. Because something has happened in the past, we have faith that it will happen in the future. Without faith, we could not function as humans. We'd be afraid to do anything. There are people who believe in something with no basis in fact. It's called *blind faith*. Eventually, they are faced with the harsh reality of whether or not their faith in that thing works. Even faith in nothing (called *nihilism*) requires faith. Nihilists place their faith in the idea that life is meaningless. They believe in the meaninglessness of life.

So the real question is: In what (or whom) will you place your faith?

Many Americans consider themselves Christians by process of elimination. We go to church every week or at least on Christmas and Easter. Our dollars bear the motto "In God We Trust." We swear our presidents in with one hand on the Bible. *"The United States was founded on Christian principles,"* we think. *"Of course, I'm a Christian. I'm not a Muslim or Buddhist. America is a Christian nation. And I'm an American. Therefore, I'm a Christian."* Almost like the Israelites of the Old Testament, to some of us Christianity is a birthright.

This book is about developing a meaningful relationship with God.[1] It's about developing a powerful faith in Him, through the man called Jesus. Christianity is about trusting God with your life. That's what *faith* means. It is a concept so simple that a child can understand it. At the same time, you can spend a lifetime developing and refining that faith.

This book isn't about that kind of Christianity.

You have probably experienced things that you don't understand. You may wonder about bigger spiritual concepts. Who or what is behind all of this? What happens after we die? If you are still wrestling with what you believe, this book will de-mystify the terminology and concepts of Christian faith. It will cause you to think more deeply about the subject.

The point of Christianity is that God wants to have a relationship with each of us. It doesn't matter who we are, what we look like, or what we've done. This includes people who didn't grow up in church. It includes alcoholics, drug addicts, and murderers.

The thing about Christianity is that once you understand it, really understand it, you can't be passive about it.

And it includes lawyers.

The Reasonable Person

In the law, we use a well-established standard to judge people's actions. It's called the *reasonable person* standard. The next time you watch a television legal commentator discussing whatever

---

1. References to God, the Father, are capitalized throughout this book. Other than Jesus' proper name, I have not capitalized references to Jesus, for the sake of simplicity and consistency.

case is the news for the week, pay attention. Sooner or later, the term is bound to come up. It's typically used in the context of, "A reasonable person would…" or perhaps, "It is reasonable to assume that…" The reasonable person standard helps us determine whether someone acted reasonably in a given situation. For the law to function effectively, must make sense. It has to be reasonable.

For Christian claims to be deemed reasonable, they must be reasonable as measured against their effect on people's lives. Reasonableness depends upon whether, based upon everything we know and have experienced, Christianity makes sense. This book will help you to decide whether Christianity makes sense. This book will help you to decide whether the claims of Christianity are reasonable.

The methods used in this book are many of the same that can be found in any lawyer's toolkit: logical and analytical reasoning, identifying assumptions within arguments, and careful review of the evidentiary record. Legal arguments are supported with the facts and the law. The stronger the support, the more persuasive the argument is. In court, *documentary evidence, eyewitness testimony*, and *circumstantial evidence* are used to help the judge or jury determine whether a party's claims are reasonable.

The Bible[2] is the foundational documentary evidence for

A discussion about Christianity that isn't based upon the Bible is incomplete at best and misleading at worst.

Christianity. If you have never read the Bible, this book will provide you with an introduction to its scope and structure. On the other hand, if you already study the Bible regularly, this book will give you a framework with which to continue your studies. It will help you to better understand where you are in

2. All references cited are to the Holy Bible, New International Version®, unless otherwise cited as "AMP," in which case such references are to the Amplified® Bible.

your Christian journey and develop a plan for continuing your Christian growth. It will help you learn to navigate the Bible without a doctorate in divinity — or a law degree, for that matter.

Christians often use scriptural "one-liners" to support claims about our faith. For example, we use the scripture John 3:16 to support the claim that Jesus was[3] the son of God. Every word in the Bible has a purpose. Nonetheless, it is unwise to come to a conclusion about anything, based upon a couple of sentences. To someone who has never read the Bible, one verse can't mean much. You have to understand the context within which it was written.

A single quote from a lengthy book doesn't really prove anything. Meaningful Bible study requires deeper reading.

You'll find footnotes at the bottom of many pages in this book. Each scriptural reference is merely a launching point for further study. The references are there if you want to understand the basis for the proposition or engage in further study. You can use them to come to your own conclusions regarding the reasonableness of Christian faith. Use the "one chapter" rule. Take the time to read the entire chapter surrounding the reference.

The Wrong Side of the Spiritual Tracks

We may have more in common than you might imagine. Church was not a regular part of my life growing up. When I finally

---

3. It is more correct to say that "Jesus is..." rather than "Jesus was..." This is because Christians believe that after he was crucified, Jesus ascended to heaven. He is still alive, and therefore "is" rather than "was." However, for the sake of clarity, I use the past tense to refer to Jesus, in terms of his life here on earth throughout this book.

started going, it seemed to be only a matter of time before they caught on to me and threw me out. I've probably done most of the same bad things you've done, and worse. I've made mistakes; plenty of them. I've made them over and over again. My spiritual road has been filled with potholes, speed bumps, and broken glass.

I became a Christian as a nine-year-old boy, as a result of a chance encounter with a kid's evangelism program. It was a puppet show, of all things. Thanks to my own stubbornness, however, my Christian growth has been a staggered and sometimes painful process. There have been many bumps and bruises, and much *backsliding*[4] along the way. These things led me to doubt the legitimacy of my conversion and caused me to question my faith. I've asked myself: *"If I really were a Christian, I wouldn't have done what I just did."*

I take great comfort in the fact that Jesus said that he didn't come to take care of folks who were well.[5] Jesus came to heal people who were sick. My relationship with God only solidified after years of bad living. The good news is that my bad life gave me an accurate perspective of what life without God is like. My life experiences include a lot of things that many "right side of the tracks" Christians haven't. It also caused me to question things that a lot of them might walk right past. It gives me an objective viewpoint on the faith.

> *We know what we were like before God touched us. We know what we are like now.*

Wrong side of the tracks Christians are special to God. We are an opportunity for Him to demonstrate His love, power and glory. We are the "before and after" photos in the spiritual rapid weight loss commercial of life. Jesus explained in the parable

---

4. *"Backsliding"* refers to Christians who return to their pre-conversion sin.
5. Matthew 9:12 (AMP).

of the prodigal son[6] that God wants a radically changed heart. When people like us change so radically, there is no other reasonable explanation for it. God is the only reasonable explanation.

There were many painful detours and side trips before reaching my ultimate destination. And yet, it is the most incredible and rewarding journey that anyone can ever experience.

To the reasonable person, the journey itself proves the point.

---

6. Luke 15:32.

CHAPTER ONE

Voir Dire

V oir dire is the first stage in a trial. Lawyers interview potential jurors to determine whether they can be fair and impartial in trial. It also gives the lawyers a chance to preview the arguments they will make at trial. Voir dire is important because it introduces the participants to each other. It sets the stage for the trial. This chapter will set the stage for this book. It's autobiographical and personal, and some of it is hard to tell. But it is a necessary part of the story.

As a threshold matter, you should understand that in trial, the lawyer cannot argue the case and also act as a witness. The lawyer/witness can unduly influence the jury. Nonetheless, in this case, I take the stand. My argument and my testimony are inseparable. The events of my life are the most convincing evidence of the validity of my faith.

If you are not a Christian, someone along the way may have encouraged you to *invite Jesus into your heart.* They said that in order to become a Christian, all you have to do is pray the so-called Christian's Prayer.[7] These people described it as an instantaneous *miraculous conversion* experience. They told you that, "Everything will take care of itself. No worries, no problems; once you give your life to God, everything is okay. Just trust in Jesus."

For some of us it can be a bit more complicated than that.

Suppose that you drop your college student off at her dorm for the first time, the week before college starts, with the sole advice, "Good luck. I know you will do well." The problem is that you never read to her when she was a child. You didn't encourage her to do her homework in high school. When she returns home for Christmas break, you can't understand why she struggled and finally ended up with a "C" average. The truth is that preparing your child for college is a lifelong project. Christianity is also a lifelong endeavor.

People *accept Jesus* and still have problems. This doesn't mean that God has abandoned them. He's still there. And yet, we have the power to choose. We can choose to do what God wants us to do. Or, we can go our own way. Becoming a Christian doesn't mean that we become perfect, though. Instead, it means we are on a path to perfection, thanks to what Jesus accomplished on the cross. The *gospel* (literally, the "good news") is, at its core, a simple concept. Jesus died so that we could live forever, with God. Everyone's story is different, but the net result is the same. The process of developing a relationship with God is a lifelong project. Until you take that first leap of faith, you can't start the journey. Until you take that first leap of faith, you can't experience the things in life that will validate it for you. The initial leap of faith in Jesus reconciles

---

7. See Chapter Eleven.

us with God. It's the daily walk in faith and dependence upon Him that makes us more like Him.

Certainly, solving the problem of one's eternal destiny is a huge accomplishment. Be that as it may, you still have to deal with the question of your remaining years of living in this world. Life is difficult. Many of us have had very difficult lives. We've had abuse and hardship. The world has not been kind to us. We're more worried about short term problems like making ends meet than esoteric things like our eternal destiny. Inviting Jesus into our hearts won't, as they say, put bread on the table.

What if you could have eternal bliss and a pretty good time in this life as well? What if all of your problems were solved, but you just couldn't see it? If you could somehow know that everything would turn out okay, it wouldn't seem so tough. You would look at the big picture and shrug off adversity, unfairness, difficulty, illness, and all of the rest of life's troubles.

It's only later, when you look back on your life, that you begin to realize that things have happened to you that can't be attributed to coincidence.

With Christianity, it might not seem that way immediately. It's only after you truly commit yourself to God that the process begins. It all comes together for good. You see God's hand in it.

The Puppet Show

It was the 1960s in Houston, Texas. Most people in Houston were connected in some way to the oil business. Big oil companies and big contractors set up offices in the Bayou City, employing thousands of people. A quick drive on the Gulf Freeway took you to Pasadena, whose skyline consisted exclusively of oil refineries. The burn-off was spectacular, especially at night when the flames could be seen for miles. The smell, however, was another story. We kids would try to hold our breath while Dad drove down the freeway. Needless to say, our breath ran out long before the smell.

It was an exciting time. Houston was one of the fastest-growing cities in America.

In those days, the family car was assuredly American-made and cost a couple of thousand dollars. Cell phones didn't exist; texting was decades away. We had a black, rotary-dial telephone that rang loudly when someone called. Personal computers, the Internet, and DVDs were years away. We trusted and listened to our government. Political scandals that would lead to the resignation of one president and impeachment proceedings against another weren't imaginable.

The country had begun to heal from the deep wound its national psyche caused by the assassination of its young president, John F. Kennedy. The escalation of the war in Vietnam hadn't begun yet. There were no real threats to our national security. Nonetheless in school, we all were familiar with the civil defense drill: crawl under the desk, double over into a ball, and wait for the big mushroom flash that never came. The cold war with the Soviet Union continued and you just never knew about the Red Menace.

I became a Christian as a nine-year-old boy in 1965. One of my school friends, Bill Goldsmith, invited me to a puppet show at the church he and his family attended. In those days before video games, a puppet show was a pretty exciting outing to a nine-year-old boy. Looking back, it is still pretty amazing to me that a puppet show could ultimately change someone's life so dramatically.

After entering the church fellowship hall, we found our way to a couple of seats directly in front of a puppet stage. Front row seats at a puppet show are about as good as it gets to a kid. The stage was decorated with vibrant colors and cartoon characters. Bill and I fidgeted with excitement. The house lights dimmed and for a brief minute, the hall was totally dark.

But then again, that's how God works. Big surprises often come in small, nondescript packages.

Suddenly, a spotlight brightly illuminated the stage. The small curtain opened. A green frog sock puppet popped up, followed quickly by a puppet made to look like a little boy.

My memory of the dialogue or even the story line of the puppet show has long faded. But the conclusion is unforgettable. At the end of the puppet show, a man stepped from behind the puppet stage and took a microphone. In another setting, you would have probably walked right past him. That night, he captivated us. He was about forty years old, with slightly graying hair and piercing blue eyes. He was otherwise nondescript. Nonetheless, he exuded an absolute sense of peace. It gave him a magnetism that is hard to describe.

The puppet man explained to the audience that all of us in that hall were, in God's eyes, sinners. In fact, he said that everyone in the entire world was a sinner. It didn't matter how good or bad we had been in our lives; we all fell short of the standard God had set for us.

Before you think, *"That's a pretty harsh message for a kid,"* you should know that even as a nine-year-old, I agreed with the puppet man. Kids know right from wrong. Everyone has done things that they know are wrong. It certainly applied to me. I had fights with my brother on a regular basis, back-talked my mom, and sometimes told lies when it was expedient. And yet, he slightly recast it. *"These things hurt God,"* is the way that he characterized them. I had done plenty of bad things that God couldn't have been happy about. I simply hadn't put it together that those things were counter to God's will. The puppet man called these bad things *sin*.

He said that God loved us, each and every one of us.[8] *"God loves me,"* flickered in my consciousness. It was intriguing that God even knew me. It didn't seem possible that God could know us on a personal level. The puppet man said that God showed His love for us by giving His only son Jesus as a sacrifice to pay for the sins of mankind. Jesus had never done anything wrong in God's eyes; he had never sinned.[9] As payment for our sins, Jesus allowed himself to be crucified — being nailed to a cross and dying what must have been the worst death imaginable. The puppet man called it a *free gift*.

He said that after Jesus died, he came back to life; he was *resurrected*. He said that it was this process, of Jesus' life, death, and resurrection that proved that Jesus was truly the son of God. The puppet man said that all we had to do to be forgiven by God for our sins was to accept the free gift. We just had to believe that Jesus was God's son and pray a prayer accepting the gift.

A hymn played in the background and the lights were dimmed. The puppet man asked everyone to bow their heads and pray. I closed my eyes and prayed. He thanked God for everything He had done for us. He then invited people in the audience to pray another prayer, in which we admitted that we were sinners, and that we believed that Jesus was God's son and had been crucified for our sins. The puppet man said that we could invite Jesus to come and live in our hearts, right then and there.

I thought about it for a minute or so. Something happened within my heart. I realized that God did love me. I just knew it. I felt it. Perhaps the enormity of what Jesus had done for me sunk

---

8. John 3:16 (AMP).
9. 2 Corinthians 5:21; Hebrews 4:14; 1 John 3:4; 1 Peter 2:22.

in. Or perhaps God didn't seem so distant to me. For whatever reason, the puppet man's words pierced straight through me. My throat tightened and tears trickled down my freckled cheeks. But somehow it wasn't embarrassing.

Simply and innocently, I prayed that prayer. *"God I am sorry for all the bad things I have done in my life. Thank you for sending Jesus to die for my sins. Please come into my heart."*

The puppet man asked the audience to hold up their hands if they had prayed the prayer. He acknowledged people in the audience, one by one, who held up their hands. With my eyes tightly closed, my little hand went up. The puppet man said simply, "God bless you." For a second, it seemed as if we were the only ones in the room. A new feeling enveloped me. It was a cleansing feeling. God was happy with me. It was a feeling of peace in my sad little soul. The puppet man said that we were *saved*[10] and *filled with God's Spirit*[11] from that moment on.

A little while later, the house lights came up. We climbed into Mr. Goldsmith's car, and they dropped me off at home. As they pulled out of our driveway and drove away, I watched the tail lights fade into the distance. I just stood there for a minute. Somehow, something very important had happened to me.

I rushed into the house, excited and wanting to tell my folks about it. The familiar bluish haze of cigarette smoke enveloped our small den, a poorly constructed addition to the house by the previous owner, a do-it-yourselfer. There were brown spots in the ceiling panels caused by rain seepage from the frequent Houston rain. I caught myself and walked into the den.

---

10. *"Saved"* is the Christian belief that we are saved from the consequences of our sins and will go to heaven after we die. (Ephesians 2:8-9).

11. The *"Holy Spirit"* is discussed throughout this book and is a fundamental concept of Christianity. Christians believe that God, in the form of a spirit, can indwell in anyone who asks. See Chapter Eight for a detailed discussion on the Holy Spirit.

My mother sat in front of the television, eating dinner. It was a "T.V. dinner." This was before microwaves; in those days meals were made from scratch. T.V. dinners were a novelty of the 1950s and 60s. These "dinners" were deeply frozen meals, prepared in aluminum pans. Several food companies offered variations on the same theme; usually beans and franks. Heated to three hundred and fifty degrees for forty-five minutes in a conventional oven, they were designed for ease, as opposed to culinary satisfaction. In our house, they were typically eaten on a "T.V. tray," which was a folding stand, about waist high, a sort of table for one. Of course, T.V. dinners, served on T.V. trays, were eaten while watching television.

Needless to say, this dining style wasn't conducive to family interaction. The irony was that we ate this way, while watching television shows featuring families gathered around the dinner table. These idealized versions of family life were subtle reminders of my wrong side of the tracks origins.

This was Mom's usual evening ritual; television and drinking beer. My brother Tommy was at a friend's house; my sister Julie was in her room. Dad had gone to bed. It was just Mom and me. She was watching a show about a family of brothers in the Old West raised only by their father. Their mother had died during childbirth. Like all shows of the era, the family had what appeared to be a perfect life. They had a nice house, very cool cowboy clothes, and horses. No one ever got mad. The father didn't get drunk (or drink at all) or smoke. Yet more irony: a family without a mother was supposed to be a sad story. I had a mother and my story was sadder.

The television screen cast a bluish glow on Mom's face as she sat there in our small den. Her auburn hair was unkempt; the red strands splayed about her head hinted at her fiery Irish nature. Tonight she was sedated; mesmerized by television and alcohol. Her normally crystalline blue eyes were glazed and red and droopy. An empty beer sat can next to her chair. Judging from the hour, it appeared to be her sixth beer. Mom was obviously and completely drunk. She slowly looked up at me. She stared vacantly at me for a few seconds. Then she slurred something unintelligible, turned back to the show, and continued to eat her dinner in front of the television.

I wished that I was back at the puppet show.

Who knows whether Mr. Goldsmith or Bill, or anyone else except the puppet man, realized that I had accepted Jesus? We never talked about it, and lost contact after my family moved away from Houston later that year. No one ever asked me about it. But something very real happened to me.

After praying that prayer, so many burdens were lifted from my little heart. For a while, something changed within me. It was a calm and cleansing feeling. At that moment, God's presence was incredibly real to me.

Although my eternal destiny changed that night, my earthly life didn't seem to change much. It took *God was always there. I just didn't always know it.* me a number of years to understand exactly what had happened to me. He protected me. He blessed me. He waited quietly and patiently for many years, when I finally reached out to Him once and for all.

Not Exactly the All-American Family

Today's talk therapists encourage us to talk about our childhoods. They say that we are a product of our environment. It seems as if everyone is carrying emotional baggage thanks to bad parenting. We blame our failures and shortcomings on our parents. We are adult children of dysfunction. We are what we are because of them.

My voir dire self-disclosure isn't for the purpose of sharing the difficulty of my childhood. My childhood, by any standards, would not be considered idyllic. Mine was a family filled with dysfunction, alcoholism, and mental illness. Nevertheless, I don't blame my parents for anything. They did the best they could, based upon who they were.

It is likely that many readers could share similar stories. We grow up with adverse circumstances that cause us shame. Our actions in response to these circumstances lead to guilt and more shame. We keep it a secret. We believe the lie that we aren't good enough. There is no point in seeking God, because we aren't good enough for Him.

You must not let your story prevent you from seeking Him. With God, there are happy endings. God loves you no matter what has happened to you or what your story is.

We are all broken in one way or another. Life is hard, and living it takes a huge toll on us.

My parents led very difficult lives. They endured a lot of deprivation and hardship, which affected them deeply. They grew up during the Great Depression in what can only be described as abject poverty. Coming of age during this era severely affected the collective psyche of their generation. Many people lost everything. Those years affected everything they did afterward. For as long as my parents were alive, the specter of that poverty haunted them both.

If you've known anyone who has gone through it, you know what I'm talking about. Simple clues like reusing aluminum foil, over and over again, and keeping clothes unworn for thirty years reveal the fragile nature of a person who is afraid that it could happen again.

About the time that the Depression ended, their generation had to deal with the threat of a world war. In the late 1930s, Hitler had begun the merciless Nazi conquest of Europe. The United States tried to stay out of it for as long as it could. But then, on December 7, 1941, and without warning, Japan bombed the American naval base at Pearl Harbor.

My father grew up in poverty in West Texas. The old photos of him show a gawky kid with dark circles under his eyes, looking hungry. When Dad was a small boy, the Great Depression completely wiped out any meager assets his family had. The change in their economic circumstances was swift and merciless. They lost their home and lived in a tent for several years.

Somehow, he made it through high school. In 1943 at the age of eighteen, Dad enlisted in the Marines, as a bomber pilot. He selflessly fought for his country. He fought a very real enemy in a very real war that would determine the fate of this country. He flew a number of missions in the South Pacific. Not much more than a boy, he found himself in the crosshairs of Japanese anti-aircraft fire on more than one occasion. Those planes were big, cumbersome, and made perfect targets. My mom told me that Dad had been wounded several times. He never talked about it.

In those days, no one had ever heard of post traumatic stress disorder. Psychology was still a novelty; arguably more akin to a magic act than medicine. Our country never understood the effects of war on those young people. Many veterans, including my dad, suffered deep psychological trauma. Although he never talked about it, he lived with it for the rest of his life. It contributed to his deep and incapacitating depression.

After World War II, Americans simply got on with their lives: they married and started families. Despite his problems, Dad got on with his life. He married Mom, and they had kids. They bought a house, got a mortgage, and began the living of their lives.

Trusting a Father

This story begins in Houston in 1969. It was a hot and oppressively humid typical July summer evening. My family was watching a live, grainy broadcast of man's first lunar landing. The window air conditioning unit was running on overtime, sputtering and coughing in an almost human way. Condensation poured from its housing. My older brother Tommy and younger sister Julie and I were glued to the family television set, a big old black and white model. The three channels came through an antenna, called "rabbit ears" because of its two elongated metal conductors, perched on top of the set. There was no remote control. You changed the channel by turning a stiff dial, which clicked loudly as you turned it. If the picture got fuzzy, as it frequently did, you tweaked the rabbit ears gingerly until it cleared up.

Dad sat in his easy chair drinking a beer and smoking a cigarette. Tommy lay on the plaid sofa, which had seen better days. Mom sat in her chair drinking a beer and smoking; middle class royalty surveying her domain. Julie and I were sprawled on the floor. The room was hazy with smoke. We watched intently, all eyes glued to the set. Astronaut Neal Armstrong stepped from the lunar landing craft onto the lunar surface. Man had conquered the moon. Those men were Americans! President Kennedy, idolized by my parents, had inspired a country with his vision of this day. Now, that vision was fulfilled. Everything seemed right with the world.

The next day, Dad tried to kill himself.

We did not have the kind of relationship depicted by television writers in the 1960s. Dad never gave me cardigan-clad life advice punctuated by a haze of pipe smoke. We never did things together that dads and sons do—fishing, hunting, catch and other such boyhood rituals. Dad left the raising of his children to his wife. Despite this, on school days at exactly 5:15 p.m., I rode my bike down to the street corner. A few minutes later, like clockwork, he drove by in his old car. I happily trailed after him, waving and pedaling as fast as my legs could go. He never waved back or even acknowledged me, but it somehow made me feel closer to him.

That day, I waited for Dad at the corner. The designated time came and went. The hands on my little wristwatch moved to 5:30 p.m., then 6:00 p.m., then 6:30. Perhaps I missed him; maybe he had already driven by. I finally rode my bike home at eight o'clock, after it started to get dark. When I walked in the house, Mom greeted me in a red-faced panic. At first I thought she was mad at me for being out late. However, my sister was crying. It wasn't about me; I relaxed. Then, I realized that Dad wasn't there. My stomach tightened up with butterflies. These were evil butterflies, not fluttering in excitement, but pounding my stomach with foreboding.

My dad was missing. No one knew where he was. A deep sense of dread filled me.

For the next three hours, Mom frantically paced all over the house. She had always been a contradiction; an incredibly strong woman with incredible frailties. When faced with a threat to her family, Mom was like a field commander. She methodically thumbed through her address book and phoned people to ask where he was. Word spread of Dad's disappearance, and neighbors dropped by to check in. Everyone was worried. It felt like a funeral without flowers or music or a minister. It was absolutely and completely terrifying.

Around midnight I fell asleep in my jeans and T-shirt, exhausted with worry. It was a dead and dreamless sleep. Around 1:00 a.m., the shrill ringing of the phone in the kitchen woke me. I crawled out of bed and made my way into our dingy little kitchen. Mom, the field commander, had answered it. She gripped the telephone tightly, exerting control over one of the few things that she could, motioning impatiently for a pen. Julie, already in the kitchen, sleepily found one and handed it to her, along with a scrap of paper. Mom wrote something down furiously and nodded her head a few times. She hung up the phone and just stared intently for a few seconds. Tommy was now awake and had shuffled into the kitchen; it had become Command Central. We all looked desperately at Mom, wanting to know whether the news was bad or good. Everything seemed to be moving in slow motion, a kind of macabre television game show. Dad's life was the grand prize.

She let out a gasp and cried out, "They found him!" In an almost figurative self-pinch, she repeated slowly, "They found him." Judging by the look on her face, they had found him *alive*. Breathtaking relief and happiness filled me. Dad was alive.

Looking back on his life now, it's easy to see his slow, gradual descent into depression. It likely started early in life, as the result of the hardships he faced. Perhaps it was part of his genetic programming. As a young husband and father, he spent most of his time working. He and Mom used alcohol to unwind. As with any emotional substitutes, they began to increasingly rely on it. Dad, rather than dealing with his issues, simply masked them. Eventually, they overcame him.

Suffering from incapacitating depression and an unfulfilled life, he had decided to end it. A massive overdose of sleeping pills was his method of choice. He had miscalculated. The security guards had found him in his car in the company parking lot. Dad was unconscious, but alive. The guard called an ambulance, and they rushed him to a hospital.

After he woke up, he wept uncontrollably as he realized his miscalculation.

Dad was admitted to a psychiatric institution for several months while receiving diagnosis and treatment. It's hard to know why people collapse in this way. Perhaps it was a combination of years of deprivation, a horrible war and the ordinary problems of life. The doctors prescribed powerful antipsychotic drugs and electroshock therapy. Until then, we didn't know how sick he was. Lurking just beneath the surface of his personality was a horribly damaged psyche that wanted to exit this world.

Despite this treatment, Dad tried to kill himself again.

His second suicide attempt was at home early one morning about a year later. It was still dark outside. Dad turned on the old gas oven, without lighting it, got on his knees, stuck his head in and began to breathe deeply. After a few minutes, he passed out. In the process, he also had filled our little house with highly volatile gas. The only thing lacking for our complete destruction was a small spark.

Waking abruptly to Mom's shrill screaming, I got out of bed and found her rushing through the house, opening windows. She was enraged and screamed hysterically at Dad, "Are you trying to kill all of us?" He stood there groggily in the kitchen in his yellowing boxer shorts, while Mom screamed at him. This wasn't something a kid was supposed to witness. Dad looked down at the floor silently, embarrassed. His brow was furrowed with deep lines and his lips were a tight, straight line across his face. You could see his disappointment at having failed again. It was hard to know what was going on behind his sad brown eyes, but to me it looked like he was thinking about how he could get this suicide thing right, once and for all.

Clearly, the drugs weren't having the desired effect.

With the initial shock of it behind her, Mom began to heave deep, emotional sobs. Like an aging circus elephant leaving the ring after a trick, Dad slowly shuffled out of the kitchen and crawled back into bed. *"Have to go to work in the morning,"* he seemed to be thinking. Mom and I opened the rest of the windows and doors. Julie made her way into the kitchen, squinting in bewilderment. She had missed the excitement. The show was over.

The sharp odor of natural gas lingered in the house for quite a while. The foul odor of the gas that almost killed all of us will remain with me forever. Whenever I smell it now, it instantly takes me back to that hot July evening in the kitchen of our little house in Houston. It fills me with a sense of tragic sadness.

A few months later, I found a loaded shotgun in Dad's car. He had never hunted; he never shot at targets. There was only one possible use for this gun. I took it and hid it under my bed. He never said anything about it.

Over the next few years, Dad was hospitalized several times for depression and psychotic episodes. The most powerful antipsychotic drugs weren't strong enough. Watching him was like watching someone waiting to die. Mom, still a Depression baby well into adulthood, was focused on one thing. When he wasn't around, she would say softly to us kids, "We need to keep Dad working." She was afraid that he would lose his job, and that we would lose everything. *It is all about keeping Dad's nose to the grindstone,* I thought. To me the more appropriate question was whether we should instead be helping him to recover from his complete mental breakdown.

The doctors finally found a workable combination of drugs. Dad stopped trying to kill himself. He kept his job. He also self-medicated. Formerly a beer drinker, Dad now began to drink cheap bourbon. The potentially lethal combination of drugs and alcohol meant that Dad was continuing his suicide quest. It meant something else, as well. Dad's deep depression coupled with alcohol became rage.

One night, Julie and I were fighting about something and had gotten loud. Silently, Dad appeared in the doorway. We had awakened him. The look in his eyes was not human. It was the dead look of a shark, whose eyes roll backward as it rips its prey in half. Without warning, he attacked. He slapped my head, sending me flying. I hit the wall and landed on the floor with a hard thud and was out cold for a couple of minutes. Coming to, I gasped for breath and tasted blood. He was still there, waiting to see if I wanted any more of it. I slumped against the wall and tried to breathe.

Saying nothing, he walked out of the room.

Adolescence for a teenage boy on its best day is difficult. The urge to leave the nest is powerful. He tries on adulthood like a new suit of clothes, and at first it feels pretty good. It means strength and independence. He soon realizes that it comes with strings attached; responsibilities and worry. Perhaps being a boy isn't so bad after all. He reverts to his boyish ways. Dad had deep issues and was haunted by the demons of the Depression, war and who knows what else. As I entered and exited adolescence, my psyche was deeply affected by my fear of my father, contrasted with an even greater fear of losing him.

One of the last times we were together as a family was at Thanksgiving when I was home from college. We were gathered around the table with turkey and dressing, and all of the rest of it. Dad led us in a prayer of thanksgiving that ended with "in Jesus' name, Amen."

The process of growing up is a constant tension and struggle between the desire for independence and the fear of it.

They were a few simple words, but words that would provide me with needed reassurance years later.

He would die shortly after that. Years of heavy medication and alcohol abuse, in combination with bad diet and no exercise claimed him. He was only fifty-seven years old, but suffering from extensive heart disease at a time before angioplasty, stents, and bypass surgery. Dad finally succeeded in killing himself. It was a self-induced heart attack.

He died on a beautiful afternoon in Houston. It was one of those perfect Houston winter days — about seventy degrees and not a single cloud in the sky. Mom was sick and he drove to the local market to pick up groceries. After checking out, Dad went out to his car and discovered that it wouldn't start; a dead battery. He began the two-mile walk home, bad heart and all, carrying about twenty-five pounds of groceries in large paper bags.

No heart patient in his right mind would take such a risk. My dad was an intelligent person. He must have intended the consequences of his actions. Of course, he couldn't have known for sure that the walk would kill him. But any reasonable person with heart problems wouldn't have done it, unless they wanted to die. Dad made it about a quarter of a mile. They found him with canned goods, soft drinks and vegetables all around him, smashed and pooling on the pavement. According to the paramedics, he was likely "dead before he hit the ground."

A neighbor phoned me at college in Austin that evening. I left my dorm at 10:00 p.m. and made the three-hour drive back to Houston. I sobbed convulsively the entire trip; it was the first time that I had cried since I was a little boy. Driving late at night had a hypnotic effect, causing me to periodically zone out and forget about the horrible news. Then, the fact that he was dead would hit me again. It was like a perverse news flash, with the same horrible story repeated over and over again.

When I got home, my mother was sitting in our small living room. It was surreal. She smoked her perpetual cigarette and stared vacantly at the cheap still life print, a portrait of roses, hanging above the old sofa. She wasn't drinking. Mom had never been this subdued. She sat there in complete silence. It had always been unclear to me whether she loved Dad. She believed that she deserved a better position than our lower middle class lot and reminded him of it constantly. That night, it was obvious that she had suffered a deep loss. My mother was suddenly a widow.

The conversations and reconciliation I hoped to have with Dad someday were now *moot*.[12] My children would never know their paw-paw, or poppy or whatever they would have called him. His death was that first peek into my own mortality, and it profoundly affected me. His death caused me to think about my

---

12. *"Moot"* is a legal term meaning "of no effect."

own life. At his funeral, I couldn't even bring myself to look into his casket. Forget what people tell you about the closure benefit of funerals. I didn't want to see him that way; lying there, cold and lifeless in makeup and a suit he never wore with his hands folded across his chest.

For many years after, my dreams were about him; haunting dreams. The dream was always same. Dad was smiling, happy, and healthy. He was free of the demons that had haunted him for most of his adult life. He was strong and confident and full of life. I found myself across the room from him, watching him engage in some intelligent conversation with someone I didn't know. A sense of admiration and excitement filled me, and I walked over to talk with him.

He looked at me, eyes alive and alert, with piercing wisdom and began to speak to me. His mouth moved but no words came out. He stared at me.

I thought, *"If I just try harder, he will speak to me."*

He just stared at me.

I woke up with a feeling of unbearable sadness.

I so wanted to talk with Dad one more time and tell him how much I loved him. Perhaps he would tell me that he loved me. It never happened in life though; it would certainly not happen now.

It took me many years to understand that all of it prevented me from trusting in a Father who loved me in a way that my father couldn't.

Seeing Through Shame

My mother was the youngest of nine children born to a poor Louisiana family. Her father died when she was twelve of alcoholism. Shortly after that, two of her older brothers died in a motorcycle accident. Mom learned deep grief at a very young age. Like a lot of middle-class alcoholics, she functioned. She fed us and clothed us and took us to school. But she needed alcohol, and it controlled her. She drank every night and got drunk. When she drank, she talked to us about current events, philosophy, and her views of the world. Sometimes, she tearfully described her childhood. She told us about walking miles and miles to get anywhere because they didn't have a car. She told us about not having store-bought clothes until she was out of high school.

Perhaps because of her chaotic childhood, Mom needed to control others. She instinctively knew how to push emotional buttons. She knew how to manipulate. Mom also had an anger problem. Living with Mom was like living with a pit bull. You never knew when she was going to lash out. It left deep scars.

One of my earliest childhood memories is of Mom and Dad, when I was about four years-old. We were all in the den watching television. They were drinking beer and arguing. The tone of the argument had quickly and unexpectedly escalated. Mom's face grew red with anger. Finding herself on the losing end of the argument, Mom played her trump card. "I want a divorce," she slurred. A lower-middle class Southern diva, she pronounced it *deeva-a-awse*. She drew my sister Julie closer to her; a potential ally and not-so subtle threat to Dad. I don't think she wasn't serious. It was simple manipulation.

The look on Dad's face proved that it had worked. He didn't say another word; the argument was over. Everyone went to bed.

Sweet dreams.

A year later, my sister and I were playing, a bit too loudly, in the kitchen. Mom yelled at us a few times to stop, to no avail. She abruptly grabbed me by my skinny arm and said, "I'm taking you to the orphanage." She grabbed Julie and dragged us both to

A child's greatest fear was being realized, then and there.

the car. The look on her face told us that she wasn't kidding. She loaded us into the car and began driving. Hers was an Oscar-worthy performance. We wailed in terror. We pleaded with her, tears streaming down our little faces, "Mommy, please don't take us to the orphanage. We'll be good; we promise." After what seem like an eternity, she turned the car around and announced that she had changed her mind.

Needless to say, we were very quiet for a long while after that.

I learned early in life not to have friends over. In sixth grade, I had invited a couple of friends to watch television after school. My mom greeted us at the door, slurring her words. It was obvious that she had been drinking. She was red-faced and smelled like a bar on the wrong side of town. It was clear from the looks on my friends' faces that their moms didn't act this way.

In the morning, Mom usually had a hangover. Tempers and hangovers don't mix well. She would bang pots and pans around in the kitchen, glaring at anyone who walked in. It became important to wake up and get out of the house as quickly as possible. Her drinking got worse when I was in high school. As she contemplated her future as an empty-nester, she became increasingly manipulative. She began to show up unannounced and drunk, at my friend's houses, the places I worked and at school.

On a date my senior year with a girlfriend, we had stopped by her house to talk with her parents. A few minutes later, with no warning, Mom was at their house, angrily ringing the door-bell. My girlfriend's mother opened the door. Mom stood there, red-faced, with a catsup stain on her blouse. If you didn't know her, you would have had a hard time taking her seriously. But I knew her and, therefore, took her very seriously. She began by dramatically slurring her concerns about "where *thish* relation-ship *ish* heading." It went downhill from there, despite the efforts of my girlfriend's mother to calm Mom down. Suddenly and characteristically, her anger turned to grief. Mom began sobbing hopelessly. She staggered off to her car and drove home. There wasn't much I could say to my girlfriend or her mother. Our relationship ended shortly after that incident. *"It's not you, it's me,"* and all that.

Mom's surprise appearances in my life continued throughout high school. One of the low points was on an October evening in 1974. Tryouts for the class play were being held in the school auditorium. About twenty students and the drama teacher, Mr. Cooke, were there. It was, ironically enough, a comedy. My part was the male lead, an All-American type, yet another ironic twist. I had learned to overachieve early in life; class president, honor society, and "most likely to succeed." Everyone thought my life was great.

At around 7:00 p.m., I was on stage, reading the lines with one of the hopeful actresses. We were at the point in the script where the male lead first meets the romantic female lead. Boy meets girl. It was as All-American as you can get. As my future co-star read her lines, for some reason I looked out beyond the stage lights. Something wasn't right. There was a dim figure in the back of the auditorium. It was hard to make her out; a small-framed woman with who looked to be in her fifties. She was out of sight from the other students waiting for their turn on the stage. She stared at me in a chilling face-off of sorts.

There was something familiar to me about her. It hadn't quite registered yet. After a minute or two, I was stunned to realize that it was my mother. It didn't seem possible that she would expose herself in this way with so many witnesses. Her pride wouldn't have allowed it. Nevertheless, alcohol is the pride antidote, especially when it is consumed in large quantities.

Mom was staggering in the back of the auditorium. It was one of those moments that you keep hoping is only a bad dream. I prayed that I would wake up. But it wasn't a dream. My stomach clenched reflexively and I started to sweat profusely. I stopped mid-sentence, absolutely speechless.

Slowly, Mom shuffled toward the stage. She was wearing her old pink house shoes. There was a large non-descript brownish stain on her yellow sleeveless knit shirt. Mom paused about halfway down the aisle between my spot onstage and the chairs where the other students sat. She squinted at the spotlight. She stood there, weaving from side to side, like a punch drunk boxer past his prime. From the stage, you could smell the alcohol on her breath. If this had been a scene from a 1970's sitcom, it would have been hysterically funny. The canned laughter would have been deafening. But it wasn't television. It wasn't funny. It was deadly serious. It was surreal. It was as if *Mom had become yet another character in this now-demented version of the comedy*. This was a new and unexpected plot twist.

Like a stereotypical drunk, she looked up at me, and then at my classmates in bewilderment, and slurred dramatically, "You *promished* that you would get a job. You *promished* me." She began to sob and shake her head slowly and tragically. There was a stunned silence among my classmates.

I looked at my mother from the stage, helpless to stop this tragedy. My body was frozen with fear. Mr. Cooke tried to intervene. Mom brushed him off and continued sobbing. She looked up at me and cried, "You said — that you — were going — to find — a job," heaving deeply between phrases. My character, the All-American type, just stood there unable to respond and looking deeply ashamed. My mother looked as if she might pass out.

After a minute, I unfroze and looked at my classmates. Maybe no one had really noticed. Maybe it was a bigger deal to me than it was to them. It was not to be the case. They all were all looking down; no one made eye contact. The look on their faces was a combination of shock and sadness. I doubt that any of them had ever witnessed anything like this before. To say that the scene was awkward would be like calling the Titanic tragedy a boating accident. Any myths about my life and likelihood of success were dispelled beyond a reasonable doubt.

I left the auditorium, drove to a grocery store parking lot, and spent the night in my car.

Fade to black.

In those short, slurred sentences she conveyed to my class-mates and teacher that the Great Depression continued for the Sedberrys.

For Mom, it all came down to money. She was still very afraid of the Great Depression.

Mom very effectively passed on those fears to her kids. She viewed her life's mission as instilling a work ethic in us. My childhood and adolescence were spent in after school and week-end jobs; selling greeting cards door-to-door while in grade school; cleaning out cages at a grooming kennel while in junior high; and in high school as a busboy, and a clerk at a grocery store. There was no time for friends. There was little time for school. Anything else and Mom erupted. Later in life, hard-core workaholism would define me.

The entire episode lasted, at most, ten minutes. Be that as it may, it is burned permanently into my memory. Deep shame doesn't even begin to describe it. The high school rumor mill is a vicious thing. It seemed certain to me that my peers had already cast votes for my latest achievement: the "most likely to end up on heroin." For the rest of that year, it was difficult to talk with anyone. I spent as little time as possible at school.

This was the classic pattern. Mom would get drunk. Mom would get angry. I would leave. In hindsight, it seems that she really thought she was doing the right thing. She had made a lot of mistakes in her life and was trying to prevent me from making the same ones. She believed in what she was doing. Even so, her actions were not evidence of her beliefs. She failed in the execu-tion of her beliefs.

My senior year, a youth minister at a local church asked me whether Jesus was my personal *savior*.[13] I answered, "Yes." He seemed perplexed. It was obvious that my life was not evidence of my faith. He walked me through the basic premises of salvation. He continued to reach out to me a few times; however, we did not stay in touch. And yet, his interest and actions led me to begin to begin to think about the apparent contradiction between my beliefs and my life. I had a hard time getting past the shame in my life.

Of course, Mom's efforts to control me backfired. I graduated and moved out at eighteen. A job as a truck driver enabled me to save for college. My goal was to get as far away from home as possible. That turned out to be Austin, about 160 miles from Houston. I enrolled at the University of Texas with enough money to get through that first year. After that, a job with the university allowed me to stay enrolled. Dad died the year of my graduation.

A Skilled Cross-Examiner

While in college, I visited a local church and tried to get closer to God. Nonetheless, the lessons from my childhood were deeply ingrained in my psyche. Dad taught me deep depression. Mom taught me rage. They both introduced me to alcohol. This led to bad behaviors. These lessons caused my spirit to constantly swim upstream, against the current of my own values. A key childhood lesson was grounded in my inability trust my parents. It was difficult to trust a father who wanted to die. It was harder to trust a mother who was untrustworthy. Sadly, it all meant that it was next to impossible for me to trust a Father who was completely trustworthy. It also meant a lot of guilt.

---

13. The term *"savior"* refers to the fundamental Christian belief that Jesus' death on the cross "saves" us from the consequences of our sin.

The guilt monologue typically went something like this: *"Who do you think you are? What makes you think God wants to have anything to do with you? Those people sitting near you in church know. They know who you really are."* Or perhaps it was along these lines: *"Surely you are not really a Christian. How can you be a true Christian and continue sinning? You're flawed. You're evil. You have no business being around good and decent Christians."*

I bought into the lies. God's standards seemed unreachable. It seemed that God would have nothing to do with me. Eventually, church became a sporadic activity for me; typically only when there was a problem.

A lot of it, in reality, came from a darker place. They were lies, asserted by a skilled cross-examiner. He is described in greater detail later in Chapter Ten.

Here's a hint. Don't think of him as a cute little guy in a red suit with a pitchfork.

After graduation, a large corporation and career beckoned me. On the outside, my life appeared to be the All-American success story. On the inside was a sad and scared person. This was a recurring theme throughout my life. People thought my life was perfect. It was far from it.

Rather than relinquishing my life to God, I did everything possible to control it. I trusted only in myself. My career was the most important thing to me. My relationships all ended as train wrecks, with emotional wreckage littering the landscape. There was a lot of carnage in my wake. Worry was my constant companion. My greatest worry was losing everything. The irony was that, without God, there wasn't much to lose.

At times, it seemed as if there was a spiritual war going on within me. My life was a vicious cycle of sin, shame, guilt, and then more sin. I was sorry for my bad acts, and yet kept on doing them.

It made no sense that Jesus had come into my heart, even though my life continued to be so bad.

This caused me to second-guess my salvation. It seemed that God hadn't changed me. The same miserable person was still there; a flawed, hurting person. Perhaps my "conversion" was illegitimate. To be clear, I never doubted that Jesus was God.[14] It was just that my bad behavior had chased him away. Maybe trying harder was the answer. It might mean that God would love me, once and for all. I invited Jesus to come into my life again, and again. It was a classic *spiritual roller coaster* existence.

As time passed, it only got worse. My problems became bigger and more far-reaching. My pain was greater. During my intermittent episodes of church attendance, no answers presented themselves. Instead of moving toward heaven, my life seemed to be gradually descending into hell.

There were many wasted years and much rationalizing. Eventually, either wisdom or defeat led me to a major crossroad. It happened to me in 1992, about twelve years after college, while living in Michigan. Lying awake in my bed early one morning, unable to sleep because of stress, worry and loneliness, I prayed: "*Father, I have made a complete mess of my life. I'm sorry. I give it all back to You. Please take control of my life. I surrender it to You.*"

Immediately, a sense of peace enveloped me. Resting in that calmness, especially after many years of unrest, is one of the greatest things we can ever experience. For the first time in a long time, sleep came to me. Jacob had a similar encounter with God early one morning.[15] He wrestled all night and somehow finally found peace. It is likely that many Christians have had similar encounters.

---

14. There are numerous references in the New Testament regarding Jesus' claim to be God. Among them: John 8:58, 10:30–33, John 14:9–11, Matthew 8:20, 9:6, 10:23 (AMP).

15. Genesis 32:24.

Very shortly after that, my life began to change for the better. The change was nothing short of miraculous. I learned more about Jesus and his life. I began to understand what it meant to have a relationship with him. I trusted more and more in him and what he accomplished on the cross. My days went from being filled with worry and struggle to being filled with peace. The more I let go, the more God blessed me time and time again, in countless ways. I prayed and my prayers were answered. Not only did He answer my prayers, He answered them in ways better than I could have ever imagined.

There were times, nonetheless, when the fear would return. The lie went like this: *"Who are you kidding? You've asked Jesus to come into your life before. It's only a matter of time before you will slip back into your old ways. What if it happened again and this change was again only temporary?"*

After a lot of prayer, wisdom beyond my spiritual years manifested itself. Rather than try and figure it out for myself, I asked God to help me understand it. A few days later while reading the Bible, a simple but profound realization occurred to me. Somehow over the years, I had forgotten about that night a long time ago in Houston, at the puppet show.

It came back to me at that moment. A young boy bowed his head and silently prayed a prayer. He meant that prayer with everything that he had.

Then it dawned on me.

We learn to listen very carefully when things "dawn" on us in this way.

All those years ago, I had through faith, accepted the *free gift* of Jesus death for my sins. The Bible says that it's by faith in Jesus that we are saved.[16] By inviting Jesus to come into my heart, the Holy Spirit indwelt in me.[17] This meant that God was living in

---

16. Ephesians 2:8.
17. The Holy Spirit is discussed in detail in Chapter Eight.

me.[18] He had been living in me all along. Even still, there was a choice to be made every single day of how my life should be lived. For me, these had been very bad choices. Bad choices typically have bad consequences. My bad choices had limited His ability to change my life.

The Holy Spirit will lead us, but only if we will let Him.[19] In other words, the decision to allow God to lead us is a daily decision. We decide each day (and arguably, each moment) whether or not we will go His way or our own way.

He will provide us with the tools to navigate life, [20] *but only if we let Him.*

My decision to become a Christian was made as a young boy. Some Christians prayer the prayer as youngsters, with results similar to my own. Things don't work out as promised. After praying that prayer, my life didn't seem to change much. But the truth is that my life changed miraculously that night. God, in the form of the Holy Spirit, came to live within me. My eternal salvation was assured.

My earthly life though, was certainly not evidence of my faith. The real problem was that through bad choices and actions, my Christian growth had stopped. There were numerous detours on my journey. After that initial step in faith, I failed to take the next step, and the next. Regardless, after my first *confession of faith* in Jesus, God was there for me. He never left me. I left Him. It seemed as though He had given up on me. Although I gave up on God at times, He never gave up on me. Although I turned my back on Him many times, He never once turned His back on me.

---

18. 1 Corinthians 6:19 (AMP).

19. Romans 8:13.

20. Galatians 5:25.

When I gave my life back to Him early that morning in Michigan, it was like starting over. God picked me up, dusted me off and helped me to continue along the way.

When Every Word Counts

Like a lot of young people, my climb up the corporate ladder yielded a tarnished gold ring at the top. I ran the race of life, mistakenly believing that the next promotion, the next house, the next relationship would make me finally happy, once and for all. Success didn't really change my life for the better. None of it made me happy.

After my early morning epiphany, I began to fully surrender my life to God. The Holy Spirit was my companion on a daily basis. For some reason, my longtime dream of going to law school resurfaced.

Unlike my prior life decisions, this one was His.

Law school beckoned after a twenty-year career in business. My dream of law school drifted in and out over the years, depending upon what else was going on in my life. However, the cost and time involved made it impossible. Regardless, I continued to pray about it. An unexpected and successful initial public offering, as part of an inadvertent career move meant new resources for me. Law school was finally within reach. I took the admissions test and was accepted to Vanderbilt in 1999. It was a lifelong dream; an answered prayer.

A legal career was my ultimate plan. My expectations were too low. That career would also lead me closer to God. Often, he does it with a wink.

Ask anyone who has had a real encounter with God. Somehow, some way, He makes it all work out for the good, no matter how badly we mess things up.

Many educated people scoff at what they believe are emotional concepts such as faith and the existence of God. They view Christianity as a belief system of simpletons. My legal education strengthened my Christian faith. It provided me with an entirely different way of thinking about God, and an entirely new way to read His Word.

My journey began that early morning in Michigan, which was filled with stress and worry. The rest stop on that road was Vanderbilt Law School. Law school ultimately helped me to understand God's Word.

The professor's job is to destroy the all of the student's preconceptions and rationalizations and force the student to identify every assumption embedded within any assertion. A skilled professor administering the Socratic Method is like a tough drill instructor in an intellectual boot camp. Law students learn to read and reason with excruciating precision. Reading was my passion. However, mine was a "business" reading style; quick and in search of main points and ideas. Law school taught me a new way of reading and a new way of thinking.

You learn to think like a lawyer by reading indecipherable materials. The mental skills required result in a courage of sorts. You acquire the courage to tackle just about any reading material and any problem. There were voluminous and technical materials, which were completely unfamiliar to me. Strange terminology required me to look things up. It required me to read the material again, and again if necessary. The deep and intense reading style is mandatory for any lawyer. In law practice, you read every single word in a document, otherwise you risk rendering bad advice to your client.

Early in my legal career a senior partner told me, "Words are the currency of lawyers. In the practice of law, every word counts." Having practiced for a number of years, it now makes sense to me. The obligations of a party to a multimillion-dollar contract can depend upon a single word. One word can change the entire meaning of a contract. Lawyers choose their words carefully and with precision. Remember President Clinton's[21] grand jury deposition testimony in 1998? When questioned about his relationship with Monica Lewinsky, a young White House intern, he carefully dissected the meaning of the word "is."

His testimony became shorthand in the American lexicon for the absurdity of over-parsing words. But he was right. He wanted clarification as to whether the question referred to the present tense or past tense before he answered it. The answer to the question depended upon what "is" meant.

I graduated in 2002, and commenced my law practice back in my hometown of Houston, Texas. Ironically, things had come full circle. God found me as a young boy in Houston. Now, my new career, my fresh start would happen there. Perhaps God had an agenda different than my own for my legal career. Or, He had his own use for my newly developed legal skills.

Icing on a Heavenly Cake

Ironic, isn't it? Becoming a lawyer only added to my credentials as a wrong side of the tracks Christian. And yet, these skills were perfectly suited to Bible study, which led me to a closer relationship with God.

One night after graduating from law school, I picked up the Bible. In those days I read the Bible regularly, but stayed strictly within the New Testament. It seemed to me that the Old Testament was too old to make much sense. Like many Christians, I simply avoided it. The *gospels*[22] were my main fare, and perhaps the

---

21. President Clinton is a Yale law graduate.
22. Matthew, Mark, Luke, and John are called the *gospels*. The gospel of Jesus Christ is described in each of these New Testament books.

occasional *epistle*[23] written by the apostle Paul. Anything beyond that was too intimidating.

That night, the Bible seemed different to me. This document was no different, at least in terms of difficulty, than anything I had read for the last three years. My law degree simply provided me with the courage to tackle it. I made up my mind to read the Bible, cover-to-cover over the course of the next year. I would read it like a lawyer. If a word or phrase did not make sense, I would read it again and again until it did. Before beginning this Bible study, I said a simple prayer.

My prayer was, *"Father, please help me to understand."*

Opening the Bible to Genesis, my journey commenced. Over the next year, the answer to my prayer manifested itself. The words made sense to me. The Bible emerged as a history of the eternal relationship between God and His followers, an instructional manual, and a description of the people, places, and events that culminated with the life, crucifixion, resurrection, and ascension of Jesus. My Christian growth accelerated beyond anything previously thought possible. I learned who God is. His relationship with mankind became clear to me. His plan for me became clear to me.

The irony is that a law degree isn't necessary for Bible study. It merely provided me with the motivation to begin. It was God's Holy Spirit that gave me the necessary tools.

Convincing Evidence

Despite the difficulties of my life, it's easy to look back now and see God, right there with me. He didn't cause my dad's mental

---

23. *Epistle* means "letter," and Paul wrote these letters to the various new Christian churches and colleagues. Romans, I and II Corinthians, Galatians, Ephesians, Philippians, Colossians, I and II Thessalonians, I and II Timothy, Titus and Philemon. There are also other New Testament epistles, written by other followers of Jesus.

illness. He didn't cause my mom to drink, or her anger. Instead, He took some suboptimal circumstances and turned them into good. My circumstances prevented me from going to law school. Nonetheless, I eventually made it. It was supposed to bring me the things in life that most people want; power, prestige and wealth. God had a better plan. My trust in Him ultimately proved to me that He can be trusted.

Before fully surrendering to God, I struggled mightily with life. The process of living beat the stuffing out of me. My life was filled with mistakes in relationships, career, family, and just about anything else that was important. My stubbornness and pride were ironic because there was nothing to be proud of. When I began to trust Jesus to deal with everything, incredibly good things began to happen to me.

My life is the best evidence for my beliefs.

That may have just been a groan from a reader—someone asking themselves, *"Isn't that a circular proposition? Good things have happened to him because he believes in Jesus. And he believes in Jesus because good things have happened to him."* What keeps this proposition from being circular is the timing of things. To be absolutely precise, my belief came first, before good things began to happen to me. My first leap of faith was that Jesus would take care of me. He did take care of me. My belief came first; the results came later.

My *Christian walk* has been full of stubbed toes and stumbles. My experience is probably the most common among Christ-followers: a struggle with sin, repentance, and forgiveness in an ongoing way as part of my lifelong journey. I prayed the Christian's prayer at an early age, but fell away from my faith soon after. It took years for me to find my way back to Him. The events of my life clearly reveal God's hand, gently leading me. No matter what I did, no matter how badly I acted, He surrounded me.

The more that we trust in Him, the less likely we are to stumble. When we *follow Jesus*, our lives are so radically changed that there is no human explanation for it. The only explanation is that something supernatural has happened to us. The proof in the proverbial pudding is in the eating. The change in our lives is the most convincing evidence of the truth of Christianity. Christianity works. It stands alone in this way among a plethora of religions, psychotherapy, and self-help doctrines. It is the world's biggest belief system because it works.

You may have a similar story. You didn't grow up in idyllic family circumstances. Instead, your life has been filled with pain, abuse, trauma and rage. You've done things that you regret. Do not buy this lie. Don't let the guilt and shame caused by your story prevent you from seeking Him. He's there, right now, waiting. No matter who you are or what you've done, God is waiting for you.

"I'm way past God now," you think. "There is no way He would have anything to do with someone like me."

God loves all of us, no matter what we have done.[24] Jesus didn't hang out with squeaky-clean people. He surrounded himself with the castoffs of Jewish society — the tax collectors, adulterers and sinners. All of these people had one thing in common. They knew they were wrong and they were sorry for it. They believed that only Jesus could make it right. Squeaky-clean Christianity is a myth. We've all sinned. We've all done what we knew was wrong.

You may think that you're not good enough for Christianity. No one is.

That's the point. God loves us anyway. He loves me. He loves you.

---

24. John 3:16.

His plan manifested reveals our own lack of imagination. I went to law school to become a lawyer. God delivered a great deal more. There was to be icing on my heavenly cake. In the end, my law degree led to a better understanding of God and ultimately, my Christian faith.

God takes our hopes and plans and supplements them with His own ingredients, which makes everything work out better than we could have imagined.

Like an eternally patient Parent, He causes everything to come together for good. It often happens when a series of seemingly random events come together and we find our-

It can't be explained away as a coincidence. Instead, it has to be God.

selves in a situation that cannot be explained by mere coincidence. In hindsight, we can see that His hand was leading us to that situation.

It's the only reasonable explanation.

CHAPTER TWO

Opening Arguments

Christian Mythology

G od loves all of us.[25] His message is crystal clear. Nonetheless, God's well-meaning and well-organized emissaries have diluted and distorted this message. Organized Christianity has created barriers, which can prevent non-believers from gaining a true understanding of the faith. This chapter and the next describe some of the mythology surrounding Christian beliefs, as well as the strange-sounding terminology used to describe those beliefs. The purpose is to explain what Christianity is, and more importantly, what it isn't.

There are three myths about Christianity that cause confusion, frustration, and misunderstanding. The first myth is that all

---

25. John 3:16; Romans 5:8 (AMP).

Christians lead happy and blemish-free lives. My voir dire in the preceding chapter should quickly disprove that one.

The second myth is that once you pray the prayer and invite Jesus into your life, all your problems are solved. In other words, after you become a Christian, you won't sin anymore. The implication is that if you do sin, then you aren't really a Christian. This myth causes us to judge high-profile Christians based upon their very public failures. It can cause new Christians to abandon their faith before it has a chance to blossom. Of course, it makes no sense. Christians sin and they have problems. The thing about Christianity is that once you begin to muster up ongoing faith in your daily life, you do begin to move in the direction of a perfect, trouble-free life.

The third myth is that Christianity is about rules and practices; a set of religious doctrines. It isn't. Christianity is about faith in Christ.

Don't Judge the Book by Its Cover

Here's a tip. Don't put a bumper sticker on your car that reads "Christians Aren't Perfect—Just Forgiven." It offends people. You may have noticed one or one with some similar phrase, or an *icthus*[26] on the back of a vehicle as it cuts you off in traffic. Or perhaps they laid on their horn as they passed you, to express their opinion of your driving skills. Frequently, these drivers are preoccupied with something much more important than driving, like texting or eating lunch, or making sure that their eyeliner is properly applied.

Conservative Christian groups condemn homosexuality, premarital sex, and other stuff that mainstream American has

---

26. An *icthus* is a Christian symbol, in the form of a fish. It was originally derived from Greek letters, which formed an acronym of the words "Jesus Christ, Son of God Savior."

convinced itself is okay. As a result, when Christians misbehave (and we all do), non-Christians tend to view us as hypocrites. We read of high-profile Christians who are caught doing things that even non-Christians consider reprehensible. Cults and groups claiming to be Christian do all kinds of horrible things in the name of God.

Some think that Christians should be held to a higher standard. People judge the entire Christian population based upon the public mistakes made by a few high-profile Christians. They pounce on the stories published by a scandal-hungry press and say, "See, I knew that Christians were just a bunch of sanctimonious hypocrites." It's the old "practice what you preach" thing. We believe one thing but do another.

If Christians repent and change, cynics claim that the change was for selfish reasons. They scoff, "Sure, he repented, but only because he got caught. His multi-million-dollar lifestyle was at risk." They shake their heads in disgust that people could be so hypocritical.

Critics close the book on Christianity because they believe that it is the religion of phonies.

Nonetheless, Christians know that like recovering alcoholics who are one drink away from alcoholism, we are one sin away from being sinners. Christian's believe that sin is part of man's DNA.[27] It was imbedded into our genetic structure as a result of our ancestors' original sin. We are constantly at war with it.

Sin comes with being human; it's part of the package.

Paul discusses the issue of Christian sin in his letter to the new Christian group in Rome.[28] He argues that if people sin when they

---

27. Romans 7:20.
28. Romans 6:6.

don't want to, then sin has essentially taken on a life of its own.[29] If you don't want to do wrong, but do it anyway, then something else must be at work.

There are most certainly hypocrites in church, just as there are hypocrites everywhere else. These people use church like others use a country club. They make social contacts. They make business contacts. Going to church makes them feel good about themselves. They have replicated the religious establishment that was created by the Pharisees and legal experts of Jesus' day. Church becomes what they can get out of it, and not in a good way. It is a mistake though, to judge Christianity by the actions of these people. We shouldn't judge a book by its cover.

Although these people may appear to be the cover, they are not the book itself.

Ironically, the people who claim that the Christian sinner is a hypocrite are likely using a double standard as a measure of hypocrisy. If we are honest with ourselves, we realize that we all do things that we know are wrong. If we do something that we know is wrong, we have violated our own standard. If we criticize others for doing something that we have done ourselves, then we have a double standard.

Expecting Christians to do good all of the time makes no more sense than expecting non-Christians to do bad all of the time.

For that matter, the outward appearances of organized Christianity can be deceiving. People grow up going to church every Sunday, with smiling faces and dressed in their Sunday best. Everyone seems so happy, so *blessed*. The testimony of their lives says, *"Be like us and you too will be blessed."* Many Christians don't talk about their past, or their mistakes or transgressions. They are afraid that confessing their past bad acts will somehow

---

29. Romans 7:17.

lead non-Christians to believe that Christianity is illegitimate. So they act as if their lives are perfect. This orchestrated joy can have the opposite effect, especially to outsiders who did not grow up going to church. We watch Christianity from the outside with our noses pressed against the glass. We mistakenly believe that because we have lived such bad lives, we could never fit in with this clean-cut, problem-free group.

Despite appearances, people who grew up going to church have problems of their own. They get used to it. It might even become a chore. They've been doing the same things the same way for so long that they have lost their perspective. Their faith has become static. Faith is supposed to be dynamic.[30]

Although there are plenty of Christians who grew up going to church every Sunday, there are plenty of others like me. These folks have seen and done things that are rarely talked about in church. Name a sin and we have committed it. In fact, if we were all completely honest with one another, we would probably realize that our sin quotient, relatively speaking, is not vastly different from anyone else's.

Every single one of our lives is short of the standard God has set for us, whether we grew up in church or not.[31]

We are all broken. We are all imperfect. We all hurt. We all struggle. It's the way life works.

Before Jesus, mankind struggled mightily to atone for sin. We presented sacrifices to God, with the hope of pleasing Him. We took it further. We decided which sins merited a sacrifice, even though it was God's sole jurisdiction. How can any human decide which sins are worthy of a sacrifice to God and which are not? For that matter, how can we make a sacrifice for each and every sin committed? We can't.

---

30. Faith is discussed in greater detail in Chapter Nine.
31. Romans 3:23 (AMP).

Many people today still have that attitude. They weigh their good deeds against their bad deeds and place their own spiritual values on those deeds. They conclude that they have a credit balance in their spiritual bank accounts. However, Christians know that we are morally bankrupt. We know that quickly after we were born, we began to accrue serious debt. Because everything we have is attributable to God, nothing that we have is legal tender that can be used to repay anything to Him. So it is impossible to ever repay our debt to God.

Without intervention, we are hopelessly lost.[32] We believe that God Himself made a deposit in our account that completely pays the debt. This is where Christianity is unique. Without a savior, how is anyone forgiven? Christianity provides mankind with payment, once and for all, for the sins of mankind. It means that the sin is wiped out forever. God doesn't see it. Another way to say it is that God sees us as perfect, thanks to the interceding perfection of Jesus.

So, the bumper sticker that reads, "Christians Aren't Perfect— Just Forgiven" is a simple acknowledgement of timing. Strictly speaking, we were forgiven before we became Christians. God made the ultimate and final sacrifice Himself. We accept by faith the forgiveness that Jesus' death provided. From God's perspective, thanks to Jesus, this makes us perfect. As a result, God no longer sees our sins. It is as if we have never sinned.

However, a bumper sticker that reads, "I'm Perfect—You Aren't" would really offend people.

No offense.

---

32. Romans 3:24 (AMP).

A Spiritual Get-Rich-Quick Scheme

Christians, in their zeal to follow Jesus' command to share the gospel,[33] can unintentionally value *conversion* quantity over quality. They measure their spiritual success by the numbers. The focus is primarily to convince non-believers to accept Jesus and *get saved*. These evangelists characterize the Christian experience as a *miraculous transformation*. They become so focused on *winning souls for Christ*, that they inadvertently omit the spiritual fine print. They don't tell you that you have to work at your faith.[34]

Typically, at the end of their message, they issue an *invitation* to their audience to pray a prayer and ask *Jesus to come into their hearts*. To be fair, in many cases, that's all it takes. A man prays the prayer and his life instantaneously, permanently, and irreversibly changes.

Still, many new believers expecting the process to be instantaneous are disappointed. To them, the change seems to be only temporary. They still have problems. They continue to struggle with sin. They begin to question the validity of their conversion. They were rushed into making a commitment that they hadn't thought about. They didn't understand the prayer that they prayed. Things haven't worked out as promised so they blame God.

Place your order, drive around to the window and pick up your soul. They were told, "Pray the prayer, God comes into your life, and all your problems are solved. Pray the prayer and God will do the rest." In a get-rich-quick spiritual scheme, these new Christians are told to sit back, enjoy the ride, and be *blessed by God* beyond comprehension. When

Their conversion was more akin to a fast-food experience.

---

33. Mark 16:35.
34. James 1:4.

life's troubles arise, as they inevitably do, these people are disappointed and perhaps embittered.

For many years, I mistakenly thought that after becoming a Christian my sinning would stop, or at least be dramatically reduced. This was based upon a series of bad assumptions that led me to bad logic. My Christian transformation was described as instantaneous. God was supposed to change me, right then and there. The first erroneous assumption was that my participation was not required; therefore, no participation was forthcoming. My second assumption was that continuing to sin after forgiveness proved that my repentance wasn't genuine. These mistaken assumptions led to the conclusion that my conversion was insincere and therefore, illegitimate.

Becoming a Christian does cause a miraculous transformation in people's lives. The Christian conversion is absolutely miraculous. And yet, it may not appear to be very miraculous. If the Creator of the universe reaches out to mankind, then a miracle has occurred. Having the opportunity to have a relationship with Him is nothing short of miraculous. It can be, but does not have to be, instantaneous. Or at least, the effects of the conversion may not be instantaneously visible.

People pray the prayer and put down the heroin needle forever. A person's life can be radically, visibly, and outwardly transformed after they accept Jesus. In other cases, it isn't. Still, in all cases, the instant we invite Jesus to come into our lives—he does. That is miraculous.

The prayer doesn't turn us into robots, though. We still have the power to choose. Anything that happens after the prayer, at least to some extent, depends on us. God will, through His Holy Spirit, work in our lives if we allow it. He's always there, lovingly working. He knows what is best for us. But we can short-circuit that work.

Christianity is about faith in Christ for our salvation, but also faith in Christ for our everyday lives.[35] We make the decision to

---

35. Romans 3:27.

change and then trust God to change us.[36] He accomplishes that change by filling us with the Holy Spirit.[37] If we try to change without fully trusting Him and allowing the Holy Spirit to operate, our lives are sub-optimized. We learn His will through prayer, Bible study, and the guidance of the Holy Spirit. It's as simple as that. The more that we trust Him with our lives, the easier it becomes to do.

As unspiritual as it may sound, an authentic Christian experience is work. You have to work at being a Christian. You have to work at your faith. We work at our faith and we work at obedience to Him. This is not to say that Christian salvation is based on our *works*. It is not.[38] Christians call it being saved by God's *grace*, which we receive through *faith*.[39] At that point, we have secured a place for ourselves in heaven. We've claimed it by believing that Jesus was who he said he was; this is faith. His sacrifice was a free and undeserved gift. That's why we call it *grace*. Yet faith that doesn't result in action isn't really faith.[40] God is ultimately responsible for the change that occurs in true Christians. That said, with human frailties what they are, letting God truly run our lives and giving it all completely to Him, is a daily effort.

Christian growth is a process. It is a lifelong process of growth that occurs through the relinquishment

It means putting eternity into perspective with your remaining time here on earth. It means understanding that since your eternity has been established, any bumps or bruises in this life are minor by comparison.

---

36. Romans 8:9.
37. Id.
38. Ephesians 2:8 (AMP).
39. Id.
40. James 2:17.

of self to God. You ask Jesus to come into your heart, declare yourself to be a Christian, and promise to follow him. The entire act of becoming a Christian takes a few seconds at most. Still, you spend the rest of your life developing this relationship through a daily, if not hourly, step-by-step process. We call it a *faith walk*.[41] You learn to give every single aspect of your life to God. You stumble. And you begin the process again.

Some Christian proselytizers avoid this fine print. The truth is that these folks intended to *lead others to Christ*, but led them only in the general vicinity of Christ. When their new converts realize that they still have problems, they may simply give up and move on to the next thing. This is not to say that these new converts are not Christians and were not miraculously transformed. They were. They were transformed by God into new sinless creatures as a result of their faith in Jesus.[42]

However, as long as these new believers wait on a miraculous tangible experience, they will delay the heavy lifting and hard work that comes with the Christian process. Worse, they may give up hope waiting for that miracle and abandon their faith. Jesus explained a long time ago that this would happen through his parable of the sower and the seed.[43] People can hear about Jesus, but things in this life get in the way of a truly fulfilling spiritual experience.

Christianity is a miraculous transformation. We are all at different stages of that transformation. Some of us approach perfection, but many of us are far from perfect. Growing as a Christian is the process of living by daily faith in God and allowing Him to miraculously transform us.

---

41. 2 Corinthians 5:7 (AMP). The Christian faith walk is discussed in detail in Chapter Nine.
42. Id.
43. Matthew 13:22 (AMP).

Rules, Rituals and Faith Seeds:
The Non-Religion Religion

I was about five years-old. It was a cool autumn day in Houston and one of the few times I remember going to church as a kid. My sister Julie and I sat on a pew near the front, next to our parents and fidgeting. My brother Tommy, being the mature seven year-old that he was, sat a few places away from the family. I was on the aisle, strategically cornered in order to insure that I would behave. We were about four rows back, facing the large stained glass windows of the church. Sunlight filtered through, giving the stained glass an almost neon-like quality. Its beauty was hypnotic.

Julie was drawing a stick figure family on a piece of paper my mom had given her. Tommy was reading the church bulletin, or at least the words that he knew. I stared at the stained glass as it shimmered with light. Music was playing, people were singing, and the preacher said something about *sowing seeds of faith*. I had no idea what he meant. As it turned out, the answer would present itself shortly.

Suddenly, a five-year-old boy's best possible dream came true. Someone handed me a plate. In that plate was money, and lots of it. There were nickels and dimes and pennies, and dollar bills. I couldn't believe my luck. In my hands was a jumble of *faith seeds* in all denominations. I held the basket with one hand and grabbed as much money as the other hand could hold. Just as suddenly, the dream abruptly ended. Mom grabbed the money-holding hand and shook it violently. Pennies and nickels flew everywhere. I heard Julie laughing as Mom pulled me out of the pew. As she dragged me down the carpeted aisle, my feet scraped along behind me. I flailed about, struggling to stay upright and keep up with her.

On that autumn day in church when they passed the plate, I had broken the rules.

You may see Christianity as a set of rules, rituals, and doctrines. There are plenty of rule-based religious systems that are happy to mandate what clothes their adherents should wear, what they should drink, how they should pray, and other similar requirements.

Rules make us feel better when we follow them. They provide consistency and predictability to our worship services. These could be rules about simple matters, such as when to stand, when to sing, and whether its *trespasses* or *debts* in the *Lord's Prayer*.[44] There may be rules about more complicated matters, such as whether we should be baptized.

My mother was mortified at my five-year-old larcenous heart, especially since the larceny had occurred in church. After all, the offering is arguably the most important practice in organized religion. It provides the means by which the church operates. Needless to say, Mom gave me memorable instruction in the etiquette of the collection plate once we got outside. I had violated one of the important rules of that particular denomination. When the plate is passed, we give; we do not receive.

The terms *religion* and *religious* mean the rules and practices that various belief systems use in the execution of their beliefs.

People spend years searching for the right religion. They become shoppers in the Philosophy Supermarket of Life, constantly comparing spiritual products, thumping doctrinal melons, seeking that perfect combination of religious precepts by which they can live. These people are rule-seekers who believe that obedience to those rules will earn them a position in eternity.

Religion, doctrine, and religious practices are not Christianity. They are merely the tools that Christians use to practice and express their faith. It is not a rule-based system. It is a faith-based

---

44. Psalm 23:1-6 (AMP).

system. Faith in Jesus Christ[45] as the Savior of mankind is the only "rule" upon which all Christian denominations are based. Religion is about faith in the rules and rituals. Christianity is about faith in Jesus and a relationship with God.

True Christianity isn't a religion. If you take a lot of comfort in rules, then true Christianity will disappoint you.

This is what separates Christianity from Islam, Judaism, Hinduism, and other world religions. Christianity says that if you believe in Jesus you will go to heaven. World religions, on the other hand, judge a person's likelihood of entering heaven against their adherence to rules. Followers of the world's various religions spend their lives appeasing their god or gods for their sins. There is no real certainty as to one's eternal destiny with these religions. One never knows for sure whether they lived good enough lives or tried hard enough to obey the rules, in order to earn their way into heaven. The harder one tries to obey rules, the harder it becomes. Paul eloquently explains this seeming paradox in his letter to the early Christian church in Rome.[46] We engage in behaviors that we know we shouldn't, but do them anyway.

That said, there are many *denominations* of the Christian faith. All are Christian and believe in fundamental Christian concepts, but they may interpret the finer principles differently. Depending upon the particular denomination, you can certainly find as many rules and rituals as you would like. Most denominations have prayer, an offering, songs of worship, some form of communion, as well as other traditions. They provide comfort to the community of believers, based upon their historical practices. Sometimes though, rituals can have the opposite effect on others.

---

45. The term "Christ" means the Messiah. *See* Chapter Five, "Examining Motive."

46. Romans 7:15 (AMP).

Unfortunately, today churches have become a pure reflection of their membership. We hang out with people who are like us. It is a sad fact that most churches in middle-class America have incredibly homogenous congregations. We worship with people that look like us and dress like us. Church members have similar educations and backgrounds. It's not exactly an inviting situation to people who don't. If you are not a Christian, you may be intimidated by the appearances of organized Christianity.

Chances are you've been to church. If you are married, you probably got married in a church. You may have gone to a funeral service at a church (or a funeral home that looked a lot like a church) in which a minister spoke about that person's life (and perhaps the afterlife). You may have spent much of your childhood in church. Or perhaps for you, church-going is sporadic. You may have gone regularly early in life, only to find more recreational uses for your Sunday mornings. You may have gotten your feelings hurt and stopped going. Possibly, you didn't get much out of it and merely faded away from it over time. Maybe you feel a bit guilty because you don't go to church now.

Suppose that you are a person who has rarely or never gone to church. You are searching for meaning in your life. You've driven past a particular church dozens of times on Sundays. People walk into the building, looking happy and healthy. You work up the courage to give it a try and visit one Sunday.

You walk in and someone hands you what appears to be a program. Although they smile, they don't know you and don't seem to want to know you. Their bearing seems to say, *"Next; keep it moving."* Rather than salvation, it's about logistics. You awkwardly walk down the aisle and find a place to sit. Unfamiliar music is playing. Everyone seems to be looking at you, and you just know they know how bad your life has been. The church has certain protocols — people stand in unison, pray some doctrinal prayer, and sing particular songs. Nothing is familiar to you.

Worse, you feel that you are the only person in the room who doesn't understand the drill.

All you want is to get through the next hour, so that you can get home and watch the game.

Even if you have grown up in church, the religious aspects of it can distract you from the real point of it all. Suppose that you have grown up in a church that is a conservative, Bible belt- leaning group. Its members go to church three times per week, and everyone dresses in their Sunday best. Among its unwritten doctrines is the idea that musical accompaniment during a church service is anti-Biblical.

One of your close friends invites you to visit her church. The church's unwritten doctrine is that we must accept people exactly as they are. We don't judge anyone, no matter what they've done. We leave the judging to God.

When you walk into the sanctuary, there is a full-blown rock band, with electric guitars, a drum kit, and all the equipment. The singer has a Goth look, eyeliner and all, and moves onstage in a spastic rhythm, not unlike one might see in a punk rock group. The band is playing rock gospel songs. Everyone has their hands up in the air and is moving in a charismatic way to the beat of the music. Even if you are able to get past the doctrine, it's just going to feel uncomfortable.

No one intentionally sets out to make visitors to their church feel this way. It just happens.

We become overly preoccupied with the protocol. All of it can make outsiders feel uncomfortable. The real problem is that this discomfort causes people to avoid church. It has nothing to do with God. They visit and simply decide it's just too awkward. They don't go back. If we get so caught up in all of it that we forget about the Object of our worship, it becomes window dressing. The façade of the building becomes more important than the One who dwells within it.

Remember: the object of Christian faith is Jesus. Faith in what he accomplished on the cross at Calvary is the central component of Christianity. Christians believe that Jesus was crucified as the ultimate payment for our sins. That payment assures our eternity in heaven. That eternal assurance enables us to live in obedience and ongoing faith in God's divine care. Faith means, every single day, giving every single aspect of our lives to Him. The real point of all of it is a meaningful relationship with God, thanks to Jesus.

The basic ideas of Christianity are simple. Much of the rest of it that has been added along the way isn't Biblical doctrine. It's the manifestation of man's interpretation of that doctrine. So whether it's *debts* or *trespasses* to you, or whether you sing a particular hymn, the core belief system in who God is, who Jesus was, what he did, and why and how you respond to it is all that matters.

To my brothers and sisters who grew up in church, the next time you see a visitor; make them feel welcome in your church. Remember that the first Christian church was composed of fishermen and tax collectors, the outcasts of society, as well as all kinds of sinners. Jesus accepted everyone; everyone was welcome.

Remember Jesus' words. It's all about loving God and loving man.[47] Think back to the time you were the visitor. Look for people who might be from the wrong side of the spiritual tracks. Help them find the right classroom. Explain the drill; the rituals, and the meaning behind the rituals. Tell them where the Bibles are. Helping someone who has come to church searching for meaning is one of the most important things we can do as Christians.

To those of you who didn't grow up in church, if you visit and don't know whether to stand or kneel, look for a friendly face and ask. Don't let the window dressing intimidate you. You might be surprised to find that they are glad you are there.

God is glad you are there.

---

47. Matthew 22:37-39 (AMP).

CHAPTER THREE

Jury Instructions

Christianspeak

My eight-year-old daughter Meredith came home from school not long ago, gave me a hug and said, "Dad, you rock." I earned this accolade by taking her and her sister Lauren to the Skate Center the weekend before. If you haven't been to a roller skating rink in a while, suffice it to say that with the disco balls, laser lights, and pop music, skating to an eight-year-old is pretty cool stuff. In the language of kids, she was saying that I was a good dad.

At a business meeting recently, one of my colleagues conspiratorially pulled me aside and invited me to play a game she called "Buzzword Bingo." The rules of the game were simple: (1) we played during the meeting; (2) players were to keep tally of the number and type of business jargon that non-players express; (3) my colleague and I were the only players; (4) no one other than the players would know that the game was being played; and (5) the winner was the unknowing participant who used the most buzzwords. The winner is pronounced the Master of Buzzwords (behind their back, of course). To the other unknowing meeting participants, it appeared to be an ordinary business meeting like any other, but they were all part of the game. Okay, I admit it's not very nice, but it made for an interesting meeting.

In that particular meeting, the winner used the terms "at the end of the day," "the bottom line is," and "we need to get to a granular level" in a single sentence! He used business jargon to such an extreme that by the end of it, my head was spinning. The speaker was a marketing person. Everyone in the room in marketing, with their common set of beliefs and information, knew what he was talking about. But the speaker left the lawyers and accountants completely befuddled.

Lawyers use Latin. Unfortunately, Latin is a *dead* language. No culture or country uses it anymore. Lawyers use it anyway. Perhaps it's because Latin is an artifact of a bygone era and old habits die hard. In law school, Latin is ubiquitous. I was confounded by phrases like *res ipsa loquitur* ("the thing speaks for itself," meaning in a negligence action the fact that the incident occurred is evidence in and of itself of negligence) and *prima facie* ("at first sight," meaning something that strongly indicates a conclusion but does not prove it). Ordinary English terms are used in extraordinary ways that are guaranteed to confuse the new law student. This confusion has its own moniker. Law students accuse law professors of *hiding the ball*.[48]

---

48. *"Hiding the ball"* refers to the alleged law professor practice of deliberately creating confusion, by asking questions only and avoiding any declarative statements regarding the state of the law. Unlike undergraduate studies, where professors spend much class time explaining the subject, in law school professors are tasked with teaching students the legal reasoning process. They do this through the *Socratic Method*. It is then up to the student to determine the state of the law, using the legal reasoning process.

Legalese can befuddle those unfamiliar with it. To lawyers, the language of the law makes great sense and enhances communication. This terminology is shorthand for deeper legal concepts. Law professors use it to efficiently convey complex doctrine. At the same time, it confuses, confounds, and fascinates most people. This is one of the reasons that jury instructions are so important. They define the terminology. Otherwise, the lawyers would hopelessly confuse the jury.

Every group has its own unique language. In most cases, the language acts as shorthand. It makes communications more efficient. Simple terms can be used to express complex ideas. They can actually impede communications. Linguistic shorthand is often confusing to outsiders. Over time, jargon becomes so tenuously related to the original concept that its meaning is lost.

Buzzwords can improve communications efficiency. But if we're not careful, they can have the opposite effect.

Washed in What?

A prediction: If aliens really can see our television broadcasts into the universe, then those on the other side of the galaxy will likely attack Earth in about ten thousand years. That is how much time it takes for our television broadcasts to reach them, at the speed of light. They will watch our programming and become convinced that Earthlings are weak, and that the planet is in serious need of a clean-up. Cable television (or satellite dish, if you prefer) has provided us with hundreds of choices in the new millennium, but somehow there are still only about two or three decent program choices at any given time.

I was channel-surfing one night not too long ago, trying to find a decent show among the hundreds of channels of jewelry infomercials, exercise programs, and sitcoms that were designed to appeal to a demographic that I'm not sure actually exists. Searching for meaningful programming in vain, I stumbled across a Christian televangelist. I landed on his show at precisely the moment that he was beseeching his viewing audience to *accept Christ.* He was nattily dressed in a tailored suit, with what was arguably the most perfect haircut I had ever seen. At the bottom of the screen a call-in number was displayed, along with a message imploring viewers to call and talk with one of the show's *prayer counselors.* The televangelist looked heavenward and then at the camera. He continued, imploring his viewing audience to *trust Jesus, accept Christ and be washed in the blood of Jesus.*

I'm not going to take any cheap shots.

There will be no commentary on the merits of televangelism or the sincerity of the televangelist's beliefs. There are all kinds of paths to God and perhaps television is one of them. Nonetheless, his credibility did not improve when he added requests for *love offerings* and *sowing the seeds of faith* to his message. In other words, "Give me your money and I'll make sure God's work is done with it." Not to mention, "God wants me to be very well-dressed and coiffed." Some might consider that a conflict of interest. Regardless, he deserves the benefit of the doubt. Televangelists have been joke fodder for late-night talk show hosts for years, and unfortunately have had more than their share of scandals. Until proven otherwise, all of these folks are my brothers and sisters.

He was speaking in code, a secret language that only people with the key could understand.

Nonetheless, I was struck by a thought: "*His audience probably has no clue what he is talking about.*" *Accepting Christ* is a term that

56

would likely make no sense to anyone but Christians. *Washed in the blood of Christ* sounds downright macabre. How can anyone *trust Jesus* when they've never met him, and especially when he died a couple of thousand years before they were born? I'm sure the televangelist knew what the terms meant. I'm equally sure that his non-Christian audience wouldn't have a clue of what most of it meant. The exuberant televangelist probably had no clue that these folks didn't have a clue.

Christians believe that we have an obligation to explain to others who we believe Jesus to be and what he accomplished on the cross.[49] Each piece of the message requires deep thought and clear communication. But in our enthusiasm to share the story of Jesus, we pass it along without being able to explain the basis of our faith. We use terms and concepts that don't make sense to people who have never been through the Christian experience.

Although the message is simple, it has incredibly complex ramifications.

Christianspeak is the shorthand terminology that Christians use to describe complex ideas. Christianspeak is terminology used by Christians, for Christians and generally, only Christians can understand it. Words and phrases like *saved, Christ follower, faith, grace,* and many others are simple terms that describe vast and life-changing concepts. It's not meant to be a secret code. To Christians, Christianspeak makes perfect sense.

Christianspeak makes sense to those who have experienced the ideas it describes; it is meaningless to those who haven't. The basic ideas in Christianity — that God became a human, brought the dead back to life and walked on water, was crucified and then

Any discussion on eternity is going to be pretty deep. Using jargon to explain it doesn't help.

---

49. 2 Timothy 4:2.

himself came back to life — are incredible. It's hard to get our intellectual arms around them. Christianspeak doesn't help. It can simply confuse.

Would-be converts shake their heads and walk away because they see it all as illogical and emotion-based. They decide that anything so complicated and mystical isn't worth the trouble. In an irony reminiscent of the Tower of Babel,[50] these people end up more confused, suspicious, and cynical than ever before. They would have been better off without such Christian enlightenment.

Christians use these terms without realizing that others might not understand their meaning. As a result, evangelism can have unintended consequences. To non-Christians, it's confusing and circular.

After I rededicated my life to God, I found myself speaking in Christianspeak frequently. I used terms like *saved*[51] (or *radically saved*), *salvation*, *believer* and others, as well as words like *sanctification* and *justification*. In some cases, I understood the meaning of the terminology. In other cases, I adopted the term without understand its meaning. That's true about a lot of things in life. We use terminology we don't understand. We describe concepts that we haven't studied. We pass along information without scrutinizing it.

It is an *ex post*, or after the fact language. Until you've been in a new car, it's hard to appreciate the term "new car smell." Until you've encountered Christ, it's hard to understand much of Christian terminology. To

The irony of Christianspeak is that we hear it long before we can understand it.

---

50. Genesis 11:4. In this story, mankind had built a large tower as a sort of monument to itself. God, in response, caused their language to be confused, which resulted in mankind scattering all over the earth.
51. Acts 4:12.

understand who Christ is, you must experience him for yourself. Unless you have been through the process, Christianspeak might as well be an ancient, dead language.

Born Again Christians

Consider the term *born again Christian*. President Jimmy Carter placed it into the American lexicon when he mentioned in an interview that he had been *born again*. His disclosure came at a time when Christianity, especially *fundamentalist* Christianity[52] was thought by many to be a religion of backwoods simpletons. People assumed that the term referred to a particular type of Christian, and especially the less sophisticated portion of the Christian population. Born again Christians were those poison-drinking, snake-handling, farm-dwelling hillbillies who built ideologies around snippets of obscure scripture. The rest of us "normal" Christians smiled and were glad we weren't one of them.

Carter, with a degree in physics from the United States Naval Academy, certainly caused people to rethink this Christian stereotype. He was educated and articulate and obviously sincere in his beliefs. And he certainly paved the way for a renaissance in professing presidential believers. At the same time, his confession of faith was misinterpreted by the media and much of mainstream America.

There is a problem with the "born again" stereotype. It assumes that these self-professed born again Christians coined the

---

52. *"Fundamentalism"* is a term used to describe Christians who believe in the literal accuracy of the Bible and of the events contained in the Bible, such as the virgin birth and the physical resurrection of Jesus. The fundamentalist movement was a response to increasing liberalism and relativism, which challenged the validity of some of these precepts.

term, to set themselves apart from the rest of Christianity. The truth is that Jesus, the founder of Christianity, coined the term.[53] He used it to describe the process by which we are conformed to God. This means that it applies to all Christians, whether we like it or not.

Jesus taught in parables and metaphors, using real world examples of things that anyone could understand. One day, he was teaching and Nicodemus, one of the leaders of the Jewish religious establishment listened. Nicodemus asked Jesus what was required in order to achieve true salvation with God.[54] The establishment was very rule-oriented and adhered strictly to *Mosaic Law*,[55] as described in the Old Testament. Jesus knew that their focus on the law distracted from the real business of faith. Nicodemus was well-educated in the law and conversant on the nuances and intricacies of it. But this vast knowledge must have left him feeling unfulfilled.

Nicodemus believed that we earn our way into heaven by practicing an intricate regimen of religious rituals. He was so caught up in his own religious trees that he couldn't see the faith forest. He wanted to know what could make him truly right with God. He turned to Jesus for the answer.[56]

Jesus replied, "Very truly I tell you, no one can see the kingdom of God unless they are born again." [57]

Jesus used the term as a metaphor for the Christian conversion experience. To be a Christian, you have to be born again. If you are not born again, you are not a Christian. Nicodemus

---

53. John 3:3.

54. John 3:2.

55. *"Mosaic Law"* refers to the Old Testament laws as described in Genesis, Exodus, Leviticus, and Deuteronomy. If you've never read them, take a quick look through them. You'll be amazed at the intricate detail found in these laws, intended to deal with a wide variety of situations in life.

56. John 3:4.

57. John 3:3.

was perplexed, and possibly shocked. He responded that Jesus couldn't possibly be talking about re-entering his mother's womb.[58] He was right. Jesus meant that in order to make it to heaven, we have to start from spiritual scratch. We must have so profound a spiritual experience that its result can only be compared to a second birth.

This rebirth is caused by the influence of the Holy Spirit, which so changes us that there is no doubt that it came from God.[59] Jesus described the transformation that occurs in one's entire being. To those who have been through it, or are going through it, a rebirth metaphor hits the nail on the head.

All Christians are born again. This transformation is an essential part of our Christianity. [60]

Once a person commits to this change and allows God to handle it, their life is so transformed, so radically changed, that it is like starting life over again, from scratch. They truly become new people. The single most important thing any Christian can point to as evidence for the reality of the Christian experience is their personal transformation—what they were like before and what they are like after encountering the notion of Jesus.

We simply can't help it. God begins to change all of us once we accept Jesus into our lives in such a way that the only way to describe it is as being born again. When we accept Jesus' doctrine of salvation, we become God's instruments through the work of the

Our changed lives are evidence of our faith.

Holy Spirit.[61] God's Holy Spirit so radically changes us that the

---

58. John 3:4.
59. Id.
60. John 3:21.
61. Romans 8:4.

only adequate way of describing this transformation is as being born again.

Saul of Tarsus

He was a well-educated Jew from Tarsus, in an area that is now Turkey. He was a Pharisee; the most Jewish among Jewish sects, that honored a strict set of religious beliefs and practices. He hated Christians. His holy work was to destroy Christianity and he was a zealous persecutor of the infant Christian church.[62] Traveling from house to house with armed guards, he mercilessly dragged Christians from their homes and put them in jail.[63] He held the coats of those who stoned Stephen, the first Christian martyr.[64] He declared that killing Stephen was a good thing.[65]

His name was Saul.

Why did Saul hate Christians? He viewed them as heretics. They believed that Jesus was the son of God. This was heresy. Worse, Jesus had criticized the Pharisees[66] for not practicing what they preached. The criticism did not sit well. This Jesus fellow needed to be dealt with. After he was crucified, they believed the problem was solved. Kill the leader and his flock will scatter. They were deeply mistaken. Strangely, Jesus' crucifixion created a bigger problem. The Christian movement grew. In a vain attempt to stop it, the establishment began widespread persecution of Christians. Saul was one of the chief persecutors.

---

62. Galatians 1:13.
63. Acts 8:3.
64. Acts 7:5-8.
65. Acts 8:1.
66. Matthew 23:15 (AMP).

One day, after Jesus had been crucified, something miraculous happened. Saul encountered the living Christ. While traveling to Damascus on a mission to persecute Jesus' followers,[67] he was struck down by a bright light coming from heaven.[68] As he lay on the ground, blinded, an unseen person asked Saul why he was persecuting him.[69] It was Jesus.[70] He healed Saul and instructed him to go into the city.[71] Saul's life was changed forever. From that moment on, he followed Jesus. Christian tradition suggests that he changed his name to Paul, to memorialize his life change. A man who shortly before had dedicated his life to killing Christians became one.

Paul arguably had more impact than any other early Christian, including Jesus' direct disciples. A very large part of the New Testament consists of the writings of Paul. These letters reflect his guidance and advice to the various newly formed churches. He began to spread the gospel to Gentiles and throughout the world. The first Christians were Jews. It was only after Paul began his ministry that the gospel was preached to the Gentiles.

His letters also describe the incredible hardships that he faced. Traveling in those days presented great difficulty and risk. Paul somehow made his way through what is now the Middle East and part of the continent of Europe preaching the gospel. He encountered numerous threats including shipwrecks, imprisonment, beatings, and a deadly snakebite. His rock-solid consistency and dedication to preaching the gospel of Jesus Christ is strong testimony to the fact that he absolutely believed it. His dedication is more impressive when you realize that Paul never met Jesus, at least in the physical sense.

---

67. Acts 9:1-3.

68. Id.

69. Id.

70. Id.

71. Id.

Why did Saul become Paul? Why did his life change so radically that it could only be described as a rebirth? How could a

Nothing temporary, such as a brain concussion, too much wine, or an encounter with aliens can adequately explain the permanent change in Paul's perspective.

man become a follower of someone he had never met? There is no easy explanation for this radical change. Further, after his encounter with Jesus on the road to Damascus, Paul was willing to risk his life in order to tell about it. Something changed him in such a way that it can only be described as being born again.

Christians believe that the Holy Spirit lives within us. [72] He is an incredible change agent from God, and is in fact, God Himself. The Holy Spirit allows us to see things differently, think differently, and believe differently than before we became Christians. If we listen to Him carefully enough and follow His will for us, He will effect dramatic change in our lives for the better. Allowing ourselves to be filled with God's Spirit, enables us to keep the slate clean. When we mess it up, He cleans it anyway. Knowing that, we can relax and focus on what is really important—knowing and fulfilling His will. This is what being a *born again Christian* means, and it is powerful evidence of the effect of our faith in Jesus.

It happened to Paul. His sins were forgiven and he was filled with the very spirit of God. His writings tell us all about it. Jesus taught that it had to happen before anyone could make it into heaven. Paul, as God's first witness, described with exquisite detail what it meant to be born again.

All true Christians are born again. Although we may be at different places in our Christian journey, the more that we trust in the assurances of His salvation, listen to the Holy Spirit, and

---

72. John 14:26 (AMP). The Holy Spirit is discussed in detail in Chapter Eight.

strive to obey His will, the more quickly God can create the change in our lives. Every Christian begins this transformation. Some Christians *backslide*, which means that for a period of time, they revert to their old ways. But every Christian is changed. The most powerful evidence of the validity of Christianity is the changed life.

There is a moral to the Christianspeak story. Whether you are on the giving or receiving end of it, for the terminology to be valid, it must have a biblical origin. Make sure that there is scriptural support for anything purporting to describe Christian beliefs. Make sure that you understand it before using it.

Anything else is hearsay evidence, guaranteed to raise an objection by opposing counsel.

CHAPTER FOUR

The Case for Christianity

The Aquarium

Once upon a time, there was a good and loving man who owned a huge aquarium filled with all kinds of tropical fish. He built the aquarium himself, with the very best materials. It was perfect. He maintained the aquarium in pristine condition. He made sure that the pump and aerator worked. It had everything that the fish could want; food, water, rocks, plants and sunken pirate ships.

The man cared deeply about his fish. He personally selected each fish. He spent countless hours admiring them and their environment. Regardless, the fish didn't reciprocate. They did not do what was right. Instead, they did whatever they felt like doing. They fought over food, although there was plenty of it. They destroyed the plants. They acted selfishly and badly, and killed each other when it was expedient. The aquarium became a violent mess.

For many years, the man tried to stop it. He separated the swordtails from the zebra danios. He added more food, with the hope that they would stop fighting over it. But there wasn't anything that worked. The man watched sadly as the fish destroyed themselves.

The man could have simply gotten rid of all of the fish and started over. But he didn't want to them to die. Instead, he believed in them and hoped that they somehow would understand and change. And yet, the nastiness was simply part of their nature. The fish either couldn't or wouldn't see it.

One day, something startling happened. The man became a fish. He gave up his own comfortable and safe environment and went to live with his fish in the aquarium. He did it because he realized that the only way to truly communicate with these fish was to become one of them. The man clearly loved the fish a great deal to be willing to make that sacrifice.

Here's the thing. The fish didn't even realize it had happened. After all, he was one of them. He looked like them. But he was different than them. He was a man who became a fish. His perspective was different. Because he had cared for them and provided for them all those years, he knew what was best for them. He was kind and loving and helped the other fish. By living with them, the man also set an example of how fish were meant to behave.

The fish didn't appreciate the man. They didn't understand that they owed their lives to him. They didn't understand his true nature and the nature of their relationship with him. They just thought he was a strange, crazy fish.

And because their nature was to hate, they killed him.

You've probably realized that this story is a metaphor for God's relationship with man. Here the metaphor breaks down. These fish will never realize that the man was more than another fish. They won't know that they are, in reality, loved and cared for by him; they will never begin to understand his character. They are so caught up in their day-to-day fish lives that they miss the most important thing. The man loves them and wants to take care of them. Of course, the metaphor breaks down because unlike the fish, we humans know and appreciate what God did for us.

Then again, perhaps the metaphor doesn't break down at all.

The Power to Choose

You can read the Bible cover-to-cover, and you will not find a single instance of God forcing anyone into anything. He could, but he doesn't. Instead, God created mankind with the power to choose. He has given each of us the power to choose. Every single day of our lives, we have the power to choose things that are consistent with His will, or those that aren't.

God could have saved himself a lot of heartache if He had made us differently and without the power to choose. However, we would have been mere robots; perhaps sinless, but robots nonetheless. How gratifying could that be to a Supreme Creator? It would be like the relationship between a car collector and his prized car. He polishes and maintains the car. The car goes where the collector steers it. It speeds up when he presses the accelerator. It slows down when he presses the brake. The collector loves the car, but the car cannot love him back.

Having a relationship with beings that can choose, even those who choose unwisely, is infinitely more interesting than with automatons that do what you program them to do. The very thing that makes us uniquely human is the thing that allows us to choose to love God. We can disagree with Him, rebel against Him, or even curse Him. He has given us free will, and that gift is completely unconditional with no strings attached. Each and every day we can choose to dedicate that day for His purposes, our own purposes, or some other purpose. We can listen to His guidance or we can ignore it.

We do things that we know are against His will. We rebel against Him. Since the very beginning, man has struggled with obedience to God. God instructed Adam and Eve to stay away from a certain tree in Eden.[73] They didn't. Ever since then, mankind has to some extent or another been in rebellion toward God.

It would seem crazy to ignore the Creator of the universe or argue with Him. But we do it all of the time.

The book of Genesis describes the first sin.[74] The story is great insight into how sin operates in all of our lives. Everything was new and good. God had just created the heavens and the earth. He created a man and a woman. He gave them all that they needed and a beautiful place to live. Say "Garden of Eden," and you don't have to say anything else.

For Adam and Eve, it wasn't enough. With a little prodding from the snake, they did what God had told them not to do. They ate the fruit. You know the rest. From then on, mankind struggled with everything. Their descendants struggled to eke out an existence, tried to find a homeland, and fought with each other. They started with a perfect relationship with the Creator of the universe and ended up sifting through the dumpster for subsistence.

The greatest believers of the Bible argued with God. Moses, one of the founding fathers of our faith, argued with God about almost everything. His biography in the book of Exodus suggests that God saved him for a special purpose. The Jews had been held as slaves in Egypt for many years. Moses started out life in a reed basket floating down the Nile, only to end up living in splendor and luxury as the Egyptian Pharaoh's adoptive son.[75]

---

73. Genesis 2 :17.

74. Genesis 3:11.

75. Exodus 2:4.

At that time, the Pharaoh ordered that all Jewish male babies be thrown into the Nile. Moses' mother waited as long as she could and finally put him in the river in the basket. He was rescued from the Nile by one of the Pharaoh's daughters.[76] Baby Moses should have drowned but instead became the adopted son of the Pharaoh! He grew into a strong young man. As the Pharaoh's son, Moses had wealth and power beyond imagination. Then one day, he lost everything. He killed an Egyptian, arguably for a good purpose — the defense of a fellow Israelite.[77] He then fled Egypt and spent many years as a nomad, living in the desert.

Moses spent most of his life in exile. He surely had moments in which he longed for the old days, praying to God to do something about his dismal situation. Suddenly, his prayers were answered.[78] The answer was delivered personally by God Himself, in the form of a burning bush.[79] God told Moses to deliver His chosen people from the Pharaoh.[80] God instructed Moses to confront Pharaoh and lead the Israelites out of captivity. This was Moses' big chance. He had marching orders from God. God wanted Moses to talk to the Pharaoh. Instead, he argued with God about whether he was the right person to carry them out.[81] He did everything he could to talk God out of it. Moses argued that he was not a great man.[82] He argued that he was not a great speaker.[83] He begged God to send someone else.[84]

---

76. Exodus 2:10.
77. Exodus 2 :15.
78. Exodus 3 :2.
79. Exodus 3:10.
80. Id.
81. Exodus 3:11
82. Id.
83. Exodus 4:10.
84. Exodus 4:13.

Moses was understandably afraid. Presumably, the Pharaoh would have heard that his adoptive son and now fugitive murderer, was actually a Jew. At the same time, it's hard to imagine a situation where it would be crazier to refuse God. Moses was clearly on the side of right. The Israelites were being held captive by the Pharaoh. The Creator of the universe was on his side. God even provided Moses with impressive equipment, just in case the Pharaoh or the Israelites didn't believe them, or if Pharaoh's magicians tried to minimize God — a walking stick that turned into a live snake and back again.[85] He gave Moses the ability to instantly inflict a disease on his own hand and cure it just as instantly.[86] He gave Moses the ability to turn the Nile River into blood.[87] All of it was guaranteed to make the Pharaoh's well-fed and highly paid magicians look like amateurs.

Regardless, Moses chose to refuse and God allowed him to refuse. He didn't turn Moses into a fat, croaking frog and say, "Let me know when you change your mind." He didn't take away Moses' free will and make him do it. Moses' brother Aaron did it instead.[88]

One of the best examples of bad choices in the Old Testament is King David. David is described as one of God's most faithful servants.[89] He knew God intimately. As a young man, he started out life as a hero.[90] He had trusted in God when he took on Goliath, against all odds. He became the king of Israel, thanks to God. But even after God had incredibly blessed him, David

85. Exodus 4 :2-8.
86. Exodus 4:6–7.
87. Exodus 4:9.
88. Exodus 4:1.
89. 1 Samuel 13 :14 (AMP).
90. *See* Chapter Five, "The Young Shepherd."

made very bad choices. He found himself in a downward spiral of sinful behavior.

David committed adultery with Bathsheba, the wife of one of his trusted commanders, Uriah the Hittite.[91] She became pregnant.[92] In order cover it up, David sent Uriah to the front lines of battle, where he was sure to be killed.[93] It's hard to imagine how a man who was one of God's special and chosen people could make such bad choices. It's harder to imagine how he could ever recover, in terms of his relationship with God.

We all make bad choices. God asks us to do things. The request might be inaudible, but He impresses it upon our hearts through His Word and the influence of the Holy Spirit. We can say, "No thanks." God allows us to do whatever we want. He will not interfere with our power to choose. He could call down to us from heaven, barking orders and admonitions. We would all be terrified and scurry to do His bidding. He won't do it. Instead, He allows us to make our own decisions about everything, including whether or not we want to have a relationship with Him.

If I were the aquarium owner, it would be a fairly simple matter to stick my hand into the tank and terrorize the fish into action. I'd flush a couple of them down the toilet and then ask the rest, "Are you ready to play ball with me now?" How gratifying would that be, except to an evil mind? Our God is a loving God, and He wants only one thing from us.

He wants us to choose to have a relationship with Him.

---

91. 2 Samuel 11:3 (AMP).
92. 2 Samuel 11:15 (AMP).
93. Id.

The Sin Problem and Winning an Unwinnable Game

Because we can choose, we can choose to sin. Sin means that a person exists in rebellion, instead of in harmony with God's will.[94] Sin means we choose to live for our own ends and for our own purposes, rather than living for Him.

God doesn't take away our power to choose. We are free to make bad choices.

A permissive god who looked the other way when man sinned would hardly be a worthy god. A god who overlooked small sins but punished big sins would be equally flawed. A god with that nature would be like a bad king, handing down imperfect law to his subjects on a whim. God must hold all of us accountable for our sins.

A just God cannot tolerate sin. He can't simply overlook sin. It would make Him unjust.

Everyone sins. Even the people we think of today as *saints* did all kinds of bad things. Jesus' followers turned their backs on him. The people who knew him the best abandoned him. They had lived with him and witnessed his incredible miracles. They knew who he was. But when he was arrested, they scattered.[95] They turned their backs on him. When he was beaten and whipped, no one defended him. Peter, the rock of the early church, denied that he even knew Jesus, three times.[96] Wouldn't it be great to read a gospel account of any of Jesus' followers' arrested for speaking up in his defense? There is no mention of anyone trying to stop any of it.

---

94. There are numerous scriptures that explain this idea, e.g. Hebrews 5:14; Matthew 5:48; James 4:17.

95. Mark 14:50.

96. Matthew 26:75 (AMP).

Things haven't changed much. Everyone sins. We do what we know we shouldn't. We still turn our backs on God, every day, especially when it's convenient. It's what humans do. It's not right, but it's what we do. Jesus is the only human who did not sin.[97]

In Old Testament days, forgiveness from God was serious stuff. Before Jesus, men spent countless hours in prayer, ritual, and sacrifice trying to right their wrong condition with God. They worked as hard as they could at it.

Today, many people don't take God seriously. We have become numb to our sinful condition. Each of us has chosen to live for ourselves, rather than for Him. Some things we simply know are bad for us. We do them anyway. We eat too much, we drink too much, and we spend too much money on things we shouldn't. Other things are a bit more subtle. We rationalize them. *"After all, I'm not hurting anyone. No one will ever know."* We self-justify our way through life because we think, *"I'm a good person. I try to do good things. I do more good things than bad things."* Conspicuously absent from this analysis is the God component.

We are confident that we are winning the game, although at times by only a slight margin. However, this perspective contains a flawed assumption. It assumes that we start life with a net-zero balance. Consider the alternative. Assume that everything you are and have comes from God. You can quickly see that you begin life with a deficit balance. You owe God from the beginning. And the debt is so great that you can

We weigh our good deeds against our bad deeds and conclude that we are good people. We view life as having a giant and eternal scoreboard.

never pay Him back. The conclusion that anyone is a good person then becomes less certain.

---

97. 2 Corinthians 5:21 (AMP); Hebrews 4:15 (AMP); 1 Peter 2:22 (AMP).

Even without a scoreboard, most of us know where we stand. We've spent much more time serving ourselves than serving others, or God. We have done more hurtful things than helpful things. If we are honest with ourselves, we will realize that we are so far behind that we can never catch up. God gave us life. God gave us the tools to achieve whatever success we have. So, even if we give Him our entire lives from day one, the best we can ever do is tie the game. The best we can do is break even.

The only way to win the game is with outside help.

A Different Kind of God

Throughout history, man has searched for and worshipped gods. We do everything we can think of to appease these gods. Generally, we look for a god when we need something. Then, when we get what we need, it's business as usual.

Ancient belief systems prescribed certain offerings and sacrifices, depending upon the particular problem one faced. Man did everything possible to try and earn a favored place in the afterlife. There was a god for just about any problem that one faced. If you were Greek and your problems involved love, you consulted with Aphrodite. Problems on the high seas? Talk with Poseidon. If you had issues requiring executive decision making, you dealt with Zeus, king of the gods. Regardless of whom you were imploring, you had better bring a goat or some other acceptable sacrifice.

Sooner or later, you had to kill another goat.

Rather than waiting for us to come to Him, He came to us. He claimed to be God's son, sent to earth for a very specific purpose. He showed us how to live; a living example. Rather than demanding

Jesus showed mankind that God was a different kind of god.

sacrifice and worship, He instead offered a gift of eternal life in heaven.

If Jesus and God are the same, then you can't get to heaven unless Jesus is part of the equation. It means that you can't get to heaven by counting up your good deeds. It made many people angry. Christian salvation is a black or white idea in a relativistic world filled with shades of grey.

Simple Christianity

The Bible's story line is surprisingly simple. God created mankind and provided an idyllic existence. He knew what was best for us. We thought we knew better. From the very beginning in Genesis, we disobeyed God and were separated from Him. We traded Eden for rebellion and ultimately, captivity. God forgave us and delivered us nonetheless. We continued to disobey Him. He continued to forgive us. This betrayal/forgiveness cycle continued for thousands of years until God sent Jesus to deliver us once and for all.

The basic premise of Christianity is so simple that a child can understand it. And yet, like the layers of an onion, each layer of Christian faith yields an ever-increasing comprehension of God and His work in our lives. We spend a lifetime learning more and more about God.

The essence of Christian faith is that: (1) Man is sinful[98] and sin requires restitution;[99] (2) God became a man, called Jesus;[100] (3) Jesus lived a sinless life, but was crucified nonetheless[101] and

---

98. Romans 3:23 (AMP).
99. Romans 6:21 (AMP).
100. 1 Corinthians 15:3.
101. Hebrews 4:15.

this crucifixion paid the price for the sins of all mankind;[102] (5) complete forgiveness of sin is available to anyone who accepts it by faith in Jesus;[103] and (6) evidence of that faith is manifested through the indwelling of the Holy Spirit[104] and obedience to God.[105]

Our slate is cleaned forever.

No matter what we have done, we are forgiven.

Jesus is God's *proxy*.[106] Another way to think about it is that Jesus provides the means by which imperfect humans can interact with a perfect God. We trust in who Jesus said that he was, and we trust in what he did for us.

Jesus' sacrifice assures us of eternal salvation. Instead of living our lives worrying about the things of this world, we begin to think about eternal things. We believe that regardless of the obstacle, with Jesus, anything is possible.[107] Rather than spending our lives waiting for the other shoe to drop, we believe that everything works together for good and that

Once our eternity is resolved, the few years we have on this planet are put into perspective.

God is going to *bless* us. He is going to make something good happen. No matter how bad the mess, Christians believe that God can fix it.

So, although there may be rules to live by, real Christianity is about trusting Jesus with our lives. Trusting in Jesus means that we surrender control to him. Surrendering control means we do what he wants us to do, rather than what we want to do.

---

102. Romans 3:23-24 (AMP).

103. 1 Peter 3:21.

104. Romans 8:4 (AMP).

105. James 2:18.

106. A "*proxy*" is someone who is authorized to act for someone else.

107. Philippians 4:13.

The sooner we surrender, the sooner God can begin to change us into new creatures, with less worry, less fear, less temptation, less anger, less angst, and less of all the rest of the bad psyche stuff.

The ironclad consistent pattern throughout the Bible is simple. God reaches out to man. He waits for us to respond. It's most noticeable when we are at our very worst. I've met countless people who found God when they had reached the very end of their emotional ropes. Drugs, alcohol, failed marriages, failed relationships, and failed hopes become the simple point at which people respond to God's gentle calling. They say, "I give up. I can't do this anymore. God, I need you. Jesus help me." He is faithful to respond. That is Christianity.

Or, we continue to fight our way through life alone. However, as we've already established, we cannot earn our way into heaven.

You either accept Christ or you reject Him.

There simply isn't any middle ground.

Faith, Ironically

In life, it is difficult to fully appreciate something until you've actually been through it. A twenty-year-old marathoner in perfect health may nod with feigned interest as the heart patient explains his bypass operation. Although if the marathoner has a heart attack, a bypass operation becomes the most important thing in her life. She will want to learn everything she can about bypass surgery. She becomes an amateur cardiologist. It has all suddenly become very real and personal.

Think about a time when someone tried to describe a place that you had never visited. Later, you visited that place. After you had seen it, the place was vastly different than you had imagined. There is almost no way to explain the vastness of the ocean to someone, unless they've seen it. Mere words to describe the

Grand Canyon are inadequate to capture its beauty and majesty. It doesn't matter how articulate you are, it's impossible to describe the grandeur of the Grand Canyon to someone who hasn't experienced it.

This is why Christianspeak is ineffective. If you haven't taken the leap, Christian ideas don't seem to make a lot of sense. Christianity seems like any other religion. Once you've taken that leap of faith and begun the Christian experience, you begin to truly understand what it means. Your faith is rewarded with conviction.

The great irony of Christianity is the leap of faith that it requires before anything observable happens.

Christians know that their decision to *trust in Jesus* was validated by the things that happened to them following that decision. It's difficult to describe it to others who have not been through it.

After you take the leap, though, it all makes sense.

The basic Christian concepts of sin and forgiveness are simple. They become complicated as we live life. Paul wrote extensively about it in the New Testament. Anyone who has accepted Jesus and continued to struggle with sin can testify to it. If people are given the opportunity to do a little *due diligence*[108] before making the decision to trust Jesus with their lives, they can avoid some of the frustration and confusion that new Christians experience. Christianity's source document is the Bible. Christians are witnesses to the effect of Christian faith. Christian due diligence happens through Bible study, and the observation of the changed life of the Christian witness. If people are allowed to look before

---

108. "Due diligence" is a business/ legal term that describes the investigation that a buyer does before making a decision to purchase. Typically, it occurs in the context of a business acquisition.

they leap, their conversion experience will be more meaningful and lasting.

Eternal Life and Earthly Life

The aquarium is a metaphor for what God did for mankind through Jesus. Mankind had fallen. God repeatedly reached out personally and through His prophets[109] to convince man to change. For a while, things would get better. Then man would return to his sinful and rebellious ways. God became human. He lived among humans, cared for them and taught them. Ultimately, he was sacrificed. Jesus died so that once and for all, we would be made right with God.[110] Jesus' provision of the Holy Spirit restores us to the relationship that Adam and Eve originally had with God. We can have a close relationship with God.

God, through Jesus and the Holy Spirit, causes two fundamental changes in our lives. The first is called *salvation*. It means, "I'm going to heaven after I die." When I was nine years-old, I was *saved*. When I prayed to Jesus and raised my hand, I accepted God's grace, the free gift through Jesus' death on the cross, through faith. I was saved from my sin, and I was saved from an eternal existence that I would rather not think about.

The second is called *sanctification*.[111] When I was thirty-seven years-old, I finally and fully surrendered my life to God. This allowed the sanctification process to begin. From the moment a Christian takes that first step of faith by accepting Christ, the

---

109. Isaiah, Ezekiel, Jeremiah, Daniel, Hoseah, Joel, Amos, Obadiah, Jonah, Micah, Nahum, Habbakuk, Zephaniah, Haggai, Zechariah, and Malachi are generally referred to as the Old Testament prophets.
110. 2 Corinthians 5:19.
111. 1 Thessalonians 5:23.

Holy Spirit indwells within them.[112] This does not mean that He takes control from you. Instead, you have to give Him control on an ongoing basis. You do that by continually giving your worries, hopes, and fears to Him and doing your best to obey Him in everything that you do. You have to allow God to occupy your entire consciousness. It's what Christians call being *filled with the Holy Spirit*.[113]

The lifelong process of trusting God results in sanctification. It is the ongoing process of becoming more like Him. Sanctification occurs as we follow God's will for us. We learn His will by reading His Word. We learn His will through prayer. It happens as we allow the Holy Spirit to work in our lives. This means turning your back on sin, worry, and other bad behaviors that you exhibited before you became a Christian.

The more we trust in God, the more that we are sanctified and move closer to Him. As we give more and more of our lives to Him, we see His increasing participation. The more that we see it, the more we realize that He will continue to do it. We begin to experience a greater and deeper faith. Simple faith results in more faith. As our faith increases, we experience ever-increasing *blessings*. These blessings come from the Holy Spirit; Christians call them the *fruits of the Spirit*.[114]

For some new believers, salvation and sanctification can be instantaneous experience. The decision to accept Jesus and surrender their life to him is one fluid step. Drug addicts and alcoholics are cured; relationships are restored in what can only be called miraculous transformations. For others, especially the harder-headed variety Christians like me, the journey toward sanctification takes longer. We can circumvent the Holy Spirit by refusing to listen to Him and by continuing to deliberately sin.

---

112. 2 Corinthians 1:22.
113. The Holy Spirit is discussed in greater detail in Chapter Eight.
114. Galatians 5:22-23 (AMP).

Christianity is the only belief system that claims that the Creator actually indwells in anyone who asks. If God is living inside of you, you have everything that you need to overcome sin or any other problem. It also stands to reason that you will have a pretty good life while on this earth. True, heartfelt and authentic Christianity means that you have made peace with God and found your eternal destiny with Him. His indwelling means that you have the ability to grow increasingly in His image, if you will let Him do His work within you.

CHAPTER FIVE

Weighing the Evidence

The Logic of Law and Faith

We've looked at the common misconceptions about Christianity, and the basics of Christian faith. We've covered what Christianity is, and what it isn't. How then do we decide whether the claims of Christianity make sense? How do we decide whether they are reasonable?

It's easy to dismiss Christianity. Some people view it as a set of beliefs that aren't based on tangible evidence. Instead, they see Christianity as a belief system that requires a great deal of faith in someone and something that they can't see. This perspective declares that faith and logic are incompatible. Faith in something unseen or intangible is viewed as illogical. They argue that Christian faith is therefore illogical and invalid.

On a superficial level, this argument makes sense. However, as with all superficial arguments, if its assumptions are exposed, the analysis doesn't hold together. In this case, the assumption is that "tangible" is limited to things that you can touch or see. In reality, there is tangible evidence of things that are imperceptible. For example, we observe a tree moving in the wind. Wind is created when high pressure air and low pressure air collide. We inflate a balloon by moving air from our lungs into a small rubber envelope, which expands as it is inflated. The same logic applies to Christian faith. We can't see God, but there is abundant evidence that He exits.

Consider the air. We can't see it or touch it. And yet, there is abundant evidence that it exists.

This chapter will explore some common arguments made against Christian faith. We will identify and explore some of the assumptions underlying these arguments. In order to do this, it is useful for you to have a framework within which to analyze them.

What follows is a quick lesson on legal logic.

Try and stay awake.

A basic understanding of these concepts will come in handy as you examine the evidence. Think of this as sort of a mini-law degree, or a lesson in learning to think like a lawyer.[115]

The law builds upon itself through the process of *legal precedent*.[116] *Stare decisis* ("the decision stands") requires a judge to rule consistently from one case to another and with the rulings of

---

115. If you are interested in learning what the phrase "think like a lawyer" means, I discuss it in greater detail in my book *Law School Labyrinth: The Guide to Making the Most of Your Legal Education* (2nd Ed., Kaplan Publishing, May 3, 2011). Essentially, it means the process of legal reasoning based upon the application of law to a prescribed set of facts.

116. *"Precedent"* is the term used to describe the law in a given situation, as determined by the judge.

other judges. Stare decisis makes the law predictable and fair and gives it its legitimacy.

In the law, the term argument describes the chain of reasoning used. It means the process of presenting opposing viewpoints in a logical and rational way.

Anyone who has seen a lawyer television series or movie understands intuitively that the key to success in *litigation*[117] is the ability of the lawyer to make reasoned and logical arguments. Similarly, when a judge determines what the law is, she uses this same reasoning process. The law relies on logic to further itself. If a judge rules illogically, it becomes increasingly difficult to enforce the law. A society has little tolerance for illogical laws. The law must make sense in order to be legitimate.

The lawyer determines the applicable precedent by comparing *judicial opinions*. These are published legal analyses, written by judges. The lawyer gathers the evidence to support the facts asserted. This can be in the form of documentary evidence, or other tangible evidence, such as ballistics evidence. Facts can be in the form of testamentary evidence—the testimony of witnesses. The lawyer then applies precedent to the facts, in order to make her argument.

A *valid* argument is one in which the premises are valid and the conclusion is legitimately based upon the premises. In addition, the argument can be based upon the *assumptions* contained within the argument. For a conclusion to be valid, it must also be consistent with any assumptions contained within the argument. An assumption is simply an unstated premise. The two forms of reasoning used are *deductive* reasoning and *analogic* reasoning. Analogic reasoning is reasoning by comparison. If something holds true in one situation, that something should also hold true in a second similar situation. For example:

---

117. *"Litigation" simply* means the process of a lawsuit or prosecution.

Premise One: Murder is a terrible thing.

Premise Two: Hating someone is the same thing as killing them in your heart.

Conclusion: Therefore, hating someone is a terrible thing.

Deductive reasoning is a kind of logic chain. If this is true and that is true, then a third thing must be true. For example:

Premise One: When the sky turns cloudy and dark, it is likely going to rain.

Premise Two: The sky has turned cloudy and dark.

Conclusion: It is likely going to rain.

If the two premises are valid, then the conclusion must be valid. However, there is also an additional step in determining the validity of an argument. Virtually every argument rests upon assumptions. In the example, the assumption is that we are referring to the sky during the daytime, and not nighttime. If this assumption is incorrect, then the sky could be cloudy and dark at night and there could be no chance of rain. The point is that in order to fully understand whether an argument is valid, you must also identify and consider the assumptions within the argument. Assumptions are implied or unstated within the argument.

Assumptions can strengthen logically weak arguments and weaken logically strong arguments. In addition, assumptions prevent an argument from being valid or invalid, based solely upon the premises. In order to determine their effect on an argument, it is important to identify them and how they are used in support of that argument.

Identifying assumptions may very well be the most critical step in evaluating the validity of any claim or argument.

The Importance of Assumptions and Inferences

In the early 1960s the United States Supreme Court held that school prayer was an improper mixing of government function and religious activities. The argument that school prayer violates the Establishment Clause of the First Amendment to the U.S. Constitution (often referred to as the *separation of church and state*), assumes that the founding fathers intended that the government would have no involvement whatsoever with any religion. It is then reasonable to conclude that religious activities by the government violate the Establishment Clause.

What if the assumption was in error? Suppose that you knew instead that the American colonists rebelled because the English king mandated that his subjects would become Anglicans. Suppose there was evidence that the vast majority of the framers of the Constitution were Christians, as clearly indicated in their letters and other writings, both within and outside of governmental office. Suppose other evidence shows clearly that the framers intertwined their Christian beliefs with their official duties.

What if the purpose of the Establishment Clause was not about government involvement in religion? What if it was about the prohibition of a government-mandated religion?

Your earlier inference that the founding fathers desired the separation of church and state would be faulty, as is your conclusion. You would then reasonably conclude that the Establishment Clause wasn't intended to prohibit governmental involvement in religion. Instead, it was intended to prohibit government-mandated religion.

So a conclusion that the Establishment Clause prohibits government involvement in religion would be based upon a faulty assumption. This would lead to a bad conclusion. We would have turned *freedom of religion* into *freedom from religion* based upon an erroneous assumption.

Eyewitness Testimony, Documentary Evidence, and Circumstantial Evidence

A woman is found dead in her apartment. There are no eyewitnesses to the crime. Her ex-husband is charged with the crime of first degree murder. The prosecution argues that the husband is guilty of the crime. The prosecution offers the following evidence to the jury: the county coroner testifies that, based upon the autopsy, he concluded that the woman died from a single gunshot to the head. During the autopsy, the bullet was recovered. A ballistics expert testifies that it was determined to be a .22 caliber bullet. The expert further testifies that, based upon the microscopic grooves on the bullet, it could only have come from one particular model of a gun. The operations manager of the gun manufacturer testifies that only three weapons of this model type were ever produced. The sales manager of the manufacturer testifies that all three were sold to one gun shop. The gun shop owner testifies that the woman's ex-husband purchased one of the guns.

It seems pretty straightforward doesn't it? The inference is that the women's husband owned the gun. This leads to the conclusion that he is the likely murderer. Granting all this, a few additional facts may lead you to an entirely different conclusion. The gun shop's documentary records show that the woman's husband purchased the gun two weeks after the woman was found dead. Or perhaps the gun shop owner is found to have had an illicit affair with the woman, who later rejected him.

Suppose there was an eyewitness to the woman's death? Her maid testifies that she saw the woman commit suicide with the husband's gun. The only question left to be decided is the maid's credibility. Most likely, the defense would present evidence of the maid's work history and stability, as well as examples of her trustworthiness and reliability. They would also examine any motivation she might have to lie, as well as any extraordinary circumstances such as her mental condition or other inability to accurately observe and relate events. If we believe the maid, then it is very likely that the husband will be acquitted. The jury would have to determine that the prosecution has not proved its case *beyond a reasonable doubt.*

In court, the judge or jury uses *eyewitness testimony, documentary evidence*, other *tangible evidence* and *circumstantial evidence* to decide whether either side's arguments are valid. We commonly refer to this as a verdict. The jury weighs the evidence, in order to reach a verdict.

The persuasiveness of eyewitness testimony is a function of the eyewitness's credibility. If we believe the eyewitness, we accept the eyewitness's testimony. The eyewitness saw what happened; there is little need for assumptions or inferences. Documentary evidence can be equally persuasive; however, it generally must be *authenticated*, which means that someone with direct knowledge has to testify under oath that the document is what it purports to be. Tangible evidence is other evidence such as DNA evidence, fiber analyses, blood spatter, and any other physical evidence that supports the presenting party's theory of the case. Tangible evidence must also be authenticated, in order to ensure that it is what it is presented to be. Often, eyewitnesses or *expert witnesses* authenticate tangible evidence.

Circumstantial evidence requires the jury to make inferences about what happened, based upon likelihoods and probabilities. Circumstantial evidence is evidence that indirectly proves an assertion. It requires the jury to put pieces of indirect evidence together, and to perhaps make assumptions about the evidence, in order to create the chain of logic necessary for the jury to arrive at a verdict. The glue that holds the logic pieces together is called an *inference*. Like the example of the air, we circumstantially prove that it exists by its effect.

A common misconception is that circumstantial evidence isn't valid evidence. However, in many cases, there is very little *direct evidence* available. There are no eyewitnesses. The jury is required to assemble the indirect pieces of evidence, in order to determine what happened. It is important to understand that many cases are won or lost, solely on the basis of circumstantial evidence.

The Case of the Galilean Who Claimed to be God

This is an unusual case. The defendant is unusual, almost a story in contradictions. He lived two thousand years ago. Had you encountered him on a road in Galilee, you might have walked right past him. His was a brief, interrupted life. He was convicted of *blasphemy*, in a hastily assembled trial of sorts. "Blasphemy" is speaking or acting in a way that is against God. It was a serious crime; a capital offense.

The defendant did not deny the charges, and he didn't speak in his own defense. He was quickly and summarily convicted, and just as quickly executed. The method of execution, a crucifixion, was horrific and intended to deter anyone from following the condemned person's path.

This case is unusual because of the nature of the evidence presented. Witnesses have testified that the defendant performed miracles that can't be easily explained by natural means. He turned water into wine.[118] These miracles became increasingly impressive over the three years that the defendant actively

---

118. John 2:9 (AMP).

taught. They became so impressive that their source couldn't be explained as anything other than coming directly from God. The defendant healed blind and seriously ill people.[119] Incredibly, he is reported to have brought the dead back to life.[120]

The defendant's execution should have ended it, once and for all. This matter has already been decided. One would expect the defendant's execution to be the end of it, once and for all. But it wasn't. He died a humiliating death two thousand years ago, and the appeals process has continued ever since.

There were only a few eyewitnesses to his life and death. They lived and worked with him; his story and teachings were later captured in writing. None of these witnesses defended him during the trial; instead, they fled. You would have expected them to move on with their lives. And yet, after the defendant's execution, something happened to them. Instead of hiding, they testified in the open. Rather than being deterred, they were emboldened. They claimed that he rose from the dead and later ascended to heaven. Many of the witnesses were also killed for continuing to testify about him, not too long after he was crucified. They died for what they believed. Nonetheless, their testimony survived through these writings.

If the defendant's death didn't end it, then these witnesses' deaths should have. That didn't happen. There are people living today, who claim to be witnesses to the defendant, although they were born long after he died. These witnesses describe incredible changes in their lives, and they attribute it all to this uneducated Galilean. They continue to testify, two thousand years after his death. There are over two billion of these witnesses.

The defendant's name was Jesus. He claimed to be God.

---

119. Mark 1:42; Luke 4:41.
120. John 11:43 (AMP).

Jesus said that he was God in an unmistakable, direct way.[121] His actions indicate that he believed that he was God. He forgave sins.[122] Under Old Testament Judaism, only God could do this. Of course, believing that you are God and being God are obviously two different things. This is the jury's charge: to decide whether Jesus who he said he was. If he was, then he is innocent of the charges.

In most cases, the verdict would be fairly simple. Most juries would quickly decide that anyone claiming to be God was insane. Regardless, there is no evidence that would tend to show that Jesus is entitled to the insanity defense. This leaves the jury with a single question. Jesus was either who he said he was, or he wasn't. If he was, then he is innocent of the charges.

Consider the evidence.

The Witnesses

Conventional wisdom would paint the early Christian movement as a cult of sorts. This characterization assumes that Jesus and his followers operated the way they did for their own purposes. They were zealots, the theory goes, determined to change the system. They elected Jesus as their leader and planned to overthrow the religious regime in power. Like rebels throughout the course of history, Jesus' followers ultimately sought power.

The assumption that early Christians operated for their own purposes isn't supported, however, by the historical record. Most groups rapidly disintegrate after their leader is removed.

---

121. There are numerous references in the New Testament regarding Jesus' claim to be God. Among them: John 8:58, 10:30–33, 14:9–11; Matthew 8:20, 9:6, 10:23 (AMP).

122. Matthew 9:2 (AMP).

Think of cults that have operated in modern history. Their leaders declare that the end times are imminent and die, typically through some sort of self-inflicted death. Still, life goes on without them. The brainwashing ceases. Cult followers gradually go back to their pre-cult lives.

Instead, those early Christians began to act very differently than before. Peter,[123] arguably one of those closest to Jesus, had previously abandoned him in his greatest time of need. At that time, Peter's courage was situational, with many ups and downs. He suffered from alternating fear, guilt, and conviction. After Jesus was arrested, Peter and the others scattered. Shortly after that, Peter regained some of courage. He wanted to find out what had happened to Jesus. He made his way to the courtyard of the home of the high priest, where Jesus was being interrogated.[124] He was spotted and accused of being one of Jesus' followers.[125] Again afraid, he denied everything.[126]

This didn't happen after Jesus died.

At that moment, Peter feared for his life, and would've done anything to save it.

Jesus was crucified shortly afterward. You would have expected that to be the end of it. Defeated and humiliated, his followers should have simply gone back to their lives before Jesus. They would have been afraid to do much else.

We see them acting in a completely different way. After Jesus was crucified, instead of scattering, the new Christian movement emerged.

The authorities moved quickly to quash this movement, torturing and killing the early Christians. These followers could

---

123. Peter is described in all of the gospels and his writings are also included in the New Testament.
124. Mark 14:66 (AMP).
125. Mark 14:67 (AMP).
126. Mark 14:68 (AMP).

have saved their own lives. They didn't. All they had to do was renounce their faith in Jesus. They didn't. Peter was crucified by Nero. James was killed by Herod Agrippa.[127] Andrew was crucified. It's hard to imagine that these people would have died for someone or something that they thought was a lie or a fraud. Many of Jesus' followers died rather than betray him. This is inconsistent with a movement which seeks power.

Something happened to Peter and the other followers. It doesn't make sense that Jesus' horrific death, without more, somehow emboldened them.

What started out as a defeated, ragtag group of followers has blossomed into a following of over two billion people who claim to know him. They call themselves Christians. These Christian *witnesses* give *testimony* to describe firsthand experiences with Jesus. Although not eyewitness to his life, they are eyewitnesses to his effect on their lives.

The Circumstantial Evidence: Impact of the Person

Conventional wisdom scoffs at the idea that Jesus was, in reality, God. In some cases, this wisdom questions whether Jesus even existed. Biblical accounts describe Jesus as being of modest means and with no formal education. He grew up in the rural area of Galilee. Galileans were thought of as backwoods commoners. He was a carpenter by trade, a manual laborer. Jesus never traveled beyond a few hundred miles of his hometown. The rich and influential people generally disliked him. He lived during a time when there were no forms of mass

---

127. Acts 12:1–2.

communication. There was no was no film or photography; there was no Internet.

How do we know Jesus existed? After he was crucified, Jesus' life story was passed along through the oral traditions of his first followers, and made its way to scrolls and crude writings. These were passed down and preserved by early Christian leaders and clergy. These writings ultimately became the Bible. Christians believe in Jesus because the Bible tells us about him. We'll explore later in this chapter why Christians believe the Bible is accurate.

But there is another way.

We look at the man's influence. Fictional people generally are only as influential as the literature describing them. In this case, we compare the man's circumstances, as well as the biblical descriptions of him, with his influence. We then determine whether Jesus can reasonably be viewed as someone whose influence exceeded what we would expect based upon those circumstances. We then consider other evidence that would tend to explain the source of that influence.

I assume that you have never met Jesus in the flesh. I have never met George Washington and yet I believe he existed. I see circumstantial evidence all around me that supports this belief. His likeness is on American money. There is a monument in Washington, D.C., named after him, as is the city itself.

If the question is whether or not Jesus existed and was who he said he was, then the same analysis should hold true. I read about Jesus in the Bible. The descriptions of him and his life are limited to a few hundred pages. His actual teachings are substantially less.

And yet, I see circumstantial evidence of his impact all around me. Other religions measure themselves against the Christian calendar. The designation used is *anno domini* or the abbreviation *A.D.*, which means "in the year of our Lord." We celebrate Jesus' birth on Christmas day and his death and resurrection at Easter.

Take a drive through your town. Chances are that you will find in a very short distance a church building, and near that another church building. If you counted the churches located within a few miles of your starting point, you might be surprised at the number. Every one of them represents the faith, work, and investment, as well as a lot of blood, sweat, and tears of a group of people who had faith enough to construct a building for the purpose of Christian worship.

Christian churches are everywhere. Christianity started as a ragtag group of Jesus followers, operating out of homes and often in secret. And yet, today it is the largest belief system in the world.

Schools and universities around the world are dedicated to understanding his teachings. Academics and scholars have studied his words and his life for hundreds of years. People have dedicated their careers and their lives to him. People have died, rather than renounce him.

Somehow the effect of Jesus' life and death are still felt today, over two thousand years later. He has billions of followers. It's hard to imagine that all of this was based upon a fictional person or a nondescript Galilean. There has to be more to the story.

Based upon this circumstantial evidence, it is reasonable to conclude that Jesus existed and was influential well beyond what he should have been. How many people can you name that have Jesus' influence today? Despite the fact that he died a criminal's death, he continues to influence our world. This leads us to the next question: "Who did Jesus believe that he was?" We look at his motive.

Examining Motive

Television lawyers argue before television juries about whether the defendant had the *motive* to commit the crime. Although, as any law student knows, motive is not actually an element of a crime. Motive is circumstantial evidence that allows the jury to infer that the accused may be guilty when faced with the lack of eyewitness testimony or other direct evidence. Motive helps us to determine why people would have done what they are alleged to have done.

The religious leaders of the time accused Jesus of blasphemy. In this case, the self-appointed representatives of God defined the crime. They decided what the precedent was. The gospels describe an ongoing effort by these leaders to get of rid of Jesus, on the basis that he preached against God.[128] Under Jewish law, blasphemy was a crime punishable by death. In an *ad hoc*[129] trial of sorts, Jesus was examined by the religious leaders[130] and the Roman government. Pilate knew that Jesus was innocent.[131] Pilate was the governor of Judea, but his constituents didn't listen to him. He wanted to free Jesus. They wanted blood. He washed his hands of the matter and allowed the crucifixion of Jesus.[132] More correctly, Jesus allowed it to happen.

What was Jesus' motive?

He had ample opportunity to avoid crucifixion. Jesus could simply have denied the charges and it is likely he could have gone free, perhaps after a good flogging. He didn't. He didn't try to argue or defend himself. He could have saved his own neck, but didn't. If Jesus had wanted to avoid death, he could have simply stopped preaching. He could have hidden until things cooled down. He didn't. He preached in the Temple, in the open,

Why did Jesus allow himself to be killed?

---

128. John 10:31–39.

129. *"Ad hoc"* means impromptu.

130. *See, e.g.* (for example) Matthew 26:59 (AMP) and Matthew 27:12 (AMP).

131. Id.

132. Matthew 27:24 (AMP).

where he was certain to be heard. Later, after he was arrested, the Roman governor over Judea, Pontius Pilate, gave him the opportunity to defend himself.[133] He could have denied everything. He could have pleaded for his life. He could have promised to stop. But he didn't.

Christians believe that they understand why.

The Bible indicates that from the very beginning, the religious authorities at the time knew what Jesus' resurrection meant. They knew that one interpretation of the Old Testament prophecies was that a *Messiah*[134] would come, be crucified, and resurrected. After Jesus was placed in the tomb, the Jewish leaders asked that Roman soldiers guard it to ensure that Jesus' followers did not steal his body and claim that Jesus was resurrected.[135] After the tomb was found empty, these same leaders bribed the soldiers to tell everyone that Jesus' followers had stolen the body.[136] Clearly, something happened that they could not control. Jesus allowed himself to be crucified because he was the Messiah. His death was part of the plan that had been prophesied from the beginning. This plan would provide the means by which man would be reconciled, once and for all, with God.

The Documentary Evidence

The Bible is the sole documentary evidence in this case. It is the evidence of Jesus' life, death and resurrection. Initially,

---

133. *See, e.g.* Matthew 27:13–14; Luke 23:4.

134. *See, e.g.* Isaiah 9:6 and Jeremiah 23:5-6. A *Messiah* is predicted throughout the Old Testament. As described in the New Testament, Christians believe that Jesus is that Messiah, and that his sinless life and crucifixion are payment for the sins of mankind.

135. Matthew 27:62–65 (AMP).

136. Matthew 28:11–15 (AMP).

Christian doctrine was passed along from person to person, by word of mouth. This eyewitness testimony was powerful and persuasive. The Bible came together as a single document in the years following Jesus' death. It consists of a significant portion of the Hebrew Bible, with the additional writings of the authors of the New Testament. The New Testament includes letters and other documents written by Jesus early followers, which record the thoughts, words, and history of the early Christian church.

In order to capture the incredible story, those early followers committed it to writing. These writings include the gospels and the various epistles and prophecies contained in the writings of Paul and other early Christians. Paul's epistles as well as the letters of the apostles John, Peter, and James make up the bulk of the rest of the New Testament. Archaeologists have found thousands of original handwritten manuscripts in Greek and other early languages that show that the New Testament was accurately transcribed into today's Bible.

The word *Bible* comes from the name of the ancient Mediterranean seaport called Byblos, which was as a trading center for papyrus. Papyrus was one of the early transportable materials used for writing. Bibles were hand-copied and used only by teachers and clergy.

But something interesting happened.

Toward the end of the Middle Ages, an inventor named Johannes Gutenberg invented a movable-type printing press. The purpose of this invention was to mass-produce the Bible. Gutenberg's invention made the Bible accessible to common people. This early, crude technology revolutionized literature. More importantly, the Bible, previously read by only a select few, ultimately became available to the common people. The Bible predated Gutenberg's press by a thousand years. Without the Gutenberg press, it would never have become the book that it has become. The printed Bible helped to spread the gospel and fuel the growth of Christianity.

While on a trip to Germany a few years ago, I visited the Gutenberg museum in Mainz and saw one of these early behemoth printing presses. In the souvenir shop, I bought a copy of the first page of the gospel of John, in the original German, which was printed on a replica of the first press. The page is simple testimony to the dedication and faith required to create it. Its beauty and intricacy are evidence of the obvious commitment of the craftsman.

Authenticating the Documentary Evidence

Christians believe that the Bible is the inspired Word of God.[137] We believe that the writers of the Bible were led by the Holy Spirit. It all came together as a single book as a result of God's guiding Hand.

Any book that is claimed to be the inspired word of God deserves very careful scrutiny.

How do we know the Bible is reliable? How do we know it is accurate? How do we authenticate this documentary evidence?

One way to authenticate this evidence is to evaluate whether the Bible's impact has been greater than we would expect from an ordinary book and great enough to support the idea that it is really God-inspired. The obvious question: Is there really anything special about the Bible? Or, is it simply some relic from an ancient past that is no longer relevant? We examine the circumstantial evidence in order to authenticate it.

The Bible was written by a series of authors, each operating independently. The Bible reflects the thoughts and writings of a wide cross section of people over thousands of years that

---

137. 2 Timothy 3:16.

somehow came together in one book. Although it was written by many people, the story told by each of them is the same.

It has been translated numerous times since it was first assembled. Any ordinary book assembled in this fashion would likely have ended up as a disjointed mess, making no sense and of no value to anyone. And yet, the Bible has arguably had a greater impact upon mankind than any other book ever written.

The early Christian writers were either eyewitnesses or heard about these events from eyewitnesses. If the events described in the New Testament were false, it is reasonable to assume that someone would have disputed them. It is likely that Christianity would have died a natural death. Obviously, that didn't happen. This Bible has survived attacks, translations, deletions, additions, and a myriad of adversity that would have caused any ordinary book to simply fade away. The Bible has not succumbed. Instead it has proliferated.

The Bible is read by millions of people each year. It continues to be the best-selling book of all time. Something about it continues to draw readership, despite the fact that it has been on the market for hundreds of years. The Bible appeals to an incredibly diverse readership. It can provide the reader with a lifetime of enlightenment. It is the only book that tells a story so simple that a child can understand it. At the same time, biblical scholars spend entire careers dissecting its meaning. The Bible has survived the test of time. *What impact has the Bible had upon mankind?* Ask yourself the following questions:

How many people do you know that have read at least a portion of the Bible?

How many people do you know that have read all of it?

How many important occasions have you witnessed or read about where a Bible was used as the basis for a promise?

Do you own a copy of the Bible? Do your friends own a copy of the Bible?

How many copies of the Bible are sold each year? How many have been sold since it was first published?

If you have read the Bible, has it helped you with life decisions? How?

Now expand the scope of these questions throughout the course of recorded history. Think about the history of the nations. Think about the founding of America and other significant historical events. Think about the Bible's use during times of crisis. Are there any other books that you can think of that have had a greater historical influence than the Bible? It's unlikely that you can name a single other book that is as ubiquitous and as part of mankind's history as the Bible. All of this circumstantial evidence when taken together leads to the reasonable inference that the Bible is indeed a special book.

Authenticating the Source

Is the Bible really God-inspired? One way to consider this question is to validate its content by comparing it with other evidence that has been authenticated itself. In other words, we compare what the Bible says with what we know to be true. If the Bible is validated by the events of our lives, we then consider whether there are any alternative non-God explanations. If we find none, then it is reasonable to conclude that God did inspire the Bible.

Random probability theory says that if you do certain things a certain number of times, it is statistically probable that something specific will happen. If something else happens, then it that occurrence is considered statistically improbable. Consider the classic statistics example: There are five colored balls in a hat. One is red, one blue, one orange, one yellow, and one is white. You draw one ball at a time, each time replacing the ball that you drew the previous time. The probability that you will draw a particular ball each time is exactly one in five. In other words, it is equally probable that you will draw a particular color each time.

Now suppose that you make five draws, each time drawing a red ball. You might be surprised, or even startled. *"What are the chances of that happening?"* You might think that this was an extremely weird coincidence or luck.

What if it happened fifty times? Each time you drew a red ball? You might think yourself a victim of someone's elaborate prank and start looking for the hidden camera. Failing that, you would likely start carefully examining the balls, the hat, and anything else you could think of to try and come up with a rational explanation for what happened. You would check to make sure that the balls are equally weighted and that the textures are the same, in order to avoid the possibility that you are somehow drawn to the red ball because it is unusual. What if it happened five hundred times? You might inspect the hat to assure yourself that it doesn't somehow trap the red ball in such a position that it becomes the only ball picked.

Once you have eliminated these possibilities, you then begin to look at external variables. But there is no rational explanation. You would conclude that there was something going on that wasn't subject to natural and earthly explanations, such as random probability, physics, and the like. One by one, you would eliminate the alternative explanations, based upon the evidence you discovered. Eventually you would run out of possibilities. That's the point when you could begin to conclude that somehow the natural order of things has been upset.

It takes little faith in the principles of random probability when things occur that are consistent with those principles.

If something defies logic and human explanation, then it is reasonable to consider that there is some sort of external superhuman influence causing it.

Once those principles are overridden, it requires a greater degree of faith to believe in those principles rather than in the alternative explanation.

Now suppose that one day, you were visiting your local library and found a book that explained everything. This book explained to you the process or phenomenon, or whatever it was that caused you to draw a red ball each and every time. You would read the book very carefully. You would read it to understand exactly what happened and why. You would also read it to confirm that the explanation was consistent with your observation. If it was inconsistent, chances are that you wouldn't keep reading.

How many times have you prayed for something that came to pass? How many times have you been faced with what appeared

Christians believe that we have found such a book.

to be an insurmountable problem and left it to Him, and it was solved somehow inexplicably? How many times have you struggled with something, faced disappointment, only to realize later that it had actually worked out for the better? How many times have you taken that leap of faith and done the right thing, made the right choice, listened to that inner voice, in spite of what you wanted to do, only to have that leap work out better than you ever could have imagined? If any of these things had happened five or ten times, you might explain them away as mere coincidence. If they happened hundreds or thousands of times it would be very difficult to call them a coincidence.

I worked my way through college and, like most college students, rarely had much money in my pocket. Unlike many college students, there were no sources of funds available to me other than wages earned through part-time jobs At the beginning of my junior year, my finances had run out. Books need to be purchased. I needed money. Desperate, my prayer was that God would provide me with money. It was a very specific prayer, in response to a very specific need. The Bible teaches that we should ask God for the things that we need.[138] The next day, an unexpected income tax refund check of about two hundred dollars arrived in the mail. To a broke college student, it was an enormous sum. It was enough money to last me for several months.

After that early morning in 1992 in Michigan and surrendering my life to God, I began to pray for something. My life had been a series of bad relationships and these relationships were growing progressively worse. As a result, my prayer was that he would find a wife for me; someone who would become my life's companion. Granted this may sound a little barbaric. After all, shouldn't the person God found for me have a choice in the matter? However, God wants us to bring everything to him in prayer; every thought, ever need, and every desire.[139] It seemed to me that he wouldn't bring me anyone who wouldn't want to be there. So I just gave it to Him.

A few days later, I was having dinner alone at a local restaurant, and suddenly had a vision. To me, it was a "vision" only because I don't know what else to call it. It was mental image of a woman. I had never seen her before. She had brown hair, hazel eyes and was about twenty-five years old. She was also beautiful. The thought crossed my mind that this might not be a sign from God. I wasn't in the habit of getting these kinds of signs. However, it was so specific and unexpected that it simply couldn't be reasonably explained any other way.

---

138. Matthew 7:7 (AMP).
139. Philippians 4:6.

I forgot about it. About six months later, I boarded a flight from Denver to Detroit. The woman taking tickets was stunningly beautiful. She kindly accepted my ticket. The rest, as they say, is history. Beth and I got married in 1994. A few years later, the vision came back to me. There is no doubt in my mind that the woman in it was Beth.

Were these coincidences? They surely could have been. Were they the only times in my life when prayers were answered, it would be easy to conclude that they were coincidences; cosmic flukes of a sort. But looking back, adding up the hundreds of answered prayers in my life, it is only reasonable to conclude that the Person to whom I pray has the ability and willingness to answer my prayers.

There are times when things happen in our lives that can only be explained by His actions. How do we know it's God? Because the Bible records God's actions and predicts how He will act. It's all described in the Bible, which leads us to conclude that it is reliable and accurate.

> *We cannot see God. We cannot hear God, at least audibly. We cannot touch God. Yet we see evidence of God all around us, in His creation.*

Arguably, the most important evidence of the validity of the Bible is the simple fact of its validation in millions of people's lives.

We check the Bible against our own life experiences.

The Bible explains them perfectly.

Authenticating the Documentary Evidence: The Prophecies

Still another way to authenticate the Bible is by evaluating the accuracy of its prophecies. The Old Testament predates the New

Testament by hundreds, and in some cases, thousands of years. For example, the book of Ezekiel is thought to have been written about five hundred years before the birth of Jesus. The Bible contains numerous Old Testament prophecies. If these prophecies are fulfilled, then the Bible can be reasonably viewed as a reliable document. Further, if Jesus fulfilled the prophecies, then it is reasonable to conclude that he was the long-awaited Messiah.

The first step is to identify the scriptures thought to be prophecies. They were written by people commonly thought to be prophets, based upon the historical record. We can then use a simple process of elimination. These scriptures are not narrative. They are not rules. They are not poetry or songs. As a result, we reasonably conclude that these scriptures are prophecy. Another way is by third party verification. These Old Testament prophecies are verified by virtue of the fact that they are contained in the Hebrew Bible. People of Jewish faith also believe that they are prophecy.

God's chosen people, the nation of Israel, had suffered long-standing oppression at the hands of its oppressors. The prophecies describe a great leader, the Messiah that would emerge from the line of King David and lead the people into a new era of peace and prosperity.[140] He would be the long-awaited savior of the nation of Israel, sent by God to rescue His people. Samuel, Isaiah,[141] Daniel, Micah and many others are Old Testament prophets who predicted the coming of the Messiah. Prophecy after prophecy describes him.[142] Scholars read these prophecies with great interest and believed that the Messiah would liberate the nation of Israel from oppression.

---

140. *See, e.g.* Isaiah 9:6 and Jeremiah 23:5-6.

141. *See, e.g.* Isaiah 53:4–6, and others. The entire book of Isaiah is a startling study in the prophecies concerning Jesus. I would encourage you to read through it. You will likely be amazed at the number of prophecies that match the events in Jesus' life.

142. *See, e.g.* Psalm 110:1; Isaiah 53:5, 59:20; ; Daniel 3:25, 7:14; Zechariah 3:8.

The first Christians were also Jews, arguably making Christianity a branch of Judaism. Where the branch diverges from the trunk is with the Christian belief that Jesus was the Messiah. Christians share the Jewish belief that God is a singular and all-powerful God who created everything. However, we believe that the Messiah was destined to be much more than a great leader.

The Jews were looking for a man to save them. Christians believe that God saved them. We believe that the Messiah was sent to deal with the God/man relationship issue, once and for all. We believe that Jesus was the Messiah prophesied in the Old Testament.[143] Nonetheless, his was a different kind of salvation. Jesus came to save each of us from the oppression of sin. God's chosen people become the people who accept this salvation. Jesus righted what was wrong with the God/man relationship. Jesus makes us right with God. His sacrifice resulted in our salvation that assures our eternal life in heaven.

The more closely Jesus' life and actions mirror the prophecies of the Old Testament, the more reasonable it is to conclude that he was the fulfillment of these prophecies. If Jesus had suddenly appeared without explanation, it would be very difficult to believe that he was who he said he was. However, his life, death, and resurrection closely reflect the prophecies contained in the Old Testament, and in some cases down to the last detail.

There are numerous prophecies[144] in the Old Testament which appear to describe Jesus' life and death. They are presented in the Bible without a great deal of fanfare and are often imbedded in an almost code-like way into scripture. The Creator of the universe doesn't need a lot of fanfare. He doesn't require a

As we examine these prophecies in their entirety, we begin to realize that they cannot be explained by mere coincidence.

---

143. *See, e.g.* Deuteronomy 18:15–19 (AMP), Isaiah 7:14, Malachi 3:1 (AMP).
144. Isaiah 52:13–53:12.

legion of angels to blow trumpets to announce him. Almost with a wink, there in the Old Testament are numerous passages describing His incredible plan, waiting to be discovered by the careful reader.

At the same time, the reader must know enough about Jesus to break the code. Some of these prophecies require the reader to have familiarity with the New Testament, in order to spot them.

You need to understand the chain of events leading to Jesus' crucifixion, in order to connect them with the prophecy. Other prophecies are so obvious and clear that anyone with a rudimentary understanding of Jesus' life and death can see them.

The Old Testament describes the relational breach that man creates with God. It also predicts the remedy for this breach.

The first in a long list of prophecies describing the remedy occurs in Genesis. Jacob gathered his sons together and predicted the future.[145] He predicted that someone from Judah will always be on the throne.[146] Jacob declared that he would wait on God for salvation.[147] Knowing the end of the story, as we do now, it resonates perfectly that Jesus, a descendant from the tribe of Judah, would provide that salvation.

Micah tells us that the savior would come from Bethlehem.[148] We know that Jesus was born in Bethlehem.[149] Christians believe in

The more Old Testament prophecy that we read, the more difficult it becomes to explain it all away as mere coincidence. The language is too specific and too identifiable with Jesus to be explained away.

145. Id.
146. Genesis 49:10.
147. Genesis 49:18.
148. Micah 5:2.
149. Luke 2:1–7 (AMP).

the virgin birth of Jesus.[150] In Isaiah, we read the prophecy of the Messiah's birth to a virgin. [151] In Psalms, we read a description of the Messiah's death.[152] Something is described that could only be the process of crucifixion. It was written many years before Jesus' birth.

I stumbled across the Twenty-Second Psalm one morning during my daily Bible study. I certainly wasn't expecting to read any prophecy in the middle of Psalms.

The passage is chilling in its description of a crucifixion.

In this Psalm,[153] we read the same statement that Jesus uttered as he died on the cross, "About three in the afternoon Jesus cried out in a loud voice, "Eli, Eli, lema sabachthani?" (which means "My God, my God, why have you forsaken me?").[154] The psalmist describes an incredibly precise description of Jesus' crucifixion experience. It is an intense first-hand experience. It is told from the viewpoint of someone who is personally going through a crucifixion. For example, there is an almost casual reference to clothing being divided up by his captors.[155] From the gospel accounts we know this happened to Jesus. The casual mention of it only adds to its believability.

Its authenticity comes from its realistic description of what we know now actually happened to Jesus.

The Psalm was written many years before Jesus' crucifixion, and yet it is clearly described from the personal perspective of the victim. It was written by someone who had been through

---

150. Luke 1:27 (AMP).

151. Isaiah 7:13.

152. Psalm 22:1.

153. Psalm 22:1.

154. Matthew 27:46.

155. Psalm 22:18.

it. It is reasonable to therefore conclude that Jesus' death on the cross was prophesied hundreds of years before it happened. The Psalm describes the crucifixion of Jesus. It's told in the first person, exactly the way it would have felt, thousands of years before it happened.

Some skeptics have argued that Jesus planned his own death, in order to fulfill Old Testament prophecy. He planned to die a martyr's death. Jesus and his followers created a *cause and effect* fulfillment of prophecy. Quoting from the Twenty-Second Psalm during his crucifixion was the *piece de resistance* of this elaborate hoax.

Suppose that it was a hoax. Never having actually experienced crucifixion, most people would describe it as unimaginable agony, and specifically in terms of their hands and feet. This obvious pain would come to most people's minds when they described crucifixion. You would expect the writing in the Psalm to focus on this pain.

And yet, after the initial and incredible pain and shock of this pain, science tells us that the longer one hangs on the cross, different variables enter into play. The victim's hands and feet would begin to hurt less as the other, deeper pain of death begins to take over. The person would begin to slip into a state of physical and mental shock. He would feel incredible thirst.[156] Joints, tendons, and ligaments would be strained beyond anything imaginable.[157] That is exactly how the psalmist describes it.

The thing about prophecy is that we often don't recognize it as such until it is fulfilled. If you were hanging on a cross, after having been scourged and beaten, and were dying a slow and agonizing death, it is unlikely that you would have the presence of mind, or the desire for that matter, to quote the psalmist. It is more likely that you would be exhausted, incoherent, and quickly moving into a state of physical shock.

---

156. Psalm 22:15.
157. Psalm 22:14.

Further, it is hard to imagine anyone engaging in a deception like this, given that they would not be around to reap any reward for the deception. There were too many variables outside of Jesus' control. He could not control the method of execution. In those days, death by stoning would have been just as likely as crucifixion. Jesus could not have predicted that the Roman soldiers would divide up his clothing.

If this was an elaborate scam, it's hard to imagine why his followers would have scattered after he was arrested. It seems more likely that they would have waited in the background, in order to be able to claim that they had seen the predicted events.

Other skeptics have posited a "swoon" theory. Jesus didn't die on the cross; he merely passed out and was later revived. It is possible. It's also possible that aliens rescued him and took him to Jupiter.

At some point, we have to simply choose what we believe, based upon all of the evidence available to us.

Despite Jesus horrible death, Christians rejoice in it. Why would anyone celebrate the horrible, humiliating death of their leader? The answer lies with the entire Christian story. The crucifixion of Jesus was the only method of execution so horrific that it would be indisputably sufficient to pay for the sins of mankind.

The psalmist explains it best. The Psalm concludes with a cry of victory, "They will proclaim his righteousness, declaring to a people yet unborn: He has done it!" [158]

Flawed Evidence?

Skeptics point to the four gospels that appear, at least in some cases, to conflict with each other. For example, the gospel of Luke is the only account of Jesus' crucifixion that includes Herod as a

---

158. Psalm 22:31.

player in the drama. The other three gospels do not. Therefore, one could conclude that at least one of the gospel accounts of Jesus' crucifixion is flawed. This conclusion assumes that each writer would have captured the same events in exactly the same way. This assumption sounds reasonable, at least on the surface. At the same time, it is more reasonable to assume that each was written from a different perspective: Matthew was a tax collector, Luke was a doctor. Each writer had a different perspective on the same Jesus.

All human memory is accomplished through the lens of perspective. Consider the circumstances surrounding President Kennedy's assassination in Dallas in 1963. There were numerous eyewitnesses watching the motorcade from Dealey Plaza. Many of their accounts differ dramatically.

Dealey Plaza is a relatively small civic square at the southern end of downtown Dallas. The Kennedy motorcade was travelling slowly. The distance between the seventh floor of the Texas Book Depository and the *grassy knoll*[159] is only a few hundred feet. Yet, there are eyewitnesses to the assassination who swear that shots came only from the Depository. Other witnesses are adamant that shots were also fired from the grassy knoll.

Each witness's testimony depends upon their perspective. The conclusion about whether there was one shooter or more depends upon the perspective of those witnesses. These are witnesses to an event that occurred only fifty years ago, and yet each has dramatically different testimony of the event. And today, despite law enforcement, presidential and congressional investigations, as well as numerous private investigations into the event, controversy remains.

We see everything through the lenses of our own experiences and biases. The Bible can be interpreted in different ways,

---

159. "Grassy knoll" refers to a small park-like patch of land in close proximity to the Texas Book Depository in Dallas.

depending upon the circumstances. Because circumstances change, each interpretation can be correct. For example, you can read a scripture on one day and get a certain nugget of wisdom out of it. You read the same scripture the next day and get an entirely different lesson. The lesson changes as your circumstances and perspective change. Both are valid.

Consider the debate about whether the Bible is literally accurate. There is no such thing as pure literal accuracy. All writing relies on figures of speech, metaphors, shorthand, and other literary devices to make their writing and speech more illustrative and interesting. The New Testament writers each wrote from a different perspective and also used these literary devices. Jesus used metaphors and parables to describe concepts to His followers for the same purpose.[160] These techniques are illustrative and are used to challenge the reader or listener to engage.

Instead, Christians believe in the inerrancy of the Bible. This means that we believe that the Bible contains no errors. Every single word, every single sentence was included for a specific reason.

Christians who argue that the Bible is literally accurate would be better served to avoid this debate. Otherwise, they risk losing the argument before it has begun.

The Bible was written by humans, and they used linguistic conventions and other literary devices, such as metaphor and figures of speech. It's unreasonable to assume that the writers of the Bible would write without these. We should not read the Bible or any document solely for its words.

They have conceded the unstated assumption that inerrancy equals literal accuracy. It doesn't.

---

160. *See, e.g.* Mark 4:14.

We should instead think critically about the Bible, how and why it was written, the context of the writings, and the perspective of the writers. The Bible will then begin to make much more sense. With respect to my literalist brothers and sisters, doing so will not undermine the inerrancy of the document.

Further, if the Bible is truly a divine document, then it only makes sense that man will have a difficult time making sense of it. We will misunderstand it and misinterpret it. This will lead to the false conclusion that the Bible contains errors. It's like an American tourist visiting a non-English-speaking country in Europe and getting frustrated with a shopkeeper who doesn't speak English. The truth though, is that responsibility for the miscommunication should fairly be borne by the American. In the same way, people read the Bible without a lot of thought, misunderstand and misinterpret it, and conclude that it is in error.

Ever since the Watergate scandal of the 1970s, the term *investigative journalist* has been a part of the American lexicon. Investigative journalists have written about every public and private scandal since then. They seek the truth, but if they can catch a politician with their hand in the proverbial cookie jar, even better. Some have made entire careers out of it. The world cannot get enough of its scandals. As any paparazzi know, there is lots of money to be made by fulfilling this appetite.

No one has presented evidence that would show that the Bible is inauthentic. No one has surfaced, claiming that "I forged the ancient manuscripts." No one has accused the Bible of being a phony document or a fraud. If the Bible were flawed, it would not have survived intact for thousands of years. Readers would discover and point out the flaws, and it would die a natural death. It would not continue to be the best-selling book of all time.

Certainly, people challenge its meaning. But the book itself has somehow remained unchallenged. The Bible has been in essentially the same form for years, quietly sitting on that bookshelf, awaiting its next reader. Generation after generation has consistently turned to the Bible for instruction, explanation, and comfort. It appeals to children and it appeals to the most hardened of criminals. It continues to be the bestselling book of all time, read by hundreds of millions, if not billions, for the insight it contains and wisdom it imparts. The Bible is perfect, assembled by many imperfect humans, at a time when perfection in literature wasn't possible. It's a book printed with earthly materials, using human processes. Despite this history, its longevity, and effectiveness are supernatural.

Millions have concluded that the Bible is inerrant exactly as it was written and translated. They've consulted it in difficult times and followed its advice. They've read it during times of fear and grief, and it has comforted them. Simply, the Bible has never failed them. After careful reading and logical and rational analysis "mistakes" turns out not to be mistakes after all. As a result, we believe that the Bible is exactly what it purports to be; the inerrant and inspired Word of God.

We believe it beyond a reasonable doubt.

A Fairy Tale?

Although the Bible's authenticity is not challenged, there are people who minimize its substance. Cynics believe that the Bible is nothing more than a series of fictional accounts, written by primitive people. They point to the stories and lessons of the Bible and conclude that these are "fairy tales." Or, they call the Bible an "inspirational book." Both are misleading.

Popular culture would have you believe that Christians are simpletons, blindly following silly doctrine. Skeptics dismiss the Bible as a fairy tale, written by people who tried to explain things they couldn't understand. They believe that the Bible is allegory. They argue that it is a series of fables written by men who worshiped a god because they couldn't explain things any other way. After all, humans don't rise from the dead. Seas do not open to allow people to escape, and then reclose and destroy entire armies. You can't feed five thousand people with a few loaves of bread and a couple of fishes.

They point to the Genesis story of the creation of man as evidence that the Bible is obviously flawed. They smirk at the notion that God literally created the universe and man in six days, as described in the Bible.[161] This has resulted in an ongoing debate between the so-called *creationists* and *evolutionists*. Evolutionists point to science and the fossil record to show that the idea that man was created by an omnipotent god is thinking for simpletons. They point to geologic and other scientific evidence showing that the earth was created over millions of years.

"Obviously," they argue, "before there was man, there were dinosaurs, and before dinosaurs, there were fish, and before there were fish, there were plankton," and so on. "For the Bible to claim that God created man from dirt, instantaneously, is silly." They conclude that the biblical description is inaccurate.

And yet, we have no way of knowing whether the writer of Genesis intended for a day to mean twenty-four hours, twenty-four million years, or something else. The conclusion that the Bible is inaccurate assumes that a "day" means twenty-four hours. For that matter, suppose that God did create the world in six, twenty-four hour days. If you begin with the assumptions that there is a God and that He is omnipotent,[162] then the debate becomes rather trivial. An omnipotent God can do anything that He wants.

Perhaps He created a fake fossil record, just to have a little fun with us.

---

161. Genesis 1:31 (AMP).

162. *See, e.g.* Genesis 1:1 (AMP); Psalm 115:3; Isaiah 14:24-27; Matthew 19:26.

Christians believe that God created man. Skeptics scoff be-

One of the biggest intellectual attacks on Christianity is that Christians attribute things to God that should be rightfully attributed to something else.

cause they believe that the universe started with a cosmic blob and that man in effect created himself, by evolving from a microorganism into a primate and from that, into a human.

Nonetheless, something or Someone had to create the blob and microorganism to begin with, or ignite the Big Bang, if you prefer. In other words, arguing that man evolved is pointless, at least as to a supreme Creator. This is unless you believe that something (the stuff of which the universe is made) can come from nothing. Otherwise, there has to be something or Someone behind it all. If one believes in an omnipotent and supreme Creator, then everything begins to make sense.

The natural tendency of things is to move in the opposite way, from order to disorder. It's called the *Second Law of Thermodynamics*, which says that over time, the total entropy of any thermodynamic system increases. Entropy means degeneration. Over time, things move from order to disorder. They degenerate. They decay. This idea has been repeatedly supported by astronomical evidence, which shows that the universe is continually expanding.

Somehow, what is happening here on earth is contrary to everything else happening in the universe. If things degenerate over time, then man evolving from amoeba would be exactly the opposite of what is supposed to happen. This means that humans are somehow an exception to the rule. The only reasonable explanation is that there is some kind of outside influence. The outside influence had to have enough power and intelligence to create a system that is contrary to the natural order of things.

It takes less faith to believe that God created the universe, than to believe that somehow organisms got together and kept getting together in an increasing orderly way. It's easier to believe that God is behind all of it.

A random series of occurrences that ultimately resulted in mankind doesn't add up.

Explaining things like the origin of life without the involvement

Believing that something can come from nothing requires huge faith.

of that Creator does as well. It takes substantially more faith to believe that life as we know it ultimately started from nothing and evolved from a protoplasmic mass, than to simply believe that there was a divine Hand behind all of it.

The fact that the earth continues to spin and the sun continues to shine is itself pretty fantastic. Science can describe it, but can't explain it. Science can't tell you what caused it. It can only offer theories. So people who put their faith in science are actually similar to people who put their faith in God. Both believe in something that can't be proven, at least directly.

Where they differ, though, is that Christians believe in God because His actions, as described in the source document of their faith, are consistent with their life experiences. They read about God's influence in the Bible, and He is validated by the testimony of their lives. Unless science followers invest the same effort in the study of science, then their faith isn't founded upon the source documents. It's founded upon hearsay evidence and speculation. Both are inadmissible in court.

An Inspirational Book?

I was on a plane not too long ago, heading to Florida on a business trip. The well-dressed woman sitting next to me and her husband were bound for a *New Age* inspirational seminar in the southern part of the state. She was tall and attractive. He was older and very scholarly looking, complete with a well-trimmed beard and an elbow-patched tweed jacket. On airplanes, people engage in conversations they might not otherwise. Perhaps it's simple nervousness or boredom. We share our innermost thoughts with complete strangers. The woman proudly told me that her husband was a New Age motivational speaker. She then noticed that I was reading the Bible.

Her face lit up and she said, "We love to read inspirational books."

I realized then and there that she had never actually read it.

Or, to be fair, I should say, *really have read it*. This claim assumes that any book purporting to be about God is inspirational.

> *Anyone who calls the Bible an "inspirational book" can't have read it.*

After all, it is inspiring to believe in God, especially if you group him into the nondescript impersonal category of a *higher power*. Higher powers are typically mindless automatons that don't require anything of you. If you haven't read the Bible, then it would be easy to misclassify it along with other books that deal with religion and self-improvement. That is a mistaken assumption.

A superficial reading of the New Testament reveals that the Bible is not an inspirational book. The God described in it is personally involved with mankind. He knows what is best for us and he knows what we are doing. The Old Testament describes the repeated pattern of mankind's rebellion against God and the resulting problems; decades of captivity, famine, and death.

Mankind fails miserably because it is selfish, greedy, dishonest, arrogant, and a bunch of other things, none of which are good. An incredible man called Jesus is born. The gospels end with him being horribly beaten, humiliated, and crucified.

Less inspirational is the fact that the Bible essentially issues an ultimatum. It requires action on our part. It warns us of the eternal consequences if we do not take that action. As opposed to "feel good" books about higher powers that mankind can control through its actions, the Bible contains simply too many absolutes to make one feel good. We cannot simply read it, feel good, and walk away from it. The Bible forces the reader to make a decision.

There are certainly a lot of good books out there that inspire me. They make me feel good. They motivate me to overcome adversity. But calling the Bible "inspirational" is like calling the *Mona Lisa* a "pretty picture." It's like referring to the Creator of the universe as one's "higher power."

> *The truth about calling the Bible an inspirational book is that nothing could be further from the truth.*

That's the irony. The Bible is inspirational, but only to those who have made the decision to commit their lives to God.

Inspirational books come and go. Pop psychobabble gurus appear on talk shows, sell books, and retire in the Cayman Islands. The Bible, on the other hand, is the same book that it has been for thousands of years. Its longevity and popularity place it in a unique position among all literature. The gospels are filled with unavoidable claims as to Jesus' true identity; you can't simply minimize them as inspirational stories. Whether you agree with them or not, the assertions of the Bible require any serious reader to come to a conclusion. That conclusion demands a personal decision from the reader. The decision is arguably the most important one that a person can ever make.

The Incontrovertible Controversy

For some people, the verdict is easy. For others, doubt remains. It's simply in our nature. Jesus had a follower who doubted. His name was Thomas. He had seen Jesus perform incredible miracles, including restoring sight to people, feeding thousands with a loaf of bread and a few fish, and raising Lazarus from the dead. And yet, when he first heard the rumors of Jesus' resurrection, he said that until he felt the nail holes in Jesus' hands for himself, he would not believe.[163]

You may have heard of the Shroud of Turin. The Shroud is a cloth purported to be the burial covering of Jesus after he was crucified. It's stored in meticulously controlled conditions at a Catholic cathedral in Turin, Italy. The Shroud contains a mysterious image of a man who bears a re-

We all have a choice. We believe what we choose to believe.

markable resemblance to Jesus. The image appears to show nail wounds in the wrists, gashes on the man's forehead consistent with a crown of thorns, and bruising and marks consistent with the beatings inflicted on Jesus as they are described in the gospels. Scientific analysis has revealed that the Shroud contains trace amounts of the spices and ingredients that were used to prepare bodies for burial in Jesus' time. Analysis of the cloth shows that it is consistent with fabric used in the time of Jesus.

Ever since the Shroud was first discovered, scientists, historians, and theologians have debated its authenticity. It has been subjected to intense scientific scrutiny and there is still no clear resolution as to its origin. It was originally carbon dated[164] as being from some time during the Middle Ages. If true, then this

---

163. John 20:25 (AMP).

164. "Carbon dating" is the process by which the presence of the isotope Carbon 14 is analyzed in order to determine the age of an object.

would of course mean that it couldn't be the burial shroud of Jesus. Still, some scientists have argued that the presence of algae on the Shroud contaminated the test. Others have theorized that the samples tested were of newer cloth pieces that were used to repair it through the ages.

The image contained in the Shroud appears to be a photographic negative. This was discovered in an almost accidental way. Photography was in its infancy. A photographer took a picture of the Shroud. When the photographic negative was developed, it revealed a positive image of the man. Scientific evidence suggests that an intense light or radiation source imparted the image upon the cloth, in a manner similar to photography. This is startling because no one disputes the fact that whatever its age, the Shroud is much, much older than photography. Some scientists have argued that the image was painted by a medieval artist, as a hoax. However, this theory simply doesn't make sense, unless that artist planning the hoax anticipated the invention of photography. Otherwise, why would he have painted the image in the negative?

The image of a crucified man is found on an ancient burial shroud. The image was created by a huge zap of energy. It is a photographic negative waiting for photography to be invented. All of the circumstantial evidence points to Jesus. To even the agnostic, it seems miraculous. Needless to say, that if the Shroud were somehow proven to indeed be the burial shroud of Jesus, it would have staggering implications. We would have photographic evidence of Jesus. The question as to Jesus' identity would be resolved.

It's not that simple.

What if you could prove that the things claimed about Jesus as they are described in the Bible were incontrovertibly true, beyond any doubt, much less a reasonable doubt? Let's take it a step

Even with incontrovertible proof, you would likely have a difficult time convincing people of the fact that Jesus was God.

further. What if you had an ancient videotape that could some-how prove that God had visited mankind two thousand years ago and provided a way out for man's sin problem? Chances are you would still be characterized as a crackpot or religious zealot. Critics would claim that you faked the videotape.

Humans focus on the here and now. We become so caught up in our own lives that we are unable to put them into an eter-nal perspective. That was the nation of Israel's problem dur-ing the exodus from slavery en route to the Promised Land. God spoke to them through Moses. He performed miracle af-ter miracle. They listened and obeyed, for a little while. But pretty soon, they were up to their old ways; disobeying and grumbling.[165]

We can't help it. It's the human way.

Suppose that God appeared today in human form. What would happen? Would we listen to Him? Would we obey His instruction? Would we commit our lives to Him? Christians believe that we already have the answer to that question. Jesus did appear. It happened two thousand years ago. And mankind not only rejected him, but mercilessly tortured and killed him.

We've come full circle in the analysis. Simply, man will be-lieve what man chooses to believe. Further, if there were incon-trovertible evidence of Jesus, then there would be no need for faith. In a sense, it would negate our power to choose. Faith is God's fundamental requirement of man. He has given us the power to choose. He will not impose His will upon us. Instead, He asks us to reach out in faith to Him.

If you examine all of the facts surrounding Jesus' life and death, it is difficult to come to any conclusion other than Jesus did what he did because he was who he said he was. Self-gain, insanity, and martyrdom aren't consistent with the description

---

165. Exodus 17:1.

of his life and ministry. We are left with only one other reasonable conclusion; that Jesus was who he claimed to be, and who the prophets predicted that he would be, and who his followers believe him to be.

In any trial, the jury is faced with a choice—whether to believe the prosecution's interpretation of the facts or the defense's. Both sides present evidence. Both sides supplement that evidence with theory. The jury must determine the truth. That is their charge. If they fail to reach a determination, we call it a *deadlocked* jury. The defendant goes free. In other words, a failure to decide is a decision in and of itself. You have to decide who Jesus is, and you have to decide whether you will follow him.

> *Once you are presented with the facts about Christianity, you are also faced with a decision.*

If you fail to decide, whether you realize it or not, you have made a decision.

The Wager

Whether a person believes that God exists, or the world is round, or anything else for that matter, is formed from hundreds and thousands of mental impressions. These impressions are caused by a variety of stimuli; what we read, see, feel, hear, and otherwise experience. These stimuli ultimately aggregate to form our view of something. Christians know that God exists and that Jesus was who he said he was based upon our lives in response to Him. We simply can't come up with a better explanation.

> *What we call a gut feeling is in reality the aggregation of a mix of inputs, many of which are so subtle as to be imperceptible.*

Perhaps you reached a verdict. Maybe you have deadlocked. In fact, let's just call it a mistrial. I'd like you to read further. And I'd like to make a wager with you. You'll need one book to participate — the Bible. Any Bible will do.

Here are the conditions of the bet: tonight or tomorrow morning (or right now, for that matter) collect your Bible and find a quiet place. Once you're settled, sit quietly for a minute. Say a simple prayer. Ask God to show you something, reveal something to you, if you will. Of course, if you don't believe in God, this will be a problem. But humor me for a minute. Say the prayer.

Now, open your Bible. It doesn't matter where. You can randomly pick a page. Now, read that page. Take your time and read it carefully. If you encounter something unfamiliar, read it again. Read the page like you would read any unfamiliar text. Read it for content. Read it for context. If you need definitions for terms, look them up in a dictionary or an online source. The point is to read it actively and not passively. Ask yourself, *"What does this mean?"*

Now, here's the wager: If you read your Bible, God will speak to you. Something that you read will strike a chord. It might be instruction. Or it could be that you've been struggling with something, and, lo and behold, an answer jumps out at you from the pages. You might realize that you need to change something in your life. Or perhaps you'll read something that will encourage you to treat someone differently.

Something will resonate for you. It might be a sentence. It might be a story. It might be a person. Or it might be something else.

That's how God speaks to us. Of course, there are many other ways He can do it. He can impress you during prayer. Or He may speak to you through the circumstances of your life. He can speak to you regularly and predictably through the Bible. That's why Christians call it His Word.

God may speak to you through a snippet of scripture. Or you may read a story and it will absolutely resonate for you. If you read the Bible, God will speak to you. He will help you to reach a verdict.

I'm betting on it.

CHAPTER SIX

The Contract

I t had been a bad week, yet another in a series of equally bad weeks. Litigation at work was consuming me. It meant many weekends of research and worry in a vain effort to resolve seemingly irresolvable issues. Litigation always means a fight. With the costs and angst involved, there are no real winners in lawsuits. Nonetheless, it's how America resolves its disputes.

Infinite loops of fear and doubt played themselves over and over again in my mind. Catastrophic results projected themselves on that large screen HDTV in my head, culminating in my complete ruination. Catastrophically worse than my own ruination, would be the ruination of my family. After you have children, the stakes in life become infinitely higher. Your gambles become their gambles. If you fail, you take them with you.

At the end of that particularly difficult week I was completely exhausted. It was a Friday night and my wife Beth and I, along with our two little girls, Meredith and Lauren were headed to the usual restaurant near our home. The girls and I were in the car, waiting for Beth. The stress had so overwhelmed me that I just sat there in the car and silently prayed. In that few seconds of pure and raw angst, my prayer said it all: *"Father, I have been holding onto this for too long. Forgive me for worrying. I give it all to you."*

After opening my eyes, that stifling weight in my spirit lifted in way that is difficult to describe. The fear was gone. I was back in the present, instead of in the future with that gnawing fear. I was simply sitting there in my car, with my two beautiful little girls.

Beth got in the car and we pulled out of the driveway of our home. As we drove off, I looked out the window to my left. It was a double rainbow; one rainbow on top of another but each separate and distinct. There was a line of dark clouds and the rainbows rose up beneath them and into them, with no apparent end. The two multicolored shafts of translucence were incredibly beautiful, and looked like a passage directly into heaven.

I pointed out the double rainbow to the girls. Neither had seen a rainbow before. Then something occurred to me that I had read in the Bible and quickly forgotten. It is called the *Great Flood*.

God's Agreement

People break promises. That is why the law of contracts came into being. The law provides confidence that certain rules and principles will be enforced between parties to an agreement. It encourages people to conduct business.

A promise is a promise. Despite that fact, the law distinguishes between promises that are legally enforceable and those that are not. A mere gratuitous promise, such as "I'll give you money if I feel like it," is not enforceable. Other promises are legally enforceable. An example of an enforceable promise is a promise made by a party: "I will sell you my house for $100,000." If the other party promises in return that she would, in fact, buy the house, then both promises are enforceable.[166] The point is that our law determines, based upon well-established precedent, which promises are legally enforceable.

With God, all promises are enforceable. God does not break promises. He does not make gratuitous promises. The foundation of God's relationship with mankind has always been the *covenant*. This covenant is described throughout the Old Testament, and in particular in the books of Genesis, Leviticus, and Deuteronomy. The covenant can be summed up as follows: *God agreed to take care of mankind*. The condition of this promise is that we must trust Him. Trust is manifested in the form of obedience. The covenant was expressed from the very beginning when God created man and woman. He created us; he would provide for us.

With the Great Flood, God caused it to rain for forty days and nights in order to destroy mankind, which had sunk to levels of depravity and evilness beyond anything imaginable.[167] The flood was the logical conclusion of events which began with Adam and Eve. We started with a perfect and unfettered relationship, in which Adam and Eve relied on God and God took care of them. He placed them in the Garden of Eden and provided everything that they needed. He took care of them. God told Adam and Eve not to eat from a certain tree.[168] They disobeyed.

Adam and Eve believed the lie. They allowed Satan to plant seeds of discontent in their hearts, which ultimately caused them to lose faith in God. This loss of faith was demonstrated through their disobedience to Him. They breached the contract.

---

166. Ordinarily, contracts for the sale of land must also be in writing, in order to be enforceable.

167. Genesis 6:11.

168. Genesis 2:16.

Their descendants perpetuated and amplified this rift with God. Abel murdered Cain.[169] The evil continued in an ever-increasing downward spiral.

God was ready to start over. He warned Noah to build an ark. The flood destroyed all of mankind, except for Noah and his family.[170] After forty days, the waters receded and God blessed Noah.[171] God provided for Noah and his family. God gave them a chance to start all over again. God and Noah entered into a new covenant, which would again reconcile God and mankind.[172]

In recognition of this new beginning of the relationship, God placed a rainbow in the sky to remind man of the covenant.[173]

Through His covenants with Noah and later Abraham, God restored His relationship with the nation of Israel. But the cycle continued and the Israelites quickly found themselves in slavery to the Pharaoh. At God's direction, Moses led them on the exodus out of Egypt, in search of the Promised Land. Moses acted as the nation of Israel's father for many years and tried to teach them God's ways. The book of Deuteronomy was his last instruction to his people. In it, he reiterated the law and reminded them of what was important as they reached their destination. Deuteronomy describes the end of the forty-year ordeal that the nation of Israel endured. They were on the verge of reaching the Promised Land. It was particularly poignant because Moses knew that he would die soon,[174] before reaching it.[175]

Moses explained to the Israelites what their relationship with God must be.[176] Moses told them that they were to love God

---

169. Genesis 4:8.

170. Genesis 7:23.

171. Genesis 9:1.

172. Genesis 9:8.

173. Genesis 9:12.

174. Deuteronomy 4:21–22.

175. Id.

176. Deuteronomy 6:13.

with everything that they had.[177] Jesus called this the *greatest commandment*.[178] Moses described what loving God means. Love requires obedience.[179] Obedience is the manifestation of our trust in God.

Jesus tells us not to worry about the things of this life.[180] God has proven time and time again that He can be trusted. He will always honor His covenant. God wants us to give Him our problems. Sometimes we simply fail to trust Him. We instinctively reach for our arsenal of intellectual weapons and begin the battle. In doing this, we are following the pattern of all mankind, beginning with Adam and Eve, who refused to simply surrender everything to Him.

Many years ago, a contract required a *seal*; a special wax imprint, which was intended to convey the seriousness of the mutual promises and provide tangible evidence of the contract's enforceability. Jesus' death on the cross fulfilled all of the law at once. We do it thanks to his efforts, through his grace. We are incapable of breaching the agreement anymore. Our faith in Jesus seals our agreement with God, once and for all.

> *When we trust in Jesus, we have fulfilled our end of the bargain for all time.*

This brings me back to the rainbow. I had always assumed that the Noah rainbow story in Genesis was a metaphor. The story had always seemed strange to me. It reminded me of some of the mythology of ancient peoples used to describe phenomena that they couldn't otherwise explain. It never occurred to me that it would have a real application in my life.

---

177. Deuteronomy 6:5.
178. Matthew 22:37 (AMP).
179. Deuteronomy 10:16.
180. Matthew 6:34 (AMP).

For weeks I had tried to emotionally and intellectually muscle my way through problem after problem. Through my own stubborn refusal to submit to Him, I had cornered myself into an infinite downward spiral of stress and despair.

During these times the Holy Spirit[181] is there with me. He speaks to me in an inaudible and yet distinct way. It's hard at times to distinguish between His words and my own self-talk.

It's can be hard to hear Him because I frequently interrupt.

If I stop and listen, He'll speak to me. It may be through a particular passage of scripture. Perhaps I've read it before. Something resonates within me and the scripture takes on a new and deeper meaning. Or, He may send someone to me; an inadvertent messenger. There have been times in my life someone came into my life and imparted a particular piece of the wisdom puzzle that helped me to deal with the issue.

On that day, sitting there in my car with my family, God showed me once again, that the Bible is absolutely accurate. When I gave it all to Him, it didn't matter anymore. God would take care of it. It would all work out for good.[182]

When I finally came to my senses and submitted to Him, He sent an incredibly beautiful rainbow. For the first time in their lives, my little girls got to see His reminder for all mankind of His covenant. He was just waiting for the right time to use it to teach me. He had shown this obstinate prodigal son, so determined to do things my own way, something that could only be described as a sign. Once we return to Him and entrust our lives to Him, He will take care of everything.

And the funny thing is that shortly after that, the litigation simply went away. The parties decided that they had better things to do than to fight.

---

181. The Holy Spirit is discussed in detail in Chapter Eight.
182. Romans 8:28 (AMP).

CHAPTER SEVEN

The Star Witness

He opened his eyes with a start, shivering, and drew a gasping breath into his tiny lungs. A flood of feelings unlike anything he had ever experienced before rushed at him, enveloping him like some awful disease. He was cold. He was hungry. He was exhausted. He was in pain. It was difficult to see. At first, he didn't know where he was. The air was damp and earthy. There was the sound of trickling water nearby. He realized that he was in a cave. The smell of smoke from the small fire wafted toward him, stinging his tiny nostrils.

Then he remembered why he was in this place.

A bearded man held him carefully and wrapped him in a rough cloth. It irritated his tender skin, but he was immediately thankful for its warmth. He felt completely helpless and out of place. These were feelings that he had never experienced before.

The man then handed him to the woman. She was so young, not much older than a child. She had incredibly kind eyes. This woman was his mother. He remembered how remarkably obedient she had been when she learned of the plan. As she held him, she parted her tunic and moved his head close to her breast. Instinctively, he suckled. He had never felt hunger before. When his tiny stomach was full, the woman held him to her chest and a little bubble parted his lips. She placed him in the feeding box to sleep. It had an animal smell. He quickly fell into a deep sleep, exhausted.

The baby became a little boy. The little boy played. He stubbed his toes and skinned his knees. He bled and he cried. The boy's mother held him and comforted him. The boy's father made little toys for him to play with. He had pets and friends. The boy learned to read.

He learned about his Father.

His father taught him to build things and use crude carpentry tools. The boy became a man. He grew stronger.

He worshipped his Father at the Temple and studied His inspired Word. His insight into the Word was beyond human comprehension. He became a rabbi, not through formal education, but through his incredible wisdom and knowledge.

Some people realized that he was different than anyone who had ever lived before. The man had no sin. God was his Father and he was God's son. He lived in complete and utter dependence upon his Father. It was as if he and his Father were somehow hardwired together. He knew God's thoughts.

He saw the evil and depravity that had polluted the perfect world his Father had created. He felt deep love for mankind and yet horror at what it had become. One day, as he stood in the line waiting to be baptized by his cousin John, [183] he knew that his time had come. He knew that the end was near—the

---

183. Matthew 3:13 (AMP).

fulfillment of His Father's will and His plan for mankind. He knew that he would soon face something that was so horrible and so incredibly evil, and yet so necessary. He knew that it would, once and for all, solve the problem of mankind's free will and sin.

We don't know much about Jesus' childhood or how he grew up. We don't know whether or not he performed miracles as a boy. We don't know exactly how or when he realized that he was God. We don't know much about Jesus' childhood or adolescence. Only his public ministry is documented in the gospels. He traveled from town to town, with the base of his ministry being in Galilee.

We might assume that he was indwelt with the Holy Spirit and divine wisdom from the beginning. He knew from the moment of his birth that he was God. Or perhaps he had a pivotal moment, when it all came together for him and he realized exactly who he was. On the other hand, it's possible that his identity dawned on him gradually, over time. It doesn't really matter. All that matters is who he said he was and whether we choose to believe it.

The Creator of everything, the Owner of all things, lived with us for a while.

Fully Man and Fully God

Christians believe that Jesus was *fully man* and yet *fully God*.[184] Jesus faced the same problems and temptations that you and I face every day, and yet Jesus never sinned.[185] How can it be that someone who is fully man never sinned?

---

184. Philippians 2:6-7.
185. 2 Corinthians 5:21.

Throughout the Old Testament, God sent the Holy Spirit to work with mankind. God selectively used the Holy Spirit to accomplish His will on earth.[186] Jesus was different. He was completely filled with the Holy Spirit. Jesus, being fully man, could have chosen to ignore the Holy Spirit. He didn't. We believe that he allowed the Holy Spirit to guide him in everything he did. After Jesus was resurrected, he promised to send the Holy Spirit so that those who follow him could have this same power available to them.[187]

The gospel of Luke describes a conversation between Jesus and his disciples, shortly after he fed the five thousand people with five loaves and two fishes.[188] Jesus asked them who the crowds thought that he was. His disciples responded that people thought he might be Elijah or one of the prophets.[189] These eyewitnesses to miracles viewed him as someone with great power.

But some did not yet view him as God. When Jesus asked his own inner circle, Luke tells us that only Peter declared that Jesus was the Messiah. The other disciples were conspicuously silent. Perhaps they were hedging their bets. The fact that these same men scattered after Jesus was arrested shows that their faith in Jesus as the Messiah was not yet complete.

Even the people who lived and worked with Jesus needed at least some degree of faith to sustain their belief that he was God's son. We have to reach a bit deeper to accept that Jesus was who he claimed to be. It requires faith. His followers had a front-row seat to the miracles he performed, yet still needed faith to believe.

It goes against our basic preconceptions that a human could also be God.

---

186. *See, e.g.* Numbers 11:25–26, 27:18; Isaiah 32:15, 63:7–14; 1 Samuel 10:10, 16:13–14; 2 Kings 2:9–10 (AMP).
187. John 14:16.
188. Luke 9:18.
189. Luke 9:19.

A Fresh Look at the Rules

The Mosaic Law had been around for a long time before Jesus' ministry. The Israelites followed an intense rules-based system, and they believed that one's likelihood of eternal life depended upon one's obedience to the rules. It was almost like a game. Religious leaders kept score. They twisted the rules for their own purposes. They engaged in great debate about how these laws should be properly honored. Not unlike lawyers of today, they dissected and parsed the meaning of the laws. However, the stakes were very high. The penalties for not following the rules were severe, up to and including death.

Jesus was frequently criticized because his followers did not strictly follow these rules.[190] The religious leaders misunderstood Jesus' perspective as laxness toward the law. They were provided to an unrepentant and rebellious people.

The rules were a mere shadow of God's desire for His creation.

He was once asked by religious leaders which commandment was the most important.[191] It was a trick question. They weren't just talking about the *Ten Commandments*.[192] There were also hundreds of other rules and requirements described in Leviticus and Deuteronomy. They asked him to pick the single most important rule out of pages and pages and hundreds of rules. Out of all of these rules, which is the most important rule to God? It was an impossible question for any man.

Jesus had clearly studied the Hebrew scripture. He used it very effectively when dealing with the religious establishment. Even the most educated rabbi would have had trouble with the

190. *See, e.g.* Mark 2:17.
191. Matthew 22:36.
192. Exodus 20:2–17 (AMP).

question. To Jesus, the answer to this impossible question was simple. His perspective was a supernatural one. He did it as only the Author of those rules could.

Jesus distilled hundreds and hundreds of arcane, intricate, and detailed rules into two rules.

He knew that the legal system was about to change. With the sacrifice that he was about to make, there wouldn't be a need for sacrifices any longer. So, he was only concerned with two things; how we would relate to each other, and how we would relate to Him. He said that we are to love God with everything we have; and love others the same way that we love ourselves.[193] This focus on loving God and loving mankind was revolutionary, given the extensive rule-based system in effect at the time. Jesus taught us a simple and profound lesson — loving God was the most important thing that a person can do. We love God through our faith in Him and our obedience to Him.

He taught his followers to turn the other cheek in dealing with their enemies.[195] He taught that following the rules for the rules' sake was simple hypocrisy.[196]

Jesus taught that the condition of one's heart was infinitely more important than a superficial obedience to the law.[195]

In some cases, his teaching meant a stricter interpretation of the rules. His view of adultery, for example, was much harsher than the strictest Jewish rules. He viewed hating someone as the same thing as murder and lust as equivalent to adultery.[197]

---

193. Matthew 22:37.
194. Matthew 23:1 (AMP).
195. Matthew 5:39 (AMP).
196. Matthew 7:5.
197. Matthew 5:28 (AMP).

Jesus was criticized as someone who wanted to do away with the legal system that had governed Israel for thousands of years. However, he spoke with the authority of someone who had authored the original rules. This is why he said that his purpose was to fulfill the law.[198] Jesus didn't want to destroy the Judaic law. He came to fulfill the law.[199]

The enforcement of any law is through a trial, conviction and punishment. For justice to prevail, disobedience merits a penalty. Jesus' death paid the price for the sins of all of mankind. His sacrifice paid the penalty for all violations of the law, past, present, and future. There was no trial because God already knew that the punishment was merited and who would accept this punishment.

His death would become the payment for all of those broken rules. It's why he taught about the intent behind the rules. He wanted us to understand what the rules really meant. They weren't about keeping score.

They were about winning the game once and for all.

The Jesus Plan

God was here. He came to this planet and lived among mankind. Jesus was the way that God told mankind exactly who He is. He was a living, breathing, in the flesh representation of God. He became a man for the purpose of showing mankind how to live, only to die in the most agonizing and humiliating way imaginable.

In an eternal human irony, mankind looked toward the heavens for God when He was there among us the entire time.

---

198. Id.
199. Matthew 5:17 (AMP)

Some view the Old Testament God is a demanding, angry and vengeful God. After all, they reason: *"Flooding the entire earth is pretty harsh, and testing Abraham by telling him to kill his only son[200] seems like the infliction of unreasonable and unnecessary emotional distress."*

But God loves us. God shows His gentle love through provision to His people. When the Israelites were wandering in the wilderness, God provided for them perfectly. It wasn't good enough. Man continued to rebel and to sin. God fixed it, once and for all, by sending His son to live in this corrupted world and to die on a cross, as payment for our sins.[201] His message of love is perfectly consistent throughout the Bible. God has provided for His creation throughout history and clearly explained how we are to live, but will not compromise one iota when it comes to self-destructive human behavior.

Jesus' ministry began simply enough, but there was clearly something different about him. He cared deeply about people. He taught forgiveness and compassion. He cured people with incurable illnesses and brought dead people back to life.[202]

His two first disciples, Peter and Andrew, dropped everything to begin their relationship with him.[203] Shortly after that, Jesus began to perform miracles. His early miracles were so great and yet so subtle that people who witnessed them may not have been aware that a miracle had occurred. Jesus turned water into wine at a big wedding in Cana.[204] These were huge urns of water, which somehow were transformed into wine. The fellow in charge of the wedding banquet didn't realize what had

---

200. *See* Chapter Nine.
201. John 3:16.
202. John 12:1.
203. Mark 1:16.
204. John 2:9.

happened. Instead, he asked the bridegroom why he had waited until the end of the wedding feast to serve the best wine.[205]

Later, Jesus taught a crowd of thousands of people on a hillside.[206] In those days, hunger was a daily companion for most people. His disciples had a few loaves of bread and a few fish.[207] One day, he taught thousands of people, many of who were likely poor and hungry. Jesus called his disciples to him and said, "I have compassion for these people; they have already been with me three days and have nothing to eat. I do not want to send them away hungry, or they may collapse on the way." [208]

Somehow, this food was miraculously extended in such a way that it fed thousands, and there was food left over.[209] The gospel accounts suggest that it simply happened between the time the first basket of food was passed around until everyone was fed.

Many of those people probably didn't fully appreciate what had happened. There wasn't a loud "Bang" or "Poof," followed by the food appearing. It just happened.

Jesus taught us to love;[210] however, he is every bit as demanding as the God is described in the Old Testament. When he encountered the money changers who were profiting from worshippers at the Temple, he chased them away.[211] They set up tables just outside the temple, so that people could exchange their money for local currency, in order to purchase sacrificial animals to make an offering. Jesus, using an improvised whip, overturned their tables and chased them

---

205. John 2:10.
206. John 6:3.
207. John 6:9.
208. Matthew 15:32.
209. John 6:11.
210. Matthew 5:44 (AMP).
211. John 2:15 (AMP).

out of the temple grounds. They turned his Father's house into a commercial venture and he couldn't stand for it.

He taught that faith in God was the most important thing that any person could have. He told his followers not to worry because God would take care of everything.[212] He taught his followers to rely on God completely. As he died on the cross, Jesus forgave his executioners and those responsible for his death.[213]

His work on the cross frees us up to be all that we can be and to do God's work during our time here on earth. Through Jesus, we can face our lives and God with certainty. We know without a doubt our eternal destiny.[214] This puts things in perspective for us. With the assurance of eternal salvation, we view our lives very differently. Our perspective changes when we measure our lives against eternity.[215]

Jesus' life and death were in fulfillment of a plan created and implemented by God. This plan was foretold thousands of years earlier, in the writings of the Old Testament prophets. Man had originally been created in God's perfect image but quickly began to diverge from that perfection. Adam and Eve took a different path than that of God. Mankind became hopelessly ensnared by sin. God, through His Spirit, reached out to man from heaven. Ultimately, He became a man and reached out personally. He allowed Himself to be sacrificed, in order to nullify the sins of mankind.[216]

The plan was simple in its elegance, but hugely expensive in its execution. In Jesus, God assumed human form and lived among humans. Despite the temptations and troubles of life, Jesus never sinned. Instead, he lived his life in perfect obedience

---

212. Luke 12:22-23 (AMP).
213. Luke 23:34 (AMP).
214. 2 Corinthians 3:4–5.
215. 2 Corinthians 4:18.
216. John 3:16.

to God. This meant that he was the perfectly qualified sacrifice, and that his life was the payment for all of the sins of humanity, forever. His resurrection proved that there was life after death and that God was in control of it. Jesus' ascension into heaven meant that he could return in a different form, a spiritual form, and that he would take his place in the hearts of anyone who asked.

God can coexist in peace with man because man's sin debt has been paid. He now lives within His followers. He can begin to truly remake them into His own perfect image.

The Sacrificial Lamb

Everyone has sinned.[217] Sin eternally separates every person from God, and therefore, without more, dooms us to eternal separation from Him.[218] The only way to avoid it is through restitution for our sin. Mankind attempted to make restitution for thousands of years under Mosaic Law through a blood sacrifice. Blood sacrifice was the atonement for sin.[219]

Rather than being an aloof and distant god, God got down on our level.

How does a perfect and rational God deal with the problem of sin? He does it by paying for that sin Himself. Rather than demanding sacrifice and worship, Jesus offered himself as the sacrifice. Christians believe that Jesus was a *perfect sacrifice* for everyone's sins. He lived a perfect and sinless life, but was

---

217. Romans 3:23–24.
218. Romans 6:23.
219. Leviticus 17:11.

crucified nonetheless.[220] He was to be the sacrifice for all of the sins of mankind.[221]

His sacrifice was a gift to mankind. The gift had three parts: (1) the gift of forgiveness for sins, past, present, and future; (2) the gift of eternal life in heaven after death;[222] and (3) the gift of the Holy Spirit. The gift was intended for everyone. Jesus' horrible death by crucifixion was restitution once and for all and ended the need for blood sacrifice.[223] We didn't do anything to earn it. It was a free gift.

We have to accept the gift. Under the principles of property law, for a gift to be valid and binding, three elements must exist: First, the gift giver or *grantor* must intend to give the gift. Second, there must be an actual transfer of the property. Finally, and most importantly, the recipient of the gift must accept the gift.

The only way to accept the gift is by faith. [224]

Jesus died so that we could live forever.[225] After Jesus, we live by faith in the saving effect of his crucifixion. Once we accept Jesus as our savior, our *personal savior* (meaning that *I* acknowledge that he died for *my* sins, as opposed to some abstract notion of his crucifixion for the sins of *all mankind*), our sins our forgiven.[226] It is essentially a spiritual "free pass." To God, our sins are no longer visible. He was sacrificed for mankind. The sacrifice provided a way, once and for all, for man to reconcile with God.

---

220. 2 Corinthians 5:21.
221. Hebrews 10:10.
222. Id.
223. 2 Corinthians 5:21.
224. Ephesians 2:8.
225. John 3:16.
226. John 3:18; Romans 3:21-26 (AMP); 2 Corinthians 5:17.

A Great Teacher?

"Okay, I'll give you that much. The Bible is a great book. Jesus was a great teacher."

Among the things one can say about Christ, simply being a great teacher is not one of them. This is because, unlike other great teachers, such as Buddha, Mohammed, and even Moses, Jesus claimed to be God's son, sent to earth directly from heaven. [227] He claimed to

The same people who call the Bible an "inspirational book" call Jesus a "great teacher." It's an almost backhanded compliment.

have a unique and special relationship with God and to speak for God.[228] "Jesus said to him, I am the Way and the Truth and the Life; no one comes to the Father except by (through) Me. If you had known Me [had learned to recognize Me], you would also have known My Father. From now on, you know Him and have seen Him." (AMP)[229]

Jesus took the Old Testament law and showed the hypocrisy of strict adherence to it to the exclusion of all else. This is why people call him a great teacher. He didn't get so caught up in the Mosaic Law that he overlooked the spiritual forest for the trees. What they don't understand is that when it came to God, Jesus was completely inflexible. He described faith in God as a "take it or leave it" proposition. He was absolutely steadfast that his way was the only way to God.

Jesus claimed that he was God.

This claim eliminates the possibility that Jesus was merely a great teacher. Instead, Jesus was who he claimed to be — or he

---

227. There are numerous references in the New Testament regarding Jesus' claim to be God. Among them: John 8:58, 10:30–33, John 14:9–11, Matthew 8:20, 9:6, 10:23 (AMP).

228. John 10:25.

229. John 14:6-7(AMP).

was crazy, or he deliberately manipulated people for personal gain. Jesus' words require you to decide who he is. They demand it. You cannot simply acknowledge him as a great teacher, and then move on.

Great teachers don't falsely claim divinity. Crazy and evil people do.

CHAPTER EIGHT

Sidebar in the Judge's Chambers

The Trinity

Christians believe that there is only one God. Religious scholars call it *monotheism*. This is in contrast with religions such as Hinduism, whose adherents believe that there are multiple gods. Hindus worship different gods for different purposes: one god who oversees crops, another god oversees relationships, and so on. This belief is referred to as *polytheism*.

Christians believe in one all-powerful God. And yet, the Bible claims that Jesus was God and that the Holy Spirit is God. Skeptics point to this as yet another example of the fallacy of the Bible.

How should we deal with it? Some Christians simply avoid it. They shrug their shoulders and say, "There are just some things that humans cannot understand." These folks would have you trust in the literal accuracy of the Bible. The Bible describes God in these three ways, therefore that's the end of it. God is God, Jesus is God, and the Holy Spirit is God because that's what the Bible says.

This is exactly the criticism that many people have of Christianity. They view it as a religion that doesn't think, but merely accepts doctrine as truth.

In reality, the Trinity is perfectly consistent with a monotheistic belief system. God, Jesus, and the Holy Spirit are the same God. Each is God manifested in a different way. One God is manifested in three ways.

If we begin with the premise that God is omnipotent and can do anything, the apparent human complications of the Trinity dissolve. Our conclusion is that He is not limited by earthly temporal references. God can be in heaven, but also on earth as a human at the same time. God can be in human form, but also in the form of Spirit at the same time. God the Father in heaven, God's son Jesus on earth, and God's Spirit anywhere and everywhere that He chooses to be, whenever He chooses it, makes perfect sense. He can also interact with each of us today in the form of a Spirit.

God can be on His throne in heaven, and walking the streets of Jerusalem as an itinerant carpenter/ preacher at the same time.

A Closer Look at the Holy Spirit

Some Christians are uncomfortable talking about the Holy Spirit. They are fine with talking about a God whom we cannot see. They are comfortable describing Jesus as our savior. But when it comes to the Holy Spirit, they get uncomfortable. They are afraid that if they articulate this belief, they risk ridicule. It sounds almost mystical. The term *holy roller* comes to mind. As with the term "born again," some Christians view matters involving the Holy Spirit as a theological artifact of more primitive days.

Whether we like it or not, the Holy Spirit is a fundamental component of Christian beliefs. It's the one thing that deeply connects us to God on a daily basis. One of the last recorded promises Jesus made to his followers before he ascended into heaven was that he would send the Holy Spirit to them. Yet, many Christians either don't or won't grasp the idea that the Holy Spirit was the next step, and a very important one, after Jesus left this earth. God lives within each of us. He is a part of our lives.[230]

Originally, man had a close and personal relationship with God. The first chapter of the book of Genesis begins with God creating the earth and the heavens, and everything in them. The second chapter describes God's creation of the first human. Seeing that the man needed a companion, God created the first woman. In the third chapter of Genesis, God visited His creation personally. God is described as physically walking in the Garden of Eden.[231] You might think this description is allegory. In this particular anecdote, the content and tone do not offer those as an option. It seems that in the beginning, God was physically present with man.

After Adam and Eve sinned, God withdrew. He stopped interacting directly with them. Instead, God's Holy Spirit became

---

230. 1 Corinthians 6:19 (AMP).
231. Genesis 3:8.

the go-between with mankind. Before Jesus, there were numerous examples of the Holy Spirit's outreach to mankind in the Old Testament.[232] David writes repeatedly in Psalms of his own encounters with the Holy Spirit.[233] Nonetheless, the Holy Spirit's interaction with man was limited. Generally, the Holy Spirit interacted only with the most righteous of people.

Christians believe that mankind was created with a void in our psyche. This void creates a longing for something (or Someone) beyond the scope of our current existence. The difference between Christians and non-Christians is how they fill this void. Many people attempt to fill it with alcohol, drugs, sex, video games, and any other excessive thing that provides temporary pleasure. We become addicted to pleasure. As any alcoholic knows though, that next drink is never enough. The alcoholic drinks to oblivion, wakes up to a horrible hangover, and starts the cycle all over again, hoping to fill the void. Without some sort of intervention, the pleasure will ultimately kill the addict.

Christians fill this void by allowing God to enter and fill us. When we make the conscious and thoughtful decision to trust Jesus for our salvation and turn our lives over to him, something incredible happens to us. God begins to live inside of us in the form of the Holy Spirit.[234] It's called it the *indwelling of the Holy Spirit*.

The Holy Spirit leads us to make the decision for Christ.[235] This is not to say that the Holy Spirit works the same way in the lives of non-believers as He does in believers. Instead, the Holy Spirit works to lead us to Christ before we become believers, and to live for Christ after we become believers.

---

232. *See, e.g.* Judges 3:10, 1 Samuel 16:13.

233. Psalm 51:11 and 139:7 are examples of David's reference to the Holy Spirit; however, arguably all of the Psalms were written by David through the influence of the Holy Spirit.

234. 1 Corinthians 3:16.

235. John 16:13 (AMP).

The prophet Joel predicted that someday, everyone could have access to the Holy Spirit.[236] Jesus fulfilled this prophecy. He explained that he had to go to heaven in order for the Holy Spirit to come. Through his crucifixion and resurrection, God provided the means for man to be reconciled with God. This restoration of the relationship meant that Holy Spirit would be available to all of Jesus' followers.[237]

The Holy Spirit is also called the *Comforter*, the *Spirit of Truth*, the *Helper* and the *Holy Ghost*. Jesus explained to his followers that he must ascend into heaven in order for the Holy Spirit to come to the new church.[238] Most Christians, through personal experience, understand the incredible power and blessings of the Holy Spirit.

The Holy Spirit to Christians is like a father to a newborn infant. Infants can recognize early on who Mama is. This is because, infants, in most cases, are immediately dependent upon their mothers. They get hungry and Mama feeds them, cooing and comforting them along the way. On the other hand, the infant has no idea (other than perhaps a vague idea) that its father exists.

And yet, the father is always in the background, protecting the infant and providing for her in other ways. Over time, the infant begins to realize that in addition to its mother, she also has a father who has been there all along.

Although our sins have been forgiven and we have been filled with the Holy Spirit, we still have choices to make. God does not remove our free will and power to

> *The Holy Spirit is always there in the background, working God's will in our lives, providing for us, guiding us and teaching us.*

---

236. Joel 2:28 (AMP).
237. 1 Corinthians 6:19-20 (AMP).
238. John 14:26, 16:7.

choose. The fact that we have the power to choose shows us how much God loves us. When we are

He gave us our lives, and also gave us the power to choose what to do with them.

filled with the Holy Spirit, He will comfort and guide us. Regardless, we still have the power to choose to follow His guidance or act upon our former desires. This is essentially the great spiritual battle.

We can choose to listen to the quiet prompting of Holy Spirit, or we can choose to yield to the daily temptations of life—the money, status, power, lust, anger, and envy that will lead ultimately to unhappiness.

The Holy Spirit provides incredible spiritual gifts to believers.[239] Christians who are filled with and controlled by the Holy Spirit lead fruitful lives that glorify God. Christians who short-circuit the Holy Spirit by choosing to go their own way lead frustrated and defeated lives.

The apostle Paul provides an example of how the Holy Spirit interacts with Christians. Paul was filled with the Holy Spirit.[240] Paul preached to the same kinds of people who had, in the not too distant past, crucified Jesus. These same people hated Paul and did everything possible to defeat his efforts to spread the gospel of Jesus. Paul was imprisoned repeatedly,[241] beaten, and flogged[242](in those days, a flogging meant the very real risk of death), stoned[243] (which he survived), shipwrecked, and bitten by a deadly snake,[244] not to mention the daily abuse and harassment he suffered at the hands of those opposed to the new Christian

---

239. *See, e.g.* Galatians 5:22, 1 Corinthians 12:7-11.

240. Acts 13:2.

241. Acts 16:23; 22:35; 24:27.

242. Acts 16:22.

243. Acts 14:19.

244. Acts 28:3.

movement. Somehow, wherever he went, he influenced people for Christ. His life was his example. His boundless energy and enthusiasm, his positive attitude and servant's heart exemplified his faith.

How could anyone suffer what Paul suffered and not turn into a bitter and defeated person? The answer lies in Paul's constant reliance on the Holy Spirit. The Holy Spirit told Paul where to go, whom to see, and what to do. Paul was willing to follow. Paul wrote to the church at Ephesus that we must prepare for spiritual battle every day.[245]

This is how the Holy Spirit works in believers' lives.

An Expert Witness

In court, lawyers often call *expert witnesses* to testify. There are medical experts, ballistics experts, and many other types of expert witnesses. The purpose of an expert witness is to help the jury to understand complex technical evidence. An expert witness acts as a translator. The expert explains complicated concepts in a way that the jury can understand.

If the Bible is the *inspired Word of God*, then it only makes sense that He is in the best position to help us interpret it. From the moment we become Christians, God occupies our hearts in the form of the Holy Spirit. The Holy Spirit helps us understand God's Word.

God has provided an expert witness, in the form of the Holy Spirit, to help us understand the Bible.

As we read His Word, the Holy Spirit is always there with the believer; watching over us and helping us understand what we are reading. If we listen carefully

---

245. Ephesians 6:12–13 (AMP).

to Him, through our obedience, He will continue to reveal to us all of the wisdom contained in the Bible.

Without the guidance of the Holy Spirit, the reader can only read the Bible at a basic, literal level. This causes the reader to conclude that the Bible is flawed. However, when read through the lenses of the Holy Spirit, the Bible functions exactly as God designed it. Under the guidance of the Holy Spirit, the Bible becomes the only book anyone could ever need. It unlocks the mysteries of the ages. It teaches us how to live. The Holy Spirit helps believers interpret and understand these deeper meanings within God's written word.[246]

A Friend in the Background

Humans crave control. Since the very beginning, we have sought control over our environment and our destiny. Giving your life to God means surrendering all control over it.[247] This goes against our nature.

Today we speak of self-control as a virtue. A *control freak* is someone who desires to control every aspect of their lives. Most of us try to control at least some aspects of our lives. Controlling some things, like our appetites and lusts, is healthy. Controlling our spending and saving our money for a rainy day is a great way to reduce stress of a personal economic catastrophe such as job loss.

On the other hand, if taken to the extreme controlling life's variables can result in stress and unhealthy behaviors. Type "A" personalities seek ever-increasing formal education in an effort to control their career options. Others sign prenuptial agreements to control who gets what in a divorce. Still others obsess about

---

246. 1 Corinthians 2:9-13(AMP).
247. Deuteronomy 10:12.

the foods they eat and the exercise they get, in order to prolong their lives for as long as possible. Psychologists refer to these excessive behaviors as *control issues*.

Perhaps it's losing your job or your spouse. Maybe it's being all alone with no friends. How would you feel about these things if you completely lost control over them? What if your worst fear actually occurred?

What are the things in life that frighten you the most?

Now imagine that you learned that you had a friend who was able to step in and miraculously save you. Although he always saved you, it might happen differently than you anticipated. In some cases, your friend's timing was such that there was short-term pain, but ultimately, it all worked out okay. In some cases, it was ultimately an better outcome than what you had hoped.

This friend was always there in the background keeping an eye on things and ready to protect you from harm. Your friend's timeframe was different than yours and his perspective was broader than yours.

Suppose that your worst fear is losing your job. Now suppose that it happens. Initially, you might wonder whether your friend was still looking out for you. In the short term, you might doubt. If you knew that he was still there, behind the scenes and helping you, you would worry less.

Imagine that you ended up with a much better job than you had before. If you stepped back and viewed the situation from a longer view, you would realize that what had happened was for good and that your friend had your best interests in mind all along.

You would begin to trust your friend more deeply, and with your increasingly important life issues. You would begin to yield control over your life to your friend.

CHAPTER NINE

Cross-Examination

My wife, Beth and were living in Monterey, California, in the late 1990s. After a successful initial public offering, my company had established its corporate headquarters there. Monterey is one of the most beautiful places in America, if not the world. The peninsula is home to incredible wildlife. Whales cruise by the Monterey Bay on their way to migratory homes in Mexico. Sea otters playfully amuse tourists. The white sandy beaches are amazingly scenic with craggy outcroppings and a constant cool ocean breeze. Pebble Beach and Carmel are small communities in the area, inhabited part-time by southern Californians and other people who are looking for some serenity in a crazy world.

I used to cycle along the coast every Saturday with a friend I'll call Dave. We met early in the morning, just before daybreak, near the "Lone Cypress" on Seventeen Mile Drive in Pebble

Beach. Typically, there was a light fog in Pebble Beach, but as we got to Carmel the sun would begin to peek through. By the time we got into town, it would be a beautiful sunny morning. The air was always cool and traffic was light. As we rode, the terrain changed from coastal to mountainous to small town Monterey, its many restaurants filling the air with short-order breakfasts cooking for the tourists.

Dave was a very successful lawyer and businessman who had made a great deal of money during the California real estate boom of the 1970s and '80s. Regardless, Dave's wealth did not prevent him from being one of the most down-to-earth people I've ever known. He was intensely intelligent and analytical. He was also one of the reasons I finally decided to go to law school. Inevitably, we engaged in deep philosophical discussions as we climbed the peninsula's vistas, sweating and huffing and puffing. I loved riding with him.

One morning we pedaled along in silence, taking in the beauty of Pebble Beach. For some inexplicable reason I shared my faith with Dave. I certainly wasn't in the habit of telling people about it. I was afraid that people who knew me would think I was a hypocrite. My life to at least some extent did not reflect my faith. Still, my relationship with God was beginning to blossom. I trusted Him more every day with everything.

As I spoke, Dave gave me a funny look. I mistakenly interpreted the look to mean that my testimony wasn't welcome. I immediately regretted raising the subject. My self-talk went something like this: *"Why did you just do that? The guy is a friend. He's smart and successful. Why did you have to bring this up?"* In hindsight, I think this was simply another example of the person who wants us all to think of him as a comic little guy in a red suit with a pitchfork. He slips these seeds of doubt into our psyche, stands back, and things just take care of themselves. I quickly resolved not to raise it again. *"Successful and intelligent people don't want to talk about your silly God."*

What I didn't understand though, was that Dave was actually interested in the subject. Like many people, he had thought deeply about it. He had just never had anyone give him a personal view on it.

We rode along for a few more minutes in silence.

Dave suddenly asked The Question.

The Question was a version of the same question that non-Christians have asked Christians for many years.

He asked, "How can a just God allow things like starvation in Africa? How can He allow things like child murders?"

I have no way of knowing, but I suspect that despite his success, something may have happened to Dave along the way that he blamed on God. People blame things on God when they can't explain it any other way. Dave was asking me a pointed question. How could I have faith in God, when the world that He created had become such a horrible place?

I thought about it for a minute. I said a quick prayer: *"Father, please give me the words."* Two words came to me.

I said simply to Dave, "Free will."

At first, he looked puzzled. Then he looked intrigued. He asked me what I meant.

I explained to Dave that his question assumed that God was responsible for everything that happened in the world. I said: "A world like that would mean a world of robots, doing the Creator's bidding." We talked for a while about the idea that God gave man free will and the power to choose. The problem was that this free will meant that mankind did things, contrary to God's will, that have ultimately resulted in the condition that the world is in today.

I told Dave: "Bad choices aren't God's fault. If we hold Him responsible for our bad choices, then it means that everything that we choose and do are preordained. This would mean that there really isn't human free will and choice. At the same time, Christians believe God solved the problem of the consequences of human choice through a plan that was executed two thousand years ago. We believe that He sent Jesus to die for our sins.

After years of struggling with bad choices, I chose to trust Jesus with everything. Once I did that, my life began to change. My problems became less important. Good things began to happen to me. I was more receptive to those things. The more they happened, the more I trusted Him. I got out of His way. The evidence of all of it is my changed life. I've changed and I can't give you any reason for it other than my faith in Jesus. You might call it 'blind faith,' but for me it's based upon the reality of my changed life."

I could have gone on for another hour, but stopped myself.

Dave looked at me intently for a few seconds and then grew silent. I thought: *"He's probably thinking: Sedberry's going to be speaking in tongues next."* We pedaled along in silence. I mentally shook my head in embarrassment.

After a few minutes, he said simply, "It's hard to argue with that."

I had expected Dave, the lawyer, to instinctively cross-examine me, or Dave, the person, to laugh at me. Instead he simply agreed with me.

Dave knew the "before" me. He knew the "after me" when I had begun to trust God with everything. He understood that we are simply victims of our own creation. We can't help it.

We get so caught up in life that we cannot view our own lives objectively. So we repeat the same destructive patterns, over and over again.

But somehow my life had changed. Unlike most life-changing events, this change was subtle. I hadn't responded to some cataclysm in my life. Instead, the change was driven by something or Someone within me. Dave could see it.

My changed life was the most powerful evidence of my faith.

The Calculus of Faith

What exactly is faith? What are Christians talking about when refer to *faith in Jesus?* Does it mean blind faith? Does it mean that we stop thinking and reasoning rationally? Does becoming a Christian mean that we should throw our intellect out the window and believe simply because we are told to do so?

Despite popular wisdom, faith and intellect aren't mutually exclusive. In fact, they are mutually dependent. Intellect is a key component of building one's faith. This is because the more we believe in something, especially if that belief is based on careful analysis, the less faith that is actually required to sustain that belief. If we understand something intimately, little faith is required to sustain a belief in it.

Math and its cousin, algebra have always been my worst enemies. My skills are woefully inadequate in both. They relentlessly lowered my grade point average in school. Despite those facts, it seems that an equation is a good way to describe this notion of faith:

> **Belief = certainty − faith**
> **Where (experience + knowledge + observation) = certainty**

For example, most of us believe that when we go to bed at night, the sun will rise the next morning. We have developed this belief, based upon years of experience, observation, as well as knowledge gained from science class. We have a great deal of certainty about it. We don't need much faith to believe that the sun will rise.

Now suppose that one morning, you woke up from a restful night's sleep. It's dark outside. You look at your alarm clock and it says 8:00 a.m. The sun should be up, but it isn't. You spend the entire day in the dark. Unless you could come up with a rational explanation, your entire belief system about sunrise would be upended. Now suppose it happens again, and again, for an entire week. Your certainty about sunrise is now reduced to zero.

After a week, the sun finally rises. It rises again the next day. You begin to feel better about things. You begin to think that perhaps the sun will rise again every day, after all. Still, you're not sure. To regain your belief that the sun will rise in the future will require at least some degree of faith. Your belief that the sun will rise has been shaken. To return to that belief requires you to accept something as true that you believe might not be true.

When I was a young boy, I used to dream that I could fly. Once, I jumped out of a tree to see whether the dream was true or not. I tried a couple of times, unsuccessfully. Despite my dream, it was clear that I could not fly. The results increased the certainty of my conclusion. Today, it doesn't take a great deal of faith for me to believe it. It doesn't take a great deal of intellect. It doesn't require an understanding of the laws of physics, to know that after jumping out of a tree (or a tall building), I will not somehow begin to float, suspended in midair.

The more certainty we have about something, the less faith that is required to sustain a belief about it. Alternatively, the less certainty we have, the greater the faith required to sustain that same belief. Faith is the portion of a set of beliefs, which is based upon something other than knowledge and experience. It is trusting in things uncertain. As the amount of knowledge decreases, the amount of faith required increases. As the degree of uncertainty in a belief increases, the amount of faith required to sustain that belief is increased.

Most of us Christians have never heard from God, at least audibly. He's never called to us from heaven with admonitions or instructions. In the Bible, we read about Him and how He works in people's lives. Our lives confirm it. Based upon our life experiences, it

We've never seen or touched God. But we believe in God. There is evidence of Him all around us.

does not require a great deal of faith to sustain this belief. On the other hand, without those experiences, it would require a great deal of faith for us to believe in God.

The apostle Paul eloquently described faith as being sure of something that we believe in but cannot see.[248] If there is anyone among the early Christians who understood the concept of faith, it was Paul. He never met Jesus in the flesh. He spent most of his adult life as a Jewish zealot, dedicated to eradicating Christianity. Somehow, he came to believe that Jesus was, in fact, the Messiah.

You might argue that if anyone had gone through what Paul did on that Damascus road, it would be easy to believe in Jesus. Think about it for a minute. Have you ever experienced things that could not be easily explained by natural means? I've had prayers answered that were so unusual and improbable, the only way I could explain them was with divine intervention. The probabilities are well beyond coincidence. At that moment, I believe in God's power in my life.

And yet, give me a few days, weeks, or months, and I will begin to write them off. My little human brain will begin to self-righteously puff its chest out and say that I'm being silly or superstitious. *"Of course those things were a coincidence,"* it will tell me.

Paul most certainly experienced the same kind of self-righteous self-talk. No matter what happened to him, Paul maintained his faith in Jesus. His faith was continually tested by adversity, deprivation, and struggles. He chose to ignore the self-talk. He kept the faith and became one of the most important writers of the New Testament.

A Leap of Faith

One way to think about Christian faith is as two distinct varieties: a leap of faith, and the faith walk. Understanding faith in this

---

248. Hebrews 11:1 (AMP).

way helps you to understand the reason why a person's initial faith in Jesus may or may not actually solve all of their problems. Whether your daily problems are solved depends upon whether you choose to practice your faith on a daily, if not an hourly (or more frequent) basis. The leap of faith and the faith walk are perfectly aligned. The second builds upon the first.

When I first believed, it took a fair amount of faith to believe in God and Jesus' salvation. We call it *childlike faith*. I didn't have a lot of information or experience upon which to base the belief. But today, many years after I first believed, I see the evidence of God throughout my life that I cannot explain any other way. So, my belief in Jesus today requires substantially less faith than when I was younger.

The first Christian step is that initial leap of faith we take when we accept Jesus as our savior. Evangelists will tell you that you must *trust Jesus*. It almost sounds like what a husband might say to his wife on their road trip, after passing the same landmark three times. "Trust me, I know where I'm going," he'll say, hopelessly lost. They ask you to trust in someone you have never seen and likely not read much about.

These people trust Jesus because they know who he is.

They've seen God work in their lives.

They know that Jesus can be trusted.

Their faith is in the fact that Jesus' death on the cross is sufficient to pay for their sins and restore them to a personal relationship with God. We are saved by our faith in Jesus and nothing else.[249]

A woman washed Jesus' feet at the home of the Pharisee.[250] Jesus said to her clearly and unequivocally that she was saved from her sins because of her belief in him.[251] There were no

---

249. Ephesians 2:8 (AMP); James 2:24.

250. Luke 7:38.

251. Luke 7:50.

additional requirements. Jesus describes faith as being the most important characteristic a person can have.[252]

People go to church for years before they take that first step in faith. Others may trust in Jesus with very little information. With little church involvement or Christian education, they decide to trust him with their lives. This pure step of faith can become more difficult, the longer we wait to do it. We lose our ability to muster faith. We lose our childlike ability to trust. We get so caught up in the troubles of this world that we become cynical, jaded, and pessimistic. On the other hand, a quick decision based upon little information can lead to the same thing.

Whatever path we choose that leads to Jesus should be a function of a cross-examination.

We examine the cross.

The Faith Walk

In order to become a lawyer, you go to law school and graduate. You pass the bar exam, and get your license. A lifelong process of developing your craft as a lawyer commences. When you accept Jesus as your *savior* through a simple *prayer of faith,* you receive a kind of license. It is a license to your eternal destiny. Still, you

After the initial Christian step in faith, we walk a daily faith walk.

must also use your license to develop and grow your faith and your relationship with Him. You practice your faith, as in "practice makes perfect."[253]

---

252. Mark 11:22-26 (AMP); Matthew 18:21(AMP).
253. 2 Corinthians 5:7 (AMP).

The faith walk is an active, ongoing belief that God is in control and will take care of us. The leap of faith and the faith walk are ultimately faith in the same thing. God is in control and will take care of us. The faith walk is the conscious act of trusting God with every single aspect of our lives.

The idea of living by faith in, and obedience to, a God that they have never seen is ludicrous to many. They consider it blind faith. It's like telling someone to

Relying on an unseen God to take care of us goes against everything in our bootstraps mentality.

jump off of a tall building because there is a safety net fifty floors below. Before any reasonable person would jump, they'd need reassurance that the net is actually in place. They would want to know how many people would be holding the net. They would carefully check the wind speed. Human nature is such that we learn to live by our wits and own cleverness.

The Christian goal is to allow God to handle all our troubles because we know that if we trust Him with our lives, He will cause it all to work together for our good.[254] We have observed empirically that He does, in fact, take care of us, and therefore conclude that He will continue to do so. It's what trusting someone all is about. We trust Him because He has shown us that He can be trusted.

The faith walk is the type of faith that Jesus talked about frequently with his followers. After he taught a large group of people on a hillside, Jesus and his followers found themselves in a furious storm in the middle of the sea.[255] Exhausted from a day filled with teaching to thousands and miraculous healing, Jesus had fallen asleep in the boat. When the storm suddenly erupted, his followers were terrified. Jesus asked

---

254. Romans 8:28 (AMP).
255. Matthew 8:23 (AMP).

them why they had so little faith. He rebuked the storm, and it dissipated.[256]

Later, during another storm, Jesus walked on the sea to join his followers on a boat.[257] Peter had seen Jesus' miracles. Seeing Jesus walking on the water, he climbed out of the boat to join him.[258] This was a leap of faith. Soon after, Peter began to doubt. He began to sink.[259] Jesus reached out and saved Peter and asked Peter why he doubted.[260] Peter could not sustain his faith walk.

Jesus had a way of turning any conversation back to the heart of the matter. Whenever anyone tried to argue the meaning of scripture with him, Jesus inevitably brought the discussion back to the real point. They wanted to split hairs. He cut to the chase.

Once Jesus was asked by the people what it was that God wanted them to do.[261] On the surface, it was a legitimate question. We should know what God wants us to do. At the same time, God has told mankind what He wants us to do for thousands of years, to no avail.

Jesus' answer exposed the question for what it was, a misunderstanding of God's basic relationship with mankind. He responded that God wanted people to believe in him.[262] We trust in who Jesus was and what he did for us. We continue to trust him with every aspect of our lives, in order to grow closer to him and become like him.

Walking in faith is like having a song playing in your head. It's there, but you can choose to change the song. Or, it's like a child who is afraid to sleep with the lights out. It might take some

---

256. Id.
257. Matthew 14:22–32 (AMP).
258. Matthew 14:29 (AMP).
259. Id.
260. Matthew 14:31.
261. John 6:28 (AMP).
262. John 6:29 (AMP).

real effort, but she can choose to not be afraid. She consciously chooses to ignore the boogeyman lurking under her bed.

We exercise our faith by conscious decision. In our daily faith walk, we encounter obstacles and issues along the way. It may be obvious, like clear temptations to lust, lie, or envy. It may be subtle, like our desire to control the things in our lives. It may be fear. But the obstacles all have one thing in common. They are, in reality, obstacles that keep us from trusting God at that particular moment.

Our faith is strengthened as a result of our relinquishment of every care, worry, hope, dream, and anything else in our lives to God and His divine intervention in our daily lives. We have the power to choose to ignore these obstacles and simply trust Him with whatever it is.

We can choose to disbelieve. Or, we can choose to trust Him every step of the way.

Early in my Christian life, I mistakenly believed that faith was something you either had or hadn't. You believed in God, or you didn't. I believed that once you took that initial the leap of faith for Jesus, everything would take care of itself.

We trust in Him and learn that He can be trusted.

Mature Christians understand that faith is a spiritual muscle. As with exercise, the more we use our faith, the stronger it grows. Faith begets more faith. We have to work at developing our faith. You can't sit on the couch, watching television and eating chips, and expect to look like a bodybuilder. You have to show up in the gym every day, work hard, and continue to push your body to its limits. The same is true with faith.

Our faith increases as we mature in our Christian understanding. Christian faith is increased as a result of life experiences. We pray for good things, and good things happen. These good things cannot be explained naturally. We pray for deliverance from troubles or catastrophe, and we are delivered. When bad things happen to us, somehow it later turns out to be for good. If one good thing happens, we can rationalize it away by calling it a coincidence. If a hundred or a thousand good things happen, something else must be at work in our lives. We can no longer explain them as mere coincidence.

As with our earthly lives, maturation occurs with the passage of time. If we experience God's grace and blessing in our lives, then we will increasingly place our trust in Him. The more jams He gets us out of, the more we will give the next jam to Him.

We believe in the power of Jesus to transform our lives, every step of the way. In doing so, we relinquish it all to him; our fears, our ambitions, our sin, our lives. The sooner we allow it, the faster our lives are transformed.

We take that first step of faith by a simple belief, but we take the next step of faith and the step after that by allowing God to miraculously transform our lives.

At its core, Christianity is a simple step of faith in Jesus. We execute upon this faith with another kind of faith; an ongoing faith in our daily lives.

Trusting Jesus is on the one hand a very simple act. It is the act of reaching out to God. But on the other hand, trusting Jesus is also an ongoing act for the rest of our earthly lives.

Faith and Works

The world's spiritual belief systems offer essentially two choices. The first choice involves a god or gods that do not reach out to us. Instead, we reach out to a them, typically with a gift, offering or sacrifice. This is a *works-based system*, where the believers have the primary control over what happens to them in life and the afterlife, based upon their actions. They control their destiny by their actions. Most of the world's religious systems fall into the category. These systems typically are rule-based, with the believers' place in eternity determined by how closely they adhere to the rules. You earn your way to heaven. You control your own destiny. In terms of life on earth, some religions call it *karma*. What goes around, comes around.

The second choice is a *faith-based* system. Christianity is based upon faith. God stepped out of heavenly perfection into an imperfect world. He suffered humiliation, torture, and crucifixion at the hands of his creatures.[263] He forgave his killers.[264]

God reached out to us. He lived and worked among his creation.

Turning the cheek is one thing; forgiving someone in this way is simply beyond human understanding. God took it one step further. He paid for our sins. His payment guarantees us a place in heaven.[265]

We reach back through faith in Jesus.

Faith means faith in Jesus. Faith is the basis for our salvation.

This is where the calculus of faith comes in. We believe in someone whom we have never met or seen. Faith comes first. We have faith that Jesus died for the sins of all mankind. Everything else in

To some, Christianity can look like a works-based system. Many denominations have more than their share of rituals and rites. Even so, the core belief has nothing to with works and everything to do with faith.

---

263. Each of the gospels describes the arrest, trumped-up charges against Jesus, illegitimate trial, torture, and murder of Jesus.
264. Luke 23:34.
265. John 3:16 (AMP).

Christianity emanates from that faith. We respond to Jesus because we have faith in him. Faith that isn't manifested in works causes us to doubt the sincerity of that faith. The good deeds that Christians do aren't because they have to; instead it's because we want to. We aren't trying to earn our way into heaven. We do good deeds in response to a loving God.

A synonym is a word that means the same thing as another word. An antonym is a word that means the opposite of another word. Synonyms for "faith" are "belief" and "trust." Antonyms for "faith" are "disbelief" and "mistrust." In Biblical terms, "works" is an antonym for "faith." *Works* is shorthand for this predisposition of man to earn his way and justify himself to God. *Faith* is shorthand for a simple belief and acknowledgment that, *"I can't do it on my own, I need a savior to make me right with God."* Anything other than this belief is an attempt to earn our way into heaven.

It is a fundamental Christian belief that we are saved by faith In Jesus and not based upon what we do. We are saved because of Jesus' work on the cross. That's it. He solved the sin problem once and for all and made a way for all of us to be saved from our sins.

Good works don't have to be a problem. After we become Christians we are definitely more disposed to do good works. We are so thankful to God for what he has done for us that we want to express our gratitude by doing good things for Him. It's only when we begin to keep a tally that we can get into trouble. Anything

Man wants to earn his way into heaven. God wants simple faith.

that keeps us from believing that it's Jesus' work on the cross that saves us, as opposed to our own works, is sin.

Faith and Obedience

James taught that faith also means putting your beliefs into action.[266] A lot of Christians are hesitant to talk about obedience because they mistakenly view it as the fine print. In their minds, the catch to this free gift is that you have to obey God. Regardless, Christianity has always been about God's free gift of salvation. It has never been about earning our way into heaven. We obey Him, based upon His Word as relayed in the Bible. We obey Him, based upon the urgings of the Holy Spirit. We obey Him to please Him. We do not obey Him in order to get to heaven.

Accepting the free gift by faith in Jesus is the priority. But receiving it will inevitably move the believer into obedience with God.

In criminal law, liability the defendant's intent is a critical factor in punishment. To the Christian, the real question is the one of our hearts. When faced with problems or stress, are we responding out of His will or our own? It's when I do what I want and not what He wants that I become like my ancestors, Adam and Eve, who started the trend of disobedience.

How can we know what He wants? We learn His will through prayer and our interaction with the Holy Spirit, that inaudible voice we can hear when we listen carefully. We learn His will through our study of His Word. We learn His will through the example of Jesus.

Everyone understands the concept of walking the talk. It means doing what you say you are going to do. It means practicing what you preach. It is a basic Christian idea that faith without action is meaningless.[267] Our beliefs are reflected in our lives. We study God's Word, in order to get better acquainted with Him.

---

266. James 2:17.
267. James 2 :14 (AMP).

We go to church because we want to worship Him. Although that first tee is beckoning on a beautiful Sunday morning, we do what we believe He wants us to do. Christians who pray regularly, study the Bible, and go to church somehow end up with stronger faith and better blessings.

Paul describes the difference between our former lives and our Christian lives in his letter to the Romans.[268] In those transitional days in which Jews who had formerly carefully followed Jewish law began to live by faith in Jesus, there was a lot of conflict about the importance of those centuries-old Jewish customs. These were customs about what they ate, who they ate with, what sacrifices they made, and how they ritually cleansed themselves. Adherence to the Jewish law was the way that Jews justified themselves before God.

There was naturally debate among new Jewish/Christian believers regarding the observances of the Mosaic Law as followers of Jesus. Paul's message was that thanks to Jesus' sacrifice, Jewish/Christians were no longer subject to the law.[269] He explained that Jesus paid the price once and for all, for the sins of mankind.[270] This means my sins and it means your sins. The sin debt has been paid in full.[271] We claim payment solely by faith in who Jesus was and what he did.[272] This is what the term *righteous* means.[273] We are righteous solely because of our faith in Jesus and what he accomplished on the cross and not because of anything we did. Anything else is "self-righteous."

At the same time, if someone were to accept the free gift as a sin pass or happy hour for sinners, we would certainly question

---

268. Romans 7:4.

269. Romans 7:1-6.

270. Romans 4:23-24.

271. Id.

272. Id.

273. Romans 3:21–23.

whether they legitimately understood the meaning of the cross. Paul explains this fallacy in Romans.[274] After we realize that we are saved, our response is to move closer and closer to God. Our obedience is in response to His love expressed to us through Jesus.

To be clear, ultimately it is all about God. Through Jesus, He did the work on the cross at Calvary. He gives us the strength and the tools to respond in faith to Him. As Paul explained, we are saved by God's grace and not by our own doing.[275] This means that God gave us something that we did not deserve. We receive this gift by accepting it in faith. We acknowledge that the gift was real, that Jesus' sacrifice was valid.[276] We receive it by accepting it. At the same time, faith that isn't put into practice is meaningless.[277] A person's faith is manifested in what they do and how they live their life. It's difficult to reconcile the beliefs of someone who claims to have faith in Christ with actions that do not follow his teachings.

Skeptics discount Christianity based upon the actions of some Christians. *"If it doesn't work for them,"* they reason, *"it certainly won't work for me."* Nonetheless, the Christian walk is a lifelong process. There are Christians who are at various stages of this walk. Some live in almost perfect faith, thanks to the work of the Holy Spirit. Others continue to grow in their faith walk. All are ultimately headed for the same destination.

Some are quicker to respond in obedience than others. Those people get it. Some of us tend to take a little longer.

Others learn to obey as a result of their spiritual bumps and bruises. Eventually, we all learn that obedience to God is the best way—the only way—to live.

---

274. Romans 6:15–18.
275. Ephesians 2:8 (AMP).
276. Id.
277. James 2 :14 (AMP).

Thanks, God, I'll Take It From Here

If works are the opposite of faith, and we are supposed to live by faith, then the biggest detour I make on the faith highway is my *"Thanks, God, I'll take it from here,"* attitude. When I run into an obstacle on the spiritual highway, I jump to my knees and begin praying to God for deliverance or the resolution of the issue. I clearly and unequivocally give it to Him. I know, in my heart of hearts, that He will take care of it. He always has and always will. There are times when it takes what seems like an eternity for God to answer my prayer. There are times when He answers the prayer so quickly that the words have barely left my lips when the answer begins to be present itself.

That's when it begins. I see the answer and I quickly take it back from Him.

After my first book was published, I frequently checked the Internet to see how it was selling, based upon the various rankings. This is a guaranteed method to drive oneself crazy. The rankings fluctuate wildly and a few sales can dramatically change them from hour to hour. The rankings were important to me because they would help to establish me as a legitimate author. This book was already in the works and it was important that future publishers to view me as a marketable author.

Finally, I gave it to God. My prayer was simple; only that He would take care of it. Miraculously and within a short period of time, my book's sales began to dramatically improve.

You've probably figured out what happened next. God had answered my prayer. What happened then? I started checking the rankings again. The whispered lie was that *"It was some sort of a fluke; my book couldn't really be doing that well."* Before long, I was once again frantically scrutinizing the rankings on an hourly basis. I had quickly forgotten Who had helped me in the first place. Of course, the *"I'll take it from here"* attitude is no different than a lack of faith when the situation began. We believe as long as the desired result is evident to us.

Peter took the initial leap of faith out of the boat. He trusted in Jesus. He walked on the water, for a while.

Once he was out and began to realize the enormity of what he had done, his human instincts took over. He tried to take control. He began to sink.

The (Pitch) Fork in the Road

Some people have a difficult time grasping the simple concept of faith. Some Christians find it almost impossible to execute on the concept. The cares, worries, and demands of this life are so great that they feel that they have to keep hold of the reins at all costs. They grip those reins so tightly that they cannot sense God's hand on their own. They are willing to trust God with their lives, but only to a point. They have faith in Jesus, faith in their salvation, and faith in their future — until something bad happens.

Many new Christians take a wrong turn in their faith journey. We take the initial step of faith. We invite God into our hearts. We are miraculously transformed into forgiven people. We begin the faith walk. We take the wrong

Then, Satan switches the road signs at the fork in the road.

path. The cares of this life cause us to doubt. Like the alcoholic who returns to the bottle, we go back to our old sinful ways because we can't wait for Him to change us. We want to do it ourselves. We try to get back on the right path. We become hopelessly confused and lost.

What we don't understand is that after that first step in faith, we must take hundreds, thousands, and hundreds of thousands of additional faith steps for the rest of our lives. This is the key to remaining filled with the Holy Spirit. Each step in faith synchronizes our lives with the will and mind of God.

In the Bible, we quickly learn that most of the principal players had very messy lives. It started with Adam and Eve, Cain and Abel and the others, and only went downhill from there. Spiritual leaders like David and Moses struggled with sin and disobedience. One of Jesus closest friends, Peter, doubted and betrayed him repeatedly. Another friend, Judas, turned him over to the authorities, and ultimately committed suicide. The rest of his friends scattered and abandoned him the only time that he really needed them.

> *For most of us, Christian or not, life is messy.*

The secret to real and lasting Christian growth is realizing that only God can change us. That realization causes us to trust Him and allow Him to change us, no matter what else is happening in our lives. If we are willing to wait on Him, we will see the change. As we see this change, our faith is increased, which allows us to trust in Him even more. We get to the emotional and spiritual point where we can trust in Him for everything, every day. Only then can we become what God wants us to be and experience the life that He wants us to have.

We believe that God is in control. We believe that He will make everything work for good for His followers. Then, we step out in that faith onto life's journey. Each and every step requires a bit more faith. Each successful step reinforces their faith. On our Christian journey, we look back and see that God has continued to walk with us, and we become less afraid to take that next step.

If we live our Christian lives in any other way, we will ride a spiritual and emotional roller coaster. We will have highs when good things happen to us, and lows when bad things happen. When we feel bad, we are more likely to do bad things that make us feel better. We become guided by our emotions rather than by God. This can delay or derail our Christian growth.

The good news of Jesus resolves our eternal destiny, but also makes our years in this world infinitely better.

We accept God's gift of salvation based upon Jesus' death on the cross, through faith. Then we live each day in faith that He will take care of us. We believe that if we trust in Jesus and obey his commands, we will be blessed by God Himself.

Abraham: the Father of Our Faith

In his letter to the new Christian believers in Rome, Paul explains that we are made righteous with God by one thing and one thing only. It is our faith in Jesus.[278] Paul uses the example of Abraham to describe exactly what faith is.[279] For the Jewish nation, Abraham was thought of as the *father of the faith* and the example of that faith in action. They attempted to live their lives modeled after the faith that Abraham showed in God. Abraham's story is described in Genesis.

Abraham was a direct descendant of Noah, and ultimately of Adam.[280] In the beginning of Genesis, everything was perfect. Within a few chapters though, mankind had left the idyllic existence in the Garden of Eden. We learned how to murder, we became violent and corrupt, and we engaged in all kinds of other behaviors abhorrent to God. God caused a great flood to wipe out most of mankind, but ultimately made peace with His creation through Noah. Abraham was part of the new generation following the flood. He was also one of the first men called specially by God.

---

278. Romans 3:22.
279. Romans 4:1.
280. Genesis 17:5.

God told Abraham to leave everything behind and go to the new land that He would show him.[281] This may not sound like much of a hardship. Consider how you would respond if you were asked to not only uproot, but to drop everything and move to a different country that you had never visited. Abraham was seventy-five years old at the time. After what was probably a pretty hard life, he was perhaps getting ready to put his feet up and relax a bit. Instead, God told him that he must leave his family, friends, and countrymen for a new place without any idea of what it would be like. In exchange, God promised to bless Abraham.[282]

What would you do in that situation? After all, how could you turn down God, the Creator of the universe? But before you respond too quickly, remember Adam and Eve? They had the closest relationship that any humans have ever had with God. God spoke directly and audibly to

You might think that if God asked, you would do anything.

Adam and Eve. He took care of them completely. They disobeyed Him nonetheless. God told Moses to go to the Pharaoh and demand that he free the nation of Israel. Moses argued with God, and more than a bit.

The sad truth is that most of us spend our entire lives arguing with God. We have all either ignored God or refused to follow His instruction. Start with Adam and you'll end up with mankind turning its back on God on a regular basis.

The Bible is full of examples of God's people ignoring Him, arguing with Him, and refusing to do what He says.

This is what makes Abraham's response so amazing. He simply

281. Genesis 12:1.
282. Genesis 12:3.

obeyed God. [283] He didn't convince himself that he was somehow delusional. He didn't argue with God about the wisdom of packing up and leaving everything.

He just obeyed.

Abraham's faith and obedience is a pattern that consistently ran through his life. God instructed Abraham and promised to bless Him. Abraham believed God, and Abraham's faith in God made him right with God.[284] This is the same kind of faith that makes us right with God today.

Abraham's faith was to be tested in a way that is almost unimaginable. God instructed Abraham to sacrifice his only remaining son, Isaac.[285]

I had read this scripture many times before we had kids but never really thought about it. After kids, my perspective was entirely different. My children are incredibly precious to me; harming them is unimaginable. God told Abraham to kill Isaac and offer him as a burnt offering.[286] More incredibly, Abraham obeyed.[287] He began methodical preparation and planning for the sacrifice of his son. While reading this scripture one morning, the enormity of what Abraham agreed to do gripped my heart in a deeply sad way.

Abraham gathered wood for the sacrifice. He gave the wood to Isaac to carry, but kept the knife and the fire himself. They slowly traveled on toward their end destination. Isaac, not suspecting anything, asked his father where the sacrificial lamb was.[288] Abraham grimly replied that God would provide it. Abraham tied up Isaac. He lifted the knife as he prepared to kill his only

---

283. Genesis 12:4.

284. Genesis 15:6.

285. Genesis 22:2.

286. Id.

287. Genesis 22:3.

288. Genesis 22:7.

son.[289] At that moment, an angel spoke to Abraham and told him to stop. He has passed this test of faith. Abraham found a male sheep tangled in the brush and sacrificed him instead of Isaac.[290]

God provided the sacrifice.

Jewish readers understand that Abraham is considered the father of the Jewish faith. Jews consider themselves his spiritual and genealogical descendants. Abraham's faith in God, as evidenced by his willingness to do whatever God asked, is the model for Christians is well. He is truly the father of our faith, in that he set the first example of man's faith in God and how we are to respond to Him.

There's another point to the story.

It has to do with another Father who sacrificed His son.

---

289. Genesis 22:10.
290. Genesis 22:13

CHAPTER TEN

Examining Capital Punishment

"I don't believe in hell." Ann, a law student friend from Pennsylvania, spoke quietly. She pointed to the Bible in front of me. We were in the law school library taking a much-needed break from many grueling hours of reading yet another arcane appellate case. My Bible had recently begun to accompany the heavy casebooks in my backpack. If there were a few extra minutes, reading it was a study break of sorts for me, and about the only non-law reading my schedule allowed. There was no time for anything else.

Ann and I had become friends and we were both a bit out of place in the law school setting. She struggled with whether she really wanted to practice law. My career path was clear; however, my perspective was different than that of my twenty-five-year-old peers. As a result, we became friends.

We often compared notes and reviewed the assigned materials together. During our study sessions, we would sometimes digress into more esoteric subjects, as students tend to do. We talked a lot about post-law school careers. My faith came up a few times, in conversation. I certainly wasn't pushing my faith on Ann, but wasn't trying to hide it either. Typically, Ann would simply nod or smile an acknowledgment and the conversation would drift to another subject.

When she saw my Bible, she visibly reacted. I stopped reading and asked her if something was bothering her. "A loving God wouldn't condemn people to hell," she continued. I didn't say anything and just listened to her. "Hell would have to be a terrible place and a loving God wouldn't send people there," she concluded. It was if she was arguing with herself. There was a lesson for me in this somewhere. She continued her soliloquy; she listed all the reasons the ideas of God and hell are incompatible. It was an argument similar in structure to The Question that Dave had asked me in Monterey.

Ann's argument assumed that God was responsible for everything that happens, regardless of the fact that He has given man the power to choose. There are consequences for our choices. If eternity is to make any sense at all, then there must always be consequences for sin. The alternative is simply too illogical and unjust.

The answer is that a just and loving God couldn't allow sin to go unpunished. A just and loving God has to deal with sin. He doesn't have to like it.

Ann told me later that she had lost both of her parents in a car accident. They were not Christians. There is no one more likely to reject the concept of hell, as well as any belief system that subscribes to the concept of hell.

The Bible teaches us about heaven and hell. [291] There are no other options. There is no spiritual halfway house. The reason many Christians are reluctant to talk about hell is that it sounds so unenlightened. Many people view a discussion on hell as a Christian scare tactic.

It's thought of as an archaic artifact of the old days of tent preaching revival, used by sweat-soaked shirt-sleeved Southern preachers upon rural uneducated country people. Hell is offensive to non-Christians. They don't appreciate the fact that someone else presumes to know their eternal destiny, especially if it involves eternal damnation.

The subject of hell is probably the single greatest reason that people accuse Christians of being judgmental and narrow minded.

For that matter, kinder and gentler Christianity doesn't like to talk about hell. After all, God is love, they reason. Perhaps, deep down inside, they can't accept the idea that a God of love would allow anyone to end up in a place of eternal damnation. So they don't think about it or talk about it.

Nonetheless, if everyone gets into heaven, then it would be populated with people who rightfully belong in hell. That would mean that there is no difference between the two. Heaven would become hell.

A kind and gentle God fits most people's view of things. And yet, we believe that there are eternal consequences of sin. How do we reconcile this seeming contradiction? The answer is simple: God is a just god. He cannot tolerate sin. He can't look the other way. He must deal with it. The Old Testament is clear in this regard as well as the consequences of living in disobedience to God. The New Testament is equally clear that Jesus paid for the sins of mankind, once and for all. After his crucifixion, there was no longer any need for future sin payment.

---

291. Romans 6:23 (AMP); Luke 16:28 (AMP); Matthew 25:31 (AMP); Revelation 14:11.

God created the world and everything in it. He established the rules of how we should live, but gave us the choice to obey. When we choose to disobey, there is a price to pay. He provided the payment.

On the one hand, God appears merciless. On the other hand, He was so full of mercy that He sent His only son to die, so that we would not have to suffer the consequences.

Unlike so many religions that thrive on relativism, Christianity is a belief system of absolutes. Without God's intervention, man is bound for eternal separation from God. That is why the subject deserves discussion in any book about Christian faith. The consequences are simply too important, too eternal, to ignore. Because Jesus died, was resurrected, and ultimately ascended into heaven, Christians believe that they will as well.[292] We believe that everyone will live eternally.

The only question is where you will live.

The Funny Little Guy with a Pitchfork

Our popular culture has reduced Satan to a funny little red guy with horns, tail, and pitchfork. He shows up in cartoons, poking someone with his pitchfork, who screams "Y-e-o-o-w-w" and runs away. He seems harmless enough.

In order to understand hell, you also have to understand who Satan is. People don't like to talk about him. Perhaps it's because they are afraid of ridicule. He is not a funny little guy. His agenda is, in reality, very serious. It has eternal consequences.

Defense lawyers will typically argue that their client did not commit the act of which he is accused.

292. Acts 2:29–31.

If that argument fails, they will argue that their clients' actions are excused because of certain extenuating circumstances, for example, temporary insanity. It's called *arguing in the alternative*. It is a kind of trap for the prosecution because in either case, the client goes free.

Satan uses the same strategy.

In Genesis, we get a good glimpse into his character, mission and methods. We read about his efforts to interfere with the relationship between God and mankind. Satan is intelligent, charming, and skilled at planting and nurturing seeds of doubt. Satan's objective is to create a wedge between us and God.

He created a wedge between God and His first children. In the Garden of Eden, Adam and Eve lived perfect lives, in perfect communion with God. They depended upon God for everything, and He provided for their every need.[293] Satan planted the seed of doubt with Eve.[294] Satan encouraged her to eat fruit from the tree that God had forbidden. He argued in the alternative: *"It must all must be some sort of misunderstanding. God couldn't have meant that you couldn't eat this fruit. It's just fruit."* He subtly challenged God's authority.[295] He questioned the wisdom of God's instruction to them to not eat the forbidden fruit. Satan began by winning her confidence. Then he went for the jugular: *"Your God is just a spoil sport. He knows that if you eat this fruit, you will become like Him."*[296]

The rest, of course, is history. Adam and Eve's idyllic existence was destroyed forever. God's relationship with mankind was critically damaged. The wedged was fixed firmly in place.

Just before he started his public ministry, Jesus fasted in the wilderness for forty days. Satan found him and launched his

---

293. Genesis 1:29.
294. Genesis 3:3.
295. Genesis 3:1.
296. Genesis 3:4.

attack.[297] He challenged Jesus' authority.[298] He attempted to cause Jesus to doubt his true identity. He suggested to Jesus that if he were hungry, he should turn stones into bread. Satan argued in the alternative. He argued that Jesus was not the Messiah; and if he were, he wasn't as powerful as a Messiah ought to be.

This was a trap for Jesus. If Jesus did nothing, then Satan would declare that Jesus was a fraud. If Jesus turned the stones into bread, then he would have allowed Satan to manipulate him into performing a miracle. Rather than taking Satan's bait, Jesus responded that the Word of God is more important than mere food.

Satan then twisted God's words by daring Jesus to leap from a cliff in order to prove that God would save him.[299] Satan again challenged the fact that Jesus was God's son. He used scripture against Jesus. Jesus refused to engage Satan in the argument. He simply responded that the scripture also prohibited testing God. Satan tried to create a wedge between Jesus and God. He tried to cause Jesus to doubt God. He attempted to use the same method he had successfully used with Adam and Eve to create a wedge between the Father and son. It didn't work.

We don't know if Satan understood Jesus' true identity. He may have thought that Jesus was a "great teacher" and that he could outwit him. Satan tried to tempt Jesus into abandoning his relationship with God, by offering him worldly power and other temptations. That is how Satan worked then, and that is how he works now. Unlike Adam and Eve, Jesus successfully resisted Satan.

Jesus proved that we can refuse to believe Satan's lies. We can choose to resist.

Some Christians don't want to risk getting the Satan's attention. They take it to the opposite extreme. They impute all kinds

---

297. Matthew 4:1 (AMP).
298. Matthew 4:3 (AMP).
299. Matthew 4:6 (AMP).

of power and control to him. They believe that, if he wants to, he can ruin their lives and create terrible pain and heartache for them and their loved ones.

What they don't fully appreciate is that Jesus has already won the war. Our sin is of no effect. It is null and void. It has been paid for. It's also important to understand that in this life we aren't powerless in the face of Satan. If we resist, he will leave us alone.[300]

Satan is real. He wants to prevent you from having a relationship with God. Perhaps this is what hell really means — a permanent void between you and God. If we were made for the purpose of having a relationship with God, it makes a lot of sense. Eternity without God would be hell. If you love God, Satan loses and God wins. Satan hates losing.

It is likely that Satan approves of our modern-day characterizations of him as a little guy in a red suit. It enables him to work in stealth. We don't worry too much about him.

Despite that, in hell all illusions about who the devil is will evaporate. Notions that Satan is a little red guy with horns and a pitchfork will be quickly dispelled. We will be faced with the reality of who he. The Bible tells us that Satan is going to spend eternity in hell.[301]

Presumably, he wants company.

But I'm a Good Person

Most of us think of ourselves as good people. Many of us don't worry about hell because we have lived basically good lives.

---

300. James 4:7.
301. Revelation 20:10.

We've raised kids, worked hard, given to charity, and tried to be kind to others. We've never cheated anyone; we've never intentionally hurt anyone, at least badly. We believe that there is a cosmic accountant who keeps track of our good and bad deeds. *"Yep, I'm a pretty good person,"* we think. As long as our good deeds outweigh our bad deeds, we will eventually make it to heaven. We rationalize: *"God is a good God, and therefore when I die I will go to heaven. It's only fair."* To many of us, it sounds like a great argument.

We watch television shows about near-death experiences in which people are propelled through a tunnel of light and greeted by departed loved ones at a place of indescribable beauty. These shows fit within our idea of a cosmic bank account. We conclude if we live a good life, it's only fair that we end up in this place, which we assume is heaven. After all, there are a lot of people who have done much worse than we have. We compare ourselves to crooks, embezzlers, and mass murderers and feel pretty good by comparison. On the surface, it sounds like justice.

Nonetheless, it is flawed logic. The premise that more good than bad deeds in your cosmic bank account makes you good enough for heaven presumes the conclusion.

It also contains an internally inconsistent premise; namely, that the rationale of an "cosmic bank account" is fair and just.

Suppose you are hit by a bus and suddenly find yourself at the pearly gates. Your only hope is that at that particular moment, your good deeds in life have outweighed your bad. What if they haven't? When you die, you run out of time to catch up. If you were condemned solely because the timing of your death was bad, it would be an unjust result.

Further, the "cosmic bank account" argument assumes that it is humanly possible to do more good than bad. The real problem with this logic is that the person is using criteria that completely lack objectivity. It's all relative. Or a person who has turned their life around might consider themselves as good, as compared with how they used to be.

A murderer might consider himself a good person, when compared to a mass murderer.

However, one's current good life may not be good enough. What you started with becomes important. For example, someone who was born in the safety and comfort of America and of relatively affluent means starts out with a big advantage over someone born into poverty in the third world. Shouldn't more be expected of the affluent American? Or shouldn't less be expected of an abused child than someone born to loving and caring parents?

This argument also assumes that what humans think is good and bad matches God's standards. It assumes that we can somehow weigh something that tends to resist weighing. A scorecard sounds reasonable to rational human beings. It appeals to our basic belief in a system of justice.[302] This belief is the framework of our society. In life, things balance out. Sooner or later, evildoers get their just rewards.

This was essentially the same rationale used by the high priests under Mosaic Law. They decided the sin. They decided the sin payment. The payment was made through ritual sacrifice, killing unblemished animals in payment for sins. On the surface it sounds reasonable. And yet, its invalidity is demonstrated by its result. Instead of getting better, people got worse.

For example, how many "helping little old ladies cross the street" would it take to offset one angry outburst? How many kind and encouraging words would it take to outweigh one slanderous

How can we ever know whether we are good enough? What is the standard?

302. Leviticus 24:19–21(AMP); Exodus 21:22–25(AMP); Deuteronomy 19:21(AMP).

remark? Does a kind act to a stranger outweigh one angry look at your spouse? How many gifts to charity can outweigh cheating on one's taxes? How many church service attendances does it take to outweigh cutting someone off in traffic? The analysis quickly becomes complicated.

Man cannot decide what is sinful in God's eyes. And we simply can't sacrifice enough lambs, goats and, chickens to compensate for the evil that we do on a daily basis. As a result, man must perpetually deal with a debit balance.

More importantly, this argument for a cosmic bank account is only valid as it relates to man's actions toward his fellow man. Your offenses against other people can reasonably be viewed in the balance. You do more good deeds than bad deeds. However, this system only applies to our deeds as it relates to other people. This means that we are no longer talking about a level playing field. The relationship is no longer horizontal, meaning human-to-human. Instead, the relationship is vertical, meaning human-to-God.

Balancing your deeds as they relate to God is a different story. In that case, your good deeds will never balance. It is because you can never give anything to an omnipotent God. Instead, you can only take from God. You can't give anything to God because He created everything anyway. Anything that you have is because God gave it to you. If you are intelligent and gifted, it's because He made you that way. If you are rich, it's because He provided you with the opportunity and means to accumulate your wealth. This is not to say that you didn't take advantage of the opportunity to maximize God's gifts. But they are still gifts.

If you take better advantage of these gifts than other people do, you still can't give God anything. Like the small child who buys a Christmas present for his dad with the dad's money, it's a sweet and wonderful gesture. And yet, from an economic perspective, the child did not give the dad new wealth. The wealth was the dad's all along.

We are accountable. If we have great wealth, then what we do with that wealth is important. We can spend it on earthly treasures or we can use it to benefit our fellow man. If we have been given a family and children, then God holds us accountable in terms of how we raise them. So, on one level, a wealthy person who establishes a charitable foundation certainly appears to be a very good person. On God's level, doing so would appear to be the minimum acceptable behavior from someone who has been given so much.

In the story of the poor widow offering her last penny, Jesus described her as giving more than the wealthy people did.[303] She gave all that she had. This means that the smallest good deed could be very great in God's eyes. It also means that people who had horrible childhoods and commit horrible crimes may not be as evil as common wisdom would indicate. The human view of good may be vastly different than God's view.

The story of Sodom and Gomorrah provides further insight into this issue.[304] God had prepared to destroy the city of Sodom. Abraham tried to bargain with God, in order to save this city. He argued that a fair God wouldn't destroy a city because the good people would be killed along with the bad. God responded that if there were fifty good people in Sodom, He would spare the city. Abraham understood the point and tried to reduce the number. Sodom was a sizable city with thousands of people. He continued to negotiate with God. Finally, God agreed that if there were ten good people in Sodom, He would not destroy it.

It is a bargain Abraham couldn't win. They both knew that there isn't anyone who qualified as good, especially in Sodom.[305]

---

303. Mark 12:42-44.
304. Genesis 18:17–33 (AMP).
305. Romans 3:12 (citing Psalms 14:1–3).

Looking through God's lenses, especially compared with Jesus, who lived a perfectly sinless life, everyone has sinned.[306] To a perfect God, all sin is abhorrent and the commission of one sin makes us unacceptable in His eyes.

If Christians are honest, we will admit that our sins continue to outweigh our good deeds each and every day. We are getting better, but we started in such a spiritual deficit, that we can never ever catch up. If we choose to do only good deeds from this day forward, we can never make up for all of our past indiscretions. Though we try our hardest, we will still disobey God. It's human nature. All of us live our lives in such a way as to be in a perpetual deficit. Our sins will always greatly outweigh our good deeds. Mankind will always be in a deficit balance to the Creator who gave us everything.

> *The Christian definition of sin means acting in a way that is contrary to God's will. It is a much broader definition than simply doing bad things. It means doing things that God doesn't want us to do.*

Becoming Good Enough

We've seen that it is impossible for our good deeds in this life to outweigh our bad. What if you are close? What if you are a really, really good person? You are still left with the difficult task of putting yourself in God's shoes, in order to decide what is "good enough" for Him. Further, if you think you've lived a life good enough to earn your way into heaven, are you willing to gamble your eternal destiny upon it?

---

306. Romans 3:23.

If there is no workable definition of "good enough" does this mean that there is no way to know for sure what it takes to get into heaven? Does it mean that everyone is hell-bound? Not necessarily. A just God could make us good enough. He could pay for sin Himself. If He pays for it Himself, then we move from a *legal* system where justice is administered, to a *gift* system whereby the Creator of everything provides payment for the sin. It's a spiritual *"get out of jail free"* card.

There is a definition of "good enough" and it is provided in the Bible. "Good enough" is defined with a single word: Jesus. This is because he was the perfect sacrifice for the sins of all mankind. He was sinless.[307] Under the Old Testament law, a perfect unblemished lamb was the appropriate sacrifice, which was made by the high priest periodically to cleanse the sins of the Israelites. Adam introduced sin into the world by disobeying God.[308] Jesus lived in perfect obedience to God but was sacrificed nonetheless.

This is why Christianity makes sense. If we believe that the God who created mankind is a just God, then we should believe that He can't simply ignore sin. A perfect God cannot tolerate sin. It has to be dealt with; it has to be nullified. This is because all sin is offensive to a perfect God. When we become Christians, we accept the payment for our sins through Jesus' death. The Bible teaches that Jesus paid the price, once and for all, for the sins of everyone, past, present, and future.[309] Because of Jesus, God no longer sees our sins.

Jesus makes us good enough for God.

And that makes us want to be good enough for God. Once we understand this, we rest in faith in Him and do our best to obey Him. This means that we become more like Jesus, who lived in complete dependence upon and obedience to his Father. Over

---

307. John 1:29.
308. Id.
309. 1 John 2:2.

the course of our lives, this results in our sanctification. If we allow it to happen, by the time our lives here on earth are at an end, we ready for eternal life.

What about the "light at the end of the tunnel" near-death experience? Relying on hearsay evidence of an alleged near-death experience is pretty risky. Perhaps the people reporting these experiences are lying, or just having a little fun. Even if they are telling the truth, what if "heaven" was actually a delusion caused by something organic, like a lack of oxygen to the brain? Or worse, what if they were deceived in the process? What if the whole thing was an orchestrated sham? What if Satan created this elaborate hoax, to fool us into thinking that the tunnel of light leads to heaven? This would be the cruel joke to end all cruel jokes, but with an eternal punchline.

It would seem more prudent to do some research, as opposed to developing one's belief in the afterlife based upon a television show.

If we are honest with ourselves, we will realize that although we have lived good lives, it is no assurance of a ticket to heaven. This is because there is no heavenly scale that weighs your deeds and no allocation of entry tickets that allow entrance to heaven. The heavenly admissions decision is not graded on a curve. Don't fall for the trap that as long as you do better than the next person, you will pass. Instead, God's decision as to your worthiness to enter heaven is completely pass/fail. Passing is based solely on your faith in Christ.

We can't earn our way into heaven. If we could, it would mean that heaven wouldn't be a lot different than life on earth. God would have to require us to surrender our free will before we enter. God who is perfect cannot tolerate imperfection. There has to be some process by which we are all perfected. This leads us right back to where we started. All of us are sinners. No one gets into heaven without some extraordinary means of access. Jesus tells us that he is that access.

All you have to do is decide to believe it.

CHAPTER ELEVEN

The Pardon

We've covered eternity. You've read about different perspectives on God. You've read about sin and its consequences. We've looked at the idea of a cosmic bank account, in terms of its effect on your eternal life. Now we move into different territory. We are going to talk about what all of it means to you. Before we go any further, you have to decide what you believe.

Many of us confront this question in times of crisis. Sooner or later, we all face our own road to Damascus. It may be the loss of a job or a loved one. It may be something worse. We wonder if there is something more than this life. We think about where we will end up after we die and where we will spend eternity. We face the question of exactly what we believe. We are faced with choosing a path that, whether we realize it or not, sets the direction of the rest of our lives.

My Damascus road experience occurred early that morning in Michigan in 1992. Unable to sleep, I tossed and turned in bed, filled with anxiety about my future. My life had been a complete waste. The harsh reality of a failed life haunted me. Controlling as much of my environment as possible was my objective. Success in the corporate world was my god. My life's landscape was littered with the debris of failed relationships. They weren't really relationships. A relationship, by definition, is a two-way street. My only relationships were those that would benefit me. Everything I had learned, accomplished, and believed hadn't worked. Although I had accepted Christ at a young age, most of my life had been spent in rebellion against God.

What I didn't understand was that God had been there all along. He had come into my heart when I prayed that prayer as a nine-year-old boy. I just was too busy living my life to listen to Him. The answer had already been given to me at the age of nine. Jesus became my savior but not my Lord. Instead, I chose to run things myself. It was only when faced with my own abject failure that I returned to Jesus and hand everything over to him.

Early that morning, it all came crashing in on me. I lay there in bed, wide awake, in a state that can only be described as pure anxiety. Like Paul, I was paralyzed. It seemed to be the end of the road. There was nowhere else to turn. The thought that kept returning to me was, *"How could someone be a Christian and have such a rotten life?"*

Like a cornered animal, it seemed as if there was nowhere to turn.

I turned to God.

At that moment, I was the nine-year-old boy who trusted in God and His plan. In that moment of complete surrender, I gave everything I was and everything I had to God.

It's certainly possible that you may never be faced with your own Damascus road. You may have grown up going to church every Sunday, or you may never have set foot inside one. Either way, you don't have a relationship with God. Life may seem pretty good right now. You live a life of relative ease and comfort. His Holy Spirit is always there in the background, gently beckoning each of us to Him. He won't ever give up on any of us until that day when we all find our way into eternity.

> *God is funny. He won't intrude; but He won't go away either.*

Decide What You Believe

The threshold question for anyone thinking about eternity is whether there is a God. By "God," we mean the omnipotent Creator of the universe. Impotent, lesser gods simply don't make sense. There is no evidence of a polytheistic universe. Instead, everything points to a common guiding Hand that is in control of the universe. If you don't believe in God, then it doesn't matter what you think about Jesus or who you think he was.

If you decide that there isn't a God, there is no point in going any further. Life is what you can see right here in front of you, and that's it. You can believe in a *higher power*, an automaton god that doesn't care if you come or go but perhaps merely periodically weighs the cosmic scales of justice. That's no different than deciding that there is no God. If God does not care about you personally, then you aren't any better off than without any god at all. Regardless, if you decide that there is no God, obviously you cannot believe that the Bible description of an "up close and personal" God is accurate.

The proof of God is in His creation.[310] We look at the life, beauty, and order around us on this earth. It becomes more difficult to believe that it is all a random occurrence. That this creation

---

310. Romans 1:18.

somehow came together in an orderly way and resulted in life without a central, guiding Hand seems beyond any calculable probability.

On the other hand, if you do believe in God, then you are faced with the question of who He is. Is he the grandfatherly bearded man that many people think of, sitting on an ancient throne in heaven? Is He an amorphous presence, hovering around the universe; a cosmic spy, eavesdropping on things that humans do? Is He an angry, vengeful God, as some believe? After all, He turned Lot's wife into a pillar of salt[311] and caused the big fish to swallow Jonah.[312] Or, is He a personal God, a vibrant omnipotent, omnipresent God, who desires to have a relationship with each of us?

In other words, is He like Jesus?

Christians believe that Jesus and God are one in the same.[313] With Christianity, we know how God manifested Himself. All we have to do is to examine the life and words of Jesus. We look to Jesus to see God.

Decide What You Will Do Next

Let's assume that you have come to the conclusion that God is real and that He loves you. There are three reasonable responses to God. First, you can ignore Him. You can close your eyes and hope that He goes away. If you feel badly about what you have done with the life He has given you, this is a reasonable, albeit short-term response.

Second, you can resent Him. This would be an entirely reasonable response, especially if you had previously thought that you were an evolutionary fluke. It is a lot easier to go through life

---

311. Genesis 19:26.
312. Jonah 1:17.
313. John 14:9 (AMP).

untroubled if you believe that you don't owe anything to anyone. Like a petulant child or rebellious adolescent, you can be angry at Him, not for what He has done, but because of what you suddenly realize you owe Him.

The third response would be to fear God. What does it mean to *fear* God? It's not what you might think. God doesn't want you to be afraid of Him. When you were oblivious to Him, life was simple. You just lived for yourself, doing what you wanted to do. When you fear Him, you realize that He is responsible for all that

Fearing God means that you now understand your place in the universe.

you have and all that you are. You defer to Him and His will for you. You respond out of thankfulness and with respect. We may respond to a small extent out of a sense of obligation to Him. But the reasonable response, to a great extent, is a sense of gratitude.

Some people say that we don't really begin to grow up until we have children. Parenthood, no matter how you look at it, requires unselfishness. A newborn is completely dependent upon its parents. As a new parent, your days of selfish living are over. You are forced to think about someone other than yourself. Relentless early morning feedings, infinite diaper changes, and the other drudgery of parenting an infant teach you what needy really is.

As your babies become toddlers their needs change, but they still need a great deal. Formula becomes solid food, but you feed the child with great care. You mash carrots and cut grapes so that your child doesn't choke. You prop them up to teach them to sit. You hold them as they progress from crawling to walking. You read and sing to your child, to comfort them and develop their minds. You begin to suspect that perhaps you are not the center of the universe, after all. You know how much you love your children.

You realize how much God loves you.

Sooner or later, you will find yourself faced with the decision about Jesus. Do we respond as Paul did, quickly and in faith? Or, do we decide to continue to fight and struggle through this life without God's help?

The question is: how we will respond?

Some people who are introduced to the gospel decide not to become Christians. They believe that Jesus was who he said he was, yet they decide that Christianity isn't worth it. It isn't worth the investment. The faith walk is too hard. It's too much work. They are too comfortable where they are. They don't want to give up certain behaviors, or decide that praying, studying the Bible, and going to church isn't worth the hassle. These folks assume that they can always change their minds later. Perhaps they get around to it. But some don't.

Others mistakenly believe that they don't measure up. In other words, they don't believe that they are good enough to become Christians. But no one measures up. Christians don't measure up. We are all sinners and don't deserve what Jesus has done for us by way of the Cross. He didn't deserve it, and yet he submitted to it. Its exquisite unfairness makes it incredibly just.

Here's the deal. God loves you. He just does. It doesn't matter what you have done or how badly you have acted, He loves you. He did not send Jesus to die just for good people. God sent Jesus to die for the sins of the entire human race. He sent him to die for us while we were sinners. Once you understand that, you're faced with a decision. You have to decide whether to respond to His love. You have to decide whether to accept the claims of Christianity.

Only Jesus measured up. That's why he was the perfect sacrifice.

Christians believe that: (1) man is sinful and sin requires punishment;[314] (2) God became a man, called Jesus;[315] (3) Jesus lived a sinless life,[316] but was crucified nonetheless and this crucifixion paid the price for the sins of all mankind;[317] (5) forgiveness of sin is available to anyone who accepts it by faith in Jesus;[318] and (6) evidence of that faith is manifested through the indwelling of the Holy Spirit[319] and obedience to God.[320]

Faith in Jesus means that we pray a prayer in which we confess that we are sinful and acknowledge that Jesus died in payment for those sins. Through that prayer, we accept God's gift in faith. We decide that we will submit ourselves to Him, as much as we possibly can, and do what we believe He wants us to do.

You may have never taken that leap of faith and asked Jesus to come into your life. If you haven't, you can do it right now. Before you do, think about it. You should fully understand what it is that you are praying. If you've read this far into the book, then you have come a long way toward understanding both.

If you ask Jesus to come into your life, then you should clearly understand who he is, and the scriptural basis for doing so.

You will have to do your own calculus of faith, or algebra, or whatever it is. Your beliefs are the sum of what you've read (the documentary evidence), what you've heard and what you've experienced (the eyewitness testimony), plus whatever faith is required to get you to the place of commitment.

---

314. Romans 3:23
315. John 3:1.
316. Hebrews 4:13.
317. John 3:16.
318. Romans 10:9.
319. Romans 8:9.
320. Romans 12:1.

If you feel uncomfortable with any of the points below, such that you simply cannot agree with them, then do some deeper reading in the Bible. Further, God's Holy Spirit will quietly and gently lead you and illuminate for you what you need to learn in order to be sufficiently convicted to make the commitment for Christ.

The following prayer outline is intended to give you a step-by-step guide, with scriptural support. You can use this outline to develop your own prayer to invite Jesus into your heart. Read the scriptures footnoted before you pray the prayer, and any other scripture that you need, until you understand what you are praying and why you are praying it. Ask yourself at each point, *"Is this what I believe?"* Once you are comfortable with each point, pray your own prayer:

Father, I am a sinner and sorry for it.[321]

My sinfulness means that I have been opposed to You.

My sin requires a sacrifice and/or punishment.[322]

I believe that Jesus was Your son.[323] I believe that Jesus' sinless life made him the perfect sacrifice for the sins of all mankind and for my own sins. I believe that Jesus died on the cross, by a horrible crucifixion, in order to act as the sacrifice for my sins. I believe that Jesus is the only way for me to have an eternal relationship with You.

---

321. Romans 3:9-19. You probably don't need scripture to decide whether or not this is true. Your heart is sufficient testimony as to the validity of this statement.

322. Romans 6:23.

323. John 3:16-19.

I accept this gift by my faith that you Jesus are my Lord and Savior and acknowledge that you now indwell in me.[324]

I will do my best to live the rest of my life for You, through faith and obedience to You.[325]

If you confessed your sinfulness, repented, and asked Jesus to come into your heart, then it's done. Your eternity is now assured. The Holy Spirit now dwells within you. God's entire plan for mankind has been personally fulfilled for you as the result of your prayer. You have accepted God's free gift and Jesus, through the form of the Holy Spirit, has come to live within you.

God can be trusted. He will always be there for you, in good times and bad. If you ever have any question about what you prayed, you can look back at this section to refresh your memory. You can review the scriptures that you read before you prayed the prayer. In the next chapter, we will cover some practical suggestions for continuing your growth as a Christian and living in faith and obedience to Him.

You've just trusted Jesus with your eternal salvation. Now, begin to trust Him with your day-to-day earthly life.

324. Ephesians 2:8.
325. James 2:14-20 (AMP).

CHAPTER TWELVE

The Defense Rests

W hat happens next? After praying that prayer as a young boy, I took a wrong turn that led to a lengthy detour in my own spiritual journey. I mistakenly believed that after praying it, all I had to do was sit back and enjoy the ride. If the book were to end here, I would have done exactly what I've criticized—dropping you off at the doorstep of Christ. This chapter is intended to help you as you begin your walk in faith, with Jesus.

Trusting God for a Lifetime

An old widow was destitute. She was ninety years old and penniless. The woman had no family; her few friends were just as poor as she was. She lived in an old, dilapidated shack on the edge of town. Every day presented the real threat of sickness and starvation. She eked out a meager existence by selling vegetables that she grew in a small garden in her little back yard. She struggled to get by; to get her basic needs met. She worried constantly about making ends meet. She lived this way for years.

One day, she was working in her garden. It was a hot day and she was parched from thirst. She had planted a row of tomato plants. One of the plants died from disease. The widow dug up the plant in order to keep the disease from spreading. She stopped to take a drink of lukewarm water from a jar. The old woman, weary from a lifetime of struggle, wiped her leathery, wizened face. As she drank, she noticed something, small and shiny and that was partially buried in the dirt. Pulling it out of the ground, she peered at it through thick glasses. She wiped off some of the dirt with her apron. She spat on her apron and wiped some more.

As she stared at the object in her hand, her eyes grew wide. For a few seconds, it seemed as if time had stopped. Her mouth gaped open involuntarily. The magnitude of it hit her like a brick. It was an ancient gold coin! She dug a bit more and found a partially decomposed canvas bag. She tugged in vain at a large bag, which was so full of these coins that she couldn't lift it!

The woman had discovered a trove of priceless gold coins buried right in her tomato garden. One coin could be sold for enough money to provide for her needs for many, many years. If she had only realized her true condition, she could have lived without fear and in abundance.

All this time, she had lived as a beggar. In reality, she had the wealth of a queen in her backyard.

You have taken the biggest step by asking Jesus to be your personal savior and to come into your heart. Perhaps the most important thing for you to understand now is that you are a child of the King; the Creator of the universe. Your inheritance is in his kingdom in heaven. You are heading to heaven!

It's easy to get caught up in the issues of this life. You have to remind yourself of your true condition. I became a Christian early in life but the problems of life quickly got in between me and God. I began to doubt the validity of my faith because it wasn't working the way other Christians had told me it should work. After accepting Jesus, my life didn't seem to change much at all. In reality, my life changed dramatically that night at the puppet show. I simply didn't understand it.

Get Out of the Way

Christians have problems like everyone else. By trusting in God to deal with them, we can have an entirely different life. Trusting God is a lifelong process.

Some view God as a distant ruler watching over mankind from His heavenly throne. Christians believe in a more up close and personal God, as shown to us originally through the life of Jesus and later through His Holy Spirit. That God is continuously causing everything to come together in the believer's life for good.[326] The Holy Spirit indwells in each of us, guiding us, giving us wisdom and special power to deal with the things of this world.

It's easy to underestimate the effect that God can have on the Christian process. As funny as it seems, many Christians tend to leave God out of it.

If, after that first step of faith, we try to go it alone, without Him, our lives will continue on the same trajectory as before. This doesn't change the fact of our salvation. Still, trusting that first

---

326. Romans 8:28.

time and then trying to muscle our way through life will yield only part of the benefits intended for Christians. Further, it likely means that you are still in rebellion to God. So, in a way, you are no better off than before. If you live as you did before, you should seriously question whether you meant the prayer that you prayed.

If you prayed the prayer and meant it, the Holy Spirit now indwells in you.

Wait a minute. I just said "If you prayed the prayer and *meant it*."

This is Christianspeak. *Mea culpa.*[327] Maybe it's even something that the funny little guy with the pitchfork would have you believe. I've heard it used by evangelists and just repeated it without thinking about it. It is a nutty thing to say. *"I prayed the prayer but did I really mean it?"* Why would anyone say a prayer to the omnipotent Creator of the universe and not mean it?

If you prayed the prayer, of course you meant it.

This means that the very God who created the universe now occupies your heart. It means listening to Him in prayer. The Holy Spirit will provide you with spiritual gifts, intended to help you walk the Christian walk.[329] We claim them by faith.

We call this state of things having a *relationship with God* or a *relationship with Jesus*. This relationship is the thing that separates Christianity from the world's religions. True Christianity requires

You need to simply get out of His way and allow Him to work within you.[328] *This means trusting in God every step of the way, every day, for everything, and doing your best to obey Him.*

---

327. *"Mea culpa"* means "I'm guilty."
328. Galatians 3:14.
329. Galatians 5:22–23.

only one thing: complete and utter faith in Jesus.[330] Faith says, "*I cannot do it, Jesus. You have to do it for me.*"

Trusting in Jesus leads to our being filled with the Holy Spirit, which leads to a close and personal relationship with God. This enables us to live by faith. Jesus has made you right with God. Once you accept the salvation provided by Jesus' work on the cross, there is another component to your Christian faith.

If you follow someone, then you follow their example. You live as you believe they want you to live. Most of us have a pretty good idea of the difference between right and wrong. You might think that obedience means doing right things rather than wrong things. There is more to obedience than doing the right things. Obedience means obeying God's will. Our faith is made complete through our obedience to His will, which we discern through His Word and through prayer.

True and consistent faith is easier said than done. There is a fine line between obedience as a result of our faith and obedience in an effort to earn our way into heaven.

Christianity is a process. From the moment we take that first step of faith, the Holy Spirit indwells in us. The Holy Spirit enables us to develop our faith. This ongoing process of Christian growth through faith and obedience, enriched by Bible study and prayer, leads us to more faith and obedience. You have to get out of God's way and let the Holy Spirit work in your life. You stop resisting Him and step into that river of faith which He created. He guides you to the ultimate destination.

Slowly but surely, we get better and better. We sin less and experience a new life. It's God's work through the Holy Spirit, but you have to participate.

---

330. Romans 3:22.

The important thing is to allow the Holy Spirit to continue to work in your life. This means consciously obeying God and deciding not to sin. It means continuously trusting Him with every aspect of your life. Christianity is a lifelong journey, a process of discovery as God, through His Holy Spirit, gently teaches and leads us. Sometimes we stumble. We make bad decisions, well-intentioned or otherwise. If we return to an attitude of submission to God, He will pick us up and help us to get back on the Christian path.

Trust God to guide you. Trust Him to do the work. Give it all to Him. And don't take it back.

Prayer

It is critically important as a new Christian that you get into the habit of prayer. You need to have regular times of prayer, but you also need to learn to pray continuously.[331] This will enable you to grow in your faith walk and rely upon God for every single thing in your life. God uses our prayers to quietly impress upon us His ideas and thoughts, ultimately for the purpose of leading us closer to Him. You will be amazed at the power of prayer. You may at times pray more out of a feeling of obligation than out of desiring to commune with God. If you simply relax and let Him quietly enter, He will unfailingly impress your heart.

It used to be that prayer was a regular part of every child's school experience. We learned to say our prayers at night before we went to bed. Many of us say some sort of prayer at holiday meals such as Thanksgiving. All of us are very familiar with the "foxhole" prayer; the prayer in times of crises. In times of stress or threat, we know how to pray and do so unabashedly. Certainly, these are the most heartfelt prayers ever uttered. We absolutely mean what we pray.

---

331. 1 Thessalonians 5:17 (AMP).

We can pray for lots of reasons, but praying to learn God's will for us is far and away the most fruitful and rewarding type of prayer. God wants us to take all of our needs to Him. And He wants us share His wisdom with us.

Prayer is more than a response to a stressful situation. Prayer is a regular, ongoing, and unceasing means of communicating with God.

Since the beginning of man, God has continually expressed His desire for a relationship with mankind. The Bible tells the stories of mankind's encounters with God. Adam and Eve experienced personal encounters with God while in the quiet peace of the Garden of Eden.[332] Moses had dialogue with God and encountered the burning bush while in the desolate wilderness. Joseph and Mary were visited by angels, God's emissaries.[333] They explained that Mary, a virgin, would become pregnant and give birth to Jesus. Paul had visions that explained to him what he should do next in his ministry.[334] Jesus is described as frequently slipping away to be alone to pray.[335]

Simply, God wants to communicate with us. He wants to hear from us. He also wants to speak to us. How does God speak to us? Some Christians say that "God told me _____," or "God talked to me and said_____." It's worse when the thing that "God told me" amounts to something for the

Non-Christians hear these Christianspeak declarations and conclude that the Christian has pretty much lost their marbles.

---

332. *See, e.g.* Genesis 3:8.
333. Matthew 1:18–24 (AMP); Luke 1: 26–38.
334. Acts 16:6–10.
335. Luke 5:16; Mark 1:35.

speaker's benefit, such as "God told me to tell you to send me your money."

There are numerous ways people speak to each other today, both audibly and inaudibly. We communicate verbally, and we communicate nonverbally through our actions. An arched eyebrow or scowl can tell a complete story. A picture is worth a thousand words, as the saying goes. In this day and age, communication channels today are many: we text, we send emails, we blog, we tweet, and we may occasionally write the old-fashioned letter. The only real variable is the effectiveness of that communication.

One can come up with credible arguments for either audible or inaudible divine communication. Does it really matter? In a sense, how God communicates to mankind is somewhat irrelevant. For that matter, why should God have to communicate audibly? He is the Creator of the universe. He can communicate any way that He wants to. Impressing something upon my mind and my heart is just as effective as if He whispered it into my ear. In fact, when I speak to God, I don't do it audibly either. But I believe that He hears me. This is not to say that God has never audibly talked to people. It just means that the communication doesn't have to be audible in order to be legitimate.

If God spoke audibly to me today and I told someone about it, they would probably call the paramedics. If God speaks inaudibly to us and we ignore it, the result is the same—God's will is frustrated. Instead of becoming preoccupied with how He speaks to us, we should focus on how we listen to Him. I am convinced that God has spoken to me. Still, he has never uttered an audible word to me. It doesn't mean that He isn't heard. He has quietly impressed my heart on many occasions.

The apostle Paul says that we are to pray continuously.[336] On the surface, this would seem to be impossible. After all, we have

---

336. 1 Thessalonians 5:17 (AMP).

jobs, kids, yard work, and all of the other things that come with living. How can we take the time to get on our knees on a daily basis, much less a continual basis?

Paul clearly led a very busy life. He spent a great deal of time walking from town to town (and being chased from many of those towns), on ships traveling to different lands, making tents (his day job),[337] teaching, and preaching. Somehow he prayed continuously.

When we are in traffic, do we allow that other car in front of us? Or, do we angrily speed up? If we ask God, we will make the right choice. Praying continuously means simply considering God's will in everything that we do. We rely on the indwelling of the Holy Spirit to reveal God's will.

The secret is in our attitude toward God. We must consider Him first in everything that we do.

In today's world, we are bombarded with media: personal communications devices, social media, wireless Internet access, DVDs, CDs, and other media beyond imagination a few short years ago. To make matters worse, time is at a premium. We are all spread too thinly between school, careers, family, and other obligations. In the rush and bombardment of life, we can easily forget about the one thing that matters. What matters is our relationship with God.

God speaks to us. He doesn't speak over us or dominate the conversation. He may occasionally grab us by the lapels in a big way, with a big plan as he did to Paul on the way to Damascus. However, in our everyday encounters with Him, we have to be willing to listen. Talk with God about everything, every minute of the day. Take special some God time for yourself. Set aside some time each day to be completely alone with God. You might be surprised at what you hear.

---

337. Acts 18:3 (AMP).

God time is like physical exercise; the more that you do it, the more that you realize how important and beneficial it is. If you don't dedicate daily time to God, you will likely find it difficult to grow your relationship with Him. You will stop growing spiritually. You may think that Christianity doesn't work. You will become like the man Jesus described who built his house upon shifting sand,[338] or the seed sowed on rocky soil.[339] In both cases, initial excitement is followed by disappointing failure.

He knows your every thought and you can know His, through prayer and Bible study. He will not impose Himself upon us. We always have the power to choose what course of action we are going to take in any given situation. If we take a course of action inconsistent with God's will, then we've sinned.

> *Through the Holy Spirit, God hardwires your heart with a direct line of two-way communication.*

Or we can instead step back, take a breath and give the issue at hand to God. If we get out of His way, and let His Holy Spirit work within us, we can be filled with the Holy Spirit. It means doing everything that you can to obey God's will. It means getting out of His way. This completely opens up the communication line between you and God. God has more influence on your lives and actions than you do.

We have to do everything we can to hear it. Because we are so easily distracted, it can be difficult to discern what He is telling us.

> *God speaks to Christians constantly through the indwelling of the Holy Spirit. The noise in our lives prevents us from hearing Him.*

---

338. Matthew 7:24–27(AMP).
339. Matthew 13:1–23 (AMP).

One way to hear Him is to put ourselves in a quiet prayerful mode and wait upon Him. If you want to hear what God has to say, you need to develop a daily habit of devoting time to studying God's Word, prayer, and reflection. The more you do it, the better the communication. It will become almost automatic. God will speak to you and you will know that it is Him.

We are indwelt with the Holy Spirit from the moment we invite Jesus into our lives. It happens automatically. Whether we are filled with the Holy Spirit is up to us.

There are those that argue that salvation and indwelling of the Holy Spirit are two separate occurrences and that one must separately invite the Holy Spirit into one's life. This is a distinction without a difference. We repent, we turn from our sins and toward God, and we let Him take care of everything else.

Investing in Your Spiritual Portfolio

Jesus told two stories about new Christians and their faith. The first is the story of the sower and the seed, in which a farmer planted seeds. [340] This parable must have resonated deeply to a people whose existence depended upon the success of their farming efforts. Although markets existed and people traded, bought, and bartered for food, in those days people were much more dependent upon their own efforts. So, if your planting was wiped out by pests, eaten by birds or rodents, or you didn't harvest, you and your family could go hungry. In the story, the farmer scattered seeds and depending upon the circumstances, the seeds either bore multiplied crops or failed to produce. The

---

340. Matthew 13:1-23 (AMP).

failures were caused by different reasons, such as birds that ate the seeds and weeds that choked the crops.

Jesus told another story about a man who built his house on a rock and another who built his upon sand.[341] The rains came and you can imagine what happened to the two houses. In those days, building a house was a lifetime effort. A person had to have either family wealth or earn enough to buy a plot of land. They had to have enough money for building materials. Then they had to actually build the house. Imagine what if would feel like to lose the effort of a lifetime as the result of a single storm. Imagine how you would feel if your home survived that same storm.

Jesus explained that the sower and the seed was a metaphor for the Christian life. He said that we can hear the gospel, but if we let the worries and distractions of this world get in the way, they can prevent us from becoming fully fruitful Christians and living the lives that God wants for us. Jesus explained that people who hear his words and put them into practice are like the man who built his house upon the rock.[342]

These stories describe the two primary components of Christian faith. The story of the man who built his house on a rock tells us that the way we engage is by learning God's Word, in order to build our spiritual foundation. The sower story tells us that once we receive the good news, we have to do something about it, we have to engage. We engage by walking in faith on a daily basis. The two components are mutually dependent. We learn about faith from God's Word; we learn about faith from our faith walk.

Our faith increases as we get to know God through his Word. The more that we study the Bible, the greater our faith will become. On one level, we respond in faith when we hear the

---

341. Matthew 7:24–27 (AMP).
342. Id.

gospel. By responding to the good news that Jesus came to save us from our sins once and for all, we take that first step of faith. We hear, we believe, and we respond. On a deeper level, as we study God's Word, we learn more about the character of God. And it gives us the desire to learn more about Him.

We learn that He can be trusted with everything. That gives us the courage to give everything to Him.

The Bible has been called an *owner's manual for humanity*. It teaches people how to act toward each other and toward God. It describes them and their lives; their hopes, their fears, their character, their needs and wants. If we follow the instructions contained in the Bible, our lives go pretty well. If we fail to heed these instructions, it usually leads to one breakdown or another (typically on a figurative darkened highway at night and without a cell phone).

Many of us form our views about Christianity largely on hearsay evidence from preachers and other folks. The tendency of some Christians is to rely on other Christians to tell us what to believe. We hang on every word of our pastors and Bible teachers, but we spend little time reading the Bible. When we do read it, we read only parts of it.

The Bible is the source document for Christian faith. If you want to become a tax attorney, it only makes sense that you would immerse yourself in the Internal Revenue Code. Likewise, if you are going to become a proficient criminal lawyer, you will spend a great deal of time in the criminal code of your jurisdiction. Accountants learn accounting rules and requirements; computer experts become intimately familiar with the source code of the programming language with which they are working. Reading the governing document will give the reader expertise, and applying what is learned will refine that expertise. We reach our own conclusions, rather than accepting those of other people.

Granted, the Bible can be an intimidating document. It was written a long time ago, in an unfamiliar language. It's a big book of small print, filled with strange names, strange places, and strange events. It is a mixture of rules and laws, anecdotes, and prophecy; a spiritual jambalaya that can require a great deal of intellectual energy to get through it. In today's world of junk food novels, social media, and video, most people have little patience to plow through a long book. We would rather read the condensed version.

After law school, I decided to read the Bible cover-to-cover. I wanted to learn for myself exactly what it said. Up until that point, I had never done what in hindsight makes perfect sense. If you want to know about a subject, you should go to the source and read it. If you read only excerpts, you will end up with a condensed perspective on the faith.

If you want to understand Christianity, you need to read the Bible.

Once you begin to read the Bible, you will learn that it is an incredibly well-organized book designed to serve a number of purposes. Most books are read once and then quickly forgotten. The Bible, on the other hand, is a lifetime read. You can read a scripture verse as a child and gain something meaningful out of it. As an adult, you can read the same verse and discern something completely different but equally meaningful from it. The Bible can be read as a narrative that describes the story of God's relationship with mankind. It can be read as a daily devotional, with scriptural guidance on how we should live. The Bible is a steadfast book, in terms of its message. It's also a flexible document, in terms of meeting the needs of a person at any point in time.

John writes that the Word was Jesus.[343] Jesus' life is a *living word*. The Word is also the written Word, the life of Jesus as

---

343. John 1:1 (AMP).

recorded in the gospels. John was telling us that when we hear the good news about Jesus, at its core, we hear it from Jesus himself. So, if faith comes by hearing about Jesus through His Word, this means that our faith comes from reading the written Word, but also from the actions and urgings of the Holy Spirit in our lives.

Can you think of any book that can satisfy the spiritual, physical, and intellectual needs of approximately two billion people? You can begin to read the Bible today. God himself, the author of your faith and the Bible, will help you to understand it. The Holy Spirit helps us to get what we need out of the Bible when we need it.

The Bible is spiritual milk for new Christians, but also spiritual nutrition for people who have been Christians for decades.

If we allow it, God will develop our faith. We allow it by simply submitting our lives to Him—from the biggest problems to the smallest details. This is where experiential faith building, reading the Bible, and the Holy Spirit's actions intersect. We can look back on our lives and say with assurance that God has always taken care of us. We conclude as a result that He always will.

The Old Testament and the New Testament

Before law school, I struggled with how to go about reading the Bible. I made it through Genesis and Exodus, which didn't seem that difficult. Both tell the story of the origin of the creation of the world and mankind. They describe mankind's fall in the Garden of Eden. God's redeems His chosen people, the Israelites, and liberates them from Egyptian slavery. It all seemed pretty straightforward.

Then Leviticus confronted me. Leviticus deals with the first rules about sacrifice and cleanliness, and other similar religious practices. You get the picture. After reading a few chapters of Leviticus, I didn't waste a lot of time reading the Old Testament. Instead, I skimmed through the Old Testament, in order to get to the important stuff in the New Testament.

Like me, some Christians avoid the Old Testament. To them, it's old news. The only thing that matters now is what Jesus did on the cross and its effect on mankind. You will learn the ending, but you will miss so much, in terms of the story that led to the ending. It's also why you should read the Bible in its entirety before you attempt to dissect scripture to prove a point.

Reading only the New Testament is like reading only the final chapter in a novel.

When I first read the Bible cover-to-cover, I was amazed. It previously seemed to be a disjointed collection of materials. In reality, it is a beautifully seamless and consistent book. The Bible's themes are simple. God loves us and wants to have a relationship with us. He wants us to trust Him. He wants to take care of us. He is righteous and just. We aren't. He took care of it anyway.

The New Testament is the fulfillment of the Old Testament. In order to truly understand the result of the New Testament, you must understand what happened in the Old Testament. The Old Testament describes the issues that ultimately led to Jesus' birth.

The Old Testament chronicles God's continual loving efforts to reach out to mankind: teaching, blessing, disciplining, and forgiving those He loves. It describes the evolution of man's relationship with God. It describes the unfortunate patterns of mankind. There is a vicious spiritual cycle. God gracefully reached out to mankind. Man accepted God's grace but then turned his back on God. Man eventually repented.

This cycle is found throughout the Old Testament. Disobeying God by trying to run things ourselves, rather than simply trusting in Him, is what humans do. Man inevitably turned his back on God, and repented. Over time, man's heart hardened once again toward God and the cycle started all over again. But God never gave up on us.

The basic problem with mankind is the same today as it was then. God wants only the best for man, but man wants to do it his own way. God reached out to Adam and Eve. He provided abundantly for them. But they knew better than God. Jealousy caused their son Cain to kill his brother Abel.[344] God delivered Lot and his wife from the destruction of Sodom and Gomorrah.[345] He told them not to look back.[346] Lot's wife turned back to look.[347] The nation of Israel, engaged in its mass exodus from Egypt complained because there was no food. God gave them manna and they grumbled about it.[348]

God gave Moses the Ten Commandments, which were the rules by which the nation of Israel was supposed to live.[349] There were rules added in the books of Leviticus and Deuteronomy. Adherence to these rules is referred to as *living under the Law*. Experts in the law and religious leaders debated the interpretation and implementation of the rules. Under the law, man was constantly worried about paying for, or *atonement* for, sin. Generally, atonement took the form of an animal sacrifice, called a *blood sacrifice*. The animal had to be unblemished and there were rules about how the sacrificial animals were to be raised, as well as very precise rules about how the sacrifice took place. The idea was that the sacrificial animal assumed the place of the sinner. The sinner deserved to die because of his sin. The animal died instead. The problem was that the sinner kept sinning.

---

344. Genesis 4:8.
345. Genesis 19:16.
346. Genesis 19:17.
347. Genesis 19 :26.
348. Numbers 11 :1.
349. Exodus 20:2.

It became apparent that only something extraordinary could fix this problem. Man had proven time and time again that, despite God's love, he would rebel. God had given mankind the power to choose, and mankind repeatedly made choices that were against God. In response, God could have done any of a number of things. He could have destroyed mankind. Or, He could have imposed His will upon mankind.

There was a third way. God accomplished it through the life, death, and resurrection of Jesus. After thousands of years of the repeated pattern of mankind—

In Jesus, God solved the sin problem once and for all.
man sins, God forgives, and man sins again—the New Testament describes how God dealt with sin and man's rebellion once and for all. He made the ultimate sacrifice by sending His son to die in our place.

The New Testament describes Jesus' life, death, and resurrection and the growth of the early Christian church. With the New Testament and Jesus, the legal system changed entirely. Jesus became the sacrifice, once and for all, for all of the sins of mankind. Without a trial, and without any legitimate charges against him, he was beaten, scourged, and crucified.

The previous sentence, if read too quickly, can deceive the reader as to the horrific nature of Jesus' death. The pre-crucifixion scourging was incredibly painful. A scourging is an extremely violent and painful whipping or flogging with a leather whip with bits of metal and bone attached to the end capable of inflicting lethal damage in and of itself. Jesus was then nailed to a cross. Crucifixion was a horrendous, excruciatingly painful death, intended to horrify onlookers and thus act as a deterrent to future offenders. There are different views as to the exact methods involved in crucifixion at that time, but suffice it to say that generally speaking, a person was nailed to a wooden cross and hung there until he died. His death was caused by a combination of shock, dehydration, and asphyxiation. Jesus died a slow, painful, and humiliating death.

Despite this, Christians believe that Jesus' crucifixion was actually a triumph for all time. More importantly, it fulfilled of God's covenant with mankind, the covenant of an eternal relationship. The chasm between God and man was closed forever.

A Suggested Approach

You don't need a law degree to read the Bible. All you need is a plan of attack. That's the purpose of the following section. It provides a methodology to use as part of your regular Bible study. Consider dedicating at least thirty minutes to a daily Bible study.

Simply begin at the beginning and read the Bible sequentially. Start with Genesis and read all the way through to Revelation. Read about the first sin and its consequences. The Old Testament describes man moving further and further away from God. Read about God's plan to deal with the problem of sin, once and for all. You'll find an incredible story. It's incredible because it resonates so perfectly with what we know about how we act. The plan is the only conceivable plan that could finally deal with sin.

Read the Bible as you would read any book. Read it cover-to-cover.

You could set a goal of reading the Bible through in one year, which works out to be between three and four chapters per day. You will start in the Garden of Eden and trace the development

Reading the Bible cover-to-cover will help you to understand its broad concepts and ideas.

of the relationship between man and God. You will begin to discern themes throughout the Old Testament, which ultimately center on mankind's disobedience and redemption. As you read the New Testament, you will learn more about Jesus. He was the fulfillment of God's plan, once and for all, for mankind through his birth, death, and resurrection.

As you read the Bible cover-to-cover, you may find it helpful to also read it selectively. This means choosing sections to read based upon your spiritual needs at that time and based upon particular issues you may be faced with. The more familiar you become with the Bible, then the more often scripture will come to mind as you approach your life. Reading the Bible cover-to-cover will allow you to understand its big picture. But reading it selectively will also enable you to extract gems of wisdom. The Bible was designed to be a lifetime read. It is probably the only book ever written that can be read in parts just as beneficially as reading the whole.

Some Christians have favorite scripture that they refer to over and over again, in times of difficulty. Many Christians find that no matter what they are going through, in their daily Bible study they somehow land on a particular passage that helps. If we listen carefully to the Holy Spirit, He will guide us to scripture that fulfills our needs at any given time.

The following are some additional suggestions:

Develop the discipline of daily study. Set aside time every day to read the Bible. There will be days when you don't feel like reading the Bible. There are times when you just want to skip it. Don't do it. It's like exercise. Make Bible study a habit. If you have ever struggled with an exercise program, you understand that the only way to stick with it is to make up your mind that it's important. In the same way, you must decide that reading the Bible is an important component of learning about God, His will and what He desires for you

Start slowly and methodically. Read deliberately and carefully. Try to grasp the big concepts first. Think of the Bible as mankind's owner's manual. If you don't read your car's owner's manual, you may have problems with the car or you may not. If you do read the manual, you will be prepared to deal with the problems.

There is a precious gold coin there, just waiting for you to find it. And you will find it. God will make sure of it.

Read in a setting conducive to learning. As a student, most likely you had a place that you set aside as your "study place." It may have been a special spot at the library, or the kitchen table, or in a nook in your room. Wherever it was, chances are that when you sat down to study, your body and mind knew that you meant business. Find a special place to read your Bible.

Begin by praying. We should always seek God's guidance and divine wisdom before we make a decision or do anything significant in our lives. Start your Bible study with a prayer. Ask God to reveal His will to you. Ask Him to grant you wisdom. In doing so, you will be following in the footsteps of greatness. When God asked King Solomon what he wanted, Solomon asked only for wisdom.[350] God gave Solomon wisdom, but also granted him riches and wealth beyond imagination.[351]

Begin at the beginning. The Old Testament describes the problem of sin and its effect on mankind. The New Testament describes the solution. Don't yield to the temptation to skip to the end of the book. Read the entire story. As early in your Bible studies as possible, begin to try to understand not only the

---

350. 1 Kings 3:5–9 (AMP).
351. 1 Kings 3:16 (AMP).

lessons contained in virtually every line in the Bible but also the "big picture" of what God is saying to you.

Spend time in the Psalms and Proverbs every day. Psalms has been described as a book on how to deal with God and Proverbs described as a book on how to deal with man. The Psalms are a great source of inspiration and comfort. The writing of the Psalms is attributed to King David, who had a special place in God's heart.[352] The Proverbs challenges us and forces us to think about things in a different way. The Proverbs are attributed to King Solomon, David's son.

There are one hundred and fifty Psalms chapters and thirty-one Proverbs chapters in the Bible. This means that you can incorporate one Proverb chapter a day in your Bible study and complete the entire book of Proverbs in a month. You can do the same with Psalms and complete the book in five months. Or instead, read five Psalms chapters for each Proverbs chapter in order to complete both books within that same month. By feeding your soul with these incredibly wise writings and allowing the Holy Spirit to help you digest them, you will be amazed at the impact they can have on your attitude and intellect.

Read for lessons. In addition to reading the Bible to understand the story that it tells, read it to learn life lessons. Pick scripture to dissect and memorize. Do it every day.

Use a concordance, commentary, or other Bible reference tool. As you study the Bible, you will encounter strange terminology. A *concordance* is a biblical reference book that will provide you with scriptural references, based upon particular Bible topics. A *commentary* is a treatise that provides the author's interpretation of particular scripture. If you don't have a lot of money to spend,

---

352. Acts 13:22.

the Internet can also be an excellent resource. There are many websites hosted by Christians with discussion and analysis of scripture.

Let me offer a *caveat*:[353] Internet biblical research may or may not be doctrinally sound. Although there are numerous good websites out there, it can be difficult to discern the good from the bad. You should conduct some due diligence before relying too heavily on any website.

Keep a journal. As you read the Bible, keep a notebook or journal handy. Make notes of your thoughts, prayers and answers to those prayers, the scriptures you read, and the lessons you learn. Describe how you might apply what you have learned. Date each entry in order to be able to review later and track your thinking, your analyses, and the things that you learned.

Periodically review your journal. You may be surprised at the lessons you've learned and then promptly forgotten. Think of the Old Testament Israelites. They rebelled against God and got into trouble. They cried out to God. He forgave them and provided a way out. Then they rebelled again. It doesn't have to be that way. You can learn from your mistakes. A journal can help you do that.

Over time, you may be surprised at the action of God in your life, with your journal being tangible evidence of that action. This is one of the great benefits of journaling. Our memories are short. We learn, forget, and then relearn lessons. With a journal you can begin to see the real and tangible evidence of God working in your life. These things become the basis for ever-increasing faith in God.

Read the Master's words. In a typical fan club, we hang on the celebrity's every word. We quote the celebrity. We act like

---

353. *"Caveat"* means caution.

them. As Christ followers, we are fans of Jesus. If we want to understand what Jesus stood for, we should take care to understand his words.

God in the human form of Jesus presents the unique opportunity for God to speak unfiltered and unvarnished. As a result, Jesus' words are incredibly powerful and more than anything else will teach us what God is like.

The following section will provide you with an overview of the organization and content of the Bible. The purpose is to give you a rough idea of the structure of the Bible. It will help you to get started in your daily Bible study.

Organization of the Bible

The Bible contains sixty-six books, which function a lot like chapters do in other literature. The New Testament has twenty-seven books and the Old Testament has thirty-nine books.

THE OLD TESTAMENT

Genesis, Exodus, Leviticus, Numbers, Deuteronomy: These books describe the creation of the world and mankind, the temptation and original sin in the Garden of Eden, God's covenant with mankind, the development of the nation of Israel and its freedom from Egyptian slavery, the Ten Commandments and other rules of cleanliness and obedience, and God's deliverance of the Israelites. They are the groundwork for Christian faith and describe the problem of sin and the character of man.

Joshua, Judges, Ruth, 1 Samuel, 2 Samuel, 1 Kings, 2 Kings, 1 Chronicles, 2 Chronicles, Ezra, Nehemiah, Esther, Job: These books describe the lives and acts of the early nation of Israel and the ongoing principles of mankind's cyclical rebellion, repentance, and obedience to God and God's continuing forgiveness.

Psalms, Proverbs, Ecclesiastes, Song of Solomon: These books contain principles and rules for man's relationship with God and with each other.

Isaiah, Jeremiah, Lamentations, Ezekiel, Daniel, Hosea, Joel, Amos, Obadiah, Jonah, Micah, Nahum, Habakkuk, Zephaniah, Haggai, Zechariah, Malachi: These books are the stories of God's prophets through the years, as well as their messages of the coming of the Messiah, who Christians believe is Jesus of Nazareth.

THE NEW TESTAMENT

Matthew, Mark, Luke, John: These gospels describe life, ministry, death and resurrection of Jesus. The gospels tell the story of Jesus and provide the basis for the Christian faith.

Acts: This book describes the acts of the early Christian apostles, including Paul, who wrote much of the remainder of the New Testament.

Romans, 1 Corinthians, 2 Corinthians, Galatians, Ephesians, Philippians, Colossians, 1 Thessalonians, 2 Thessalonians, 1 Timothy, 2 Timothy, Titus, Philemon, Hebrews: This volume of works was written by the apostle Paul. These epistles are letters to the early Christian churches and describe some of the foundational principles followed by believers today.

James 1, James 2, 1 Peter, 2 Peter, 1 John, 2 John, 3 John, Jude: These books were written by early followers of Christ, and describe Christian principles and instruction.

Revelation: This book is the final chapter of the Bible and describes in apocalyptic terms, the second coming of Jesus and the end times for earth.

The Bible is waiting to instruct you. All you have to do is open it up and begin reading it with an open mind. Reading God's Word is an important part of your Christian growth. Starting your day with Bible study, before the onslaught of that day's problems, will lessen the onslaught. The Holy Spirit will help you. Start your study with prayer and ask Him to guide you.

As you begin your faith walk, you should continue to invest in your Christian growth. Bible study is a core component of your investment portfolio. It will help you continue to give yourself to God in faith. Ultimately, you will live the life that God intended for you to live.

Church and Christian Fellowship

These Christians can be found on the front pew every Sunday, surrounding themselves with other Christians, and spending much of their time in church-related activities. They become caught up in the activity because it makes them feel good about themselves. They begin to think that this work is earning them a special place in heaven.

A lot of Christians get so caught up in Christian ritual that they begin to substitute activity for faith in a misguided effort to earn their way into heaven.

It can also lead to them judging others who don't work as hard as they do.

It's difficult to tell the difference between these workers and Christians living in a true faith-based relationship with Jesus.

They are so wrapped up in the Christian lifestyle that they have fooled themselves into thinking that it will get them into heaven. It's easy to see how they can fool other people. The reality is that there is absolutely nothing that we can do to earn our way into heaven. Jesus' work on the cross accomplished that. It is our faith in Jesus and nothing more that gets us into heaven. Our desire to do the Christian stuff is a response to that faith, not the other way around.

You might ask, *"Why we should go to church anyway?"* We go to church to grow spiritually. We go to church to praise and worship God. We go to church to learn more about Him. We go to church to spend time with other *Christ followers*, who share our common beliefs. The tragedy is that the people running the church can short circuit all of it because they unintentionally make visitors feel like outsiders.

Early in my Christian walk, I struggled with regular church attendance. I didn't particularly enjoy going. The church wasn't welcoming, and I always felt like an outsider. There were a few church folks in those years who weren't what I would call stellar ambassadors of the faith. Some people operated in cliques and seemed to care less if I came or went. Further, notably absent from the scene was anyone who looked like they did anything other than make six figures, live in a nice suburban home, and drive an expensive SUV.

Church for its own sake seemed to be a type of legalism. There seemed to be plenty of hypocrisy and spiritual snobbery. To me, church was more than a building. I wanted to engage in my own worship at the location of my choosing. As a result, I shopped around a great deal for a church and somehow found a problem with all of them.

One day, out of the blue, something occurred to me.

This is another example of a thought occurring to me that is difficult to explain as arising from within my own intellect.

These ideas come from Him.

It occurred to me that one of the primary purposes of any church service is simply to worship God. We go to church to show God that we love Him. You can debate all day about whether church is an effective place of worship, but the truth is that, worship is between you and God. Although I'm surrounded by cliquish Christians, if I sing my loudest in a genuine desire to show God how much I love Him and appreciate Him, then mission accomplished. To a great extent, the rest of it simply doesn't matter. Whether the church stands when singing or sits, whether the singing is a cappella or not, whether it's trespasses or debts, the important thing is that I'm sitting there or standing, singing, praying, and worshipping Him.

Paul explained it best in his letter to the church in Corinth. He wrote that there are different kinds of spiritual gifts but that they all come from the same God.[354] He uses the human body as an analogy.[355] Every body part works differently, but together for the good of the body. In the same way, Christians have different gifts of the Holy Spirit, but they all work together for good for the Christian community.

There is another reason why church is so important for new Christians. It's because a church is generally the best place to find other believers.

God has given each of us spiritual gifts. Some of us have the power to discern things that others cannot. Others are able to read scripture and teach the Word to the benefit of others. Still others have the gift of compassion for others. God has given you gifts. He wants you to use them for the benefit of His church. The best way to determine your gifts is to pray about it. Ask God to help you understand His will for you. Talk with other believers;

---

354. 1 Corinthians 12:4–11 (AMP).
355. 1 Corinthians 12:12–14 (AMP).

they may be closely in tune with the Holy Spirit and can offer some insight as well. Sooner or later, that small, still voice of the Holy Spirit will enlighten you. It may be a subtle message at first. But stay faithful and keep trying to understand it. Your faith will be rewarded with wisdom, and you will learn what your gifts and purpose are while on this earthly journey.

You may have to sift through a few relationships (and get your feelings hurt), but you need to be around other believers. If you find the right crowd, you will grow, compare notes, share thoughts and prayers, and have a solid support group when things go south, as they sometimes will. From the days of the first Christian church, believers have relied upon other believers to help them strengthen their faith. Further, your fellow believers will help you to stay on the right path and hold you accountable if you stray.

Baptism

The Old Testament contains many rituals and ceremonies, each of which was followed precisely in order for the participant to have a chance at salvation. There were rules about what one could eat and who they could eat it with. There were rules about worship, who could go into the temple and when. Some very specific rules about sacrifices required atonement of sin through blood sacrifice. After Jesus was crucified, atonement became obsolete. He was the ultimate blood sacrifice. His death was the atonement for all sin and for all time. There was no longer any need for the ritualistic sacrifices in the Temple.

The New Testament describes only two rituals. The first is the Lord's Supper. We take part in this ritual with the elements (usually a small bread wafer and a thimbleful of grape juice), to commemorate Jesus' last supper on earth with his disciples. The gospel accounts describe this supper and that Jesus instructed his followers to do it in his memory.[356] The second ritual is baptism. Jesus was baptized,[357] as were many of his followers. Neither is a condition for salvation; however, many Christians participate in these rituals. They are performed in as many ways as there are denominations.

Some Christians will tell that you need to be baptized in order to get to heaven. They point to certain scripture to show that water baptism is essential to salvation.[358] After rededicating my life to Christ, I began to feel led toward baptism. However, I was resistant to doing it because I had heard people preach that it was a prerequisite to salvation. I knew that I was already saved.

I spoke with my dear father-in-law, who is a minister with a denomination where some believe that baptism is a requirement for salvation. He gave me a wise and balanced answer. He said that although some of his peers believe that baptism is essential to salvation, his view was that making it so would mean salvation by works.

A works salvation is in conflict with scripture, which tells us that we are saved by faith and not works.[359] There isn't anything else we need to do, other than simply believe, in order to go to heaven. It's hard to imagine that a belief system that relies upon faith in Jesus as its central component would require immersion in water to complete one's salvation. It just doesn't seem reasonable. Instead, it seems legalistic. After much prayer and thought, I decided to be baptized at the age of forty. I made the decision for the right reason. It was out of love for God, as opposed to fear.

We should be baptized, not because it will assure our salvation, but simply because Jesus did it. We don't know why He

---

356. *See, e.g.* Luke 22.
357. Matthew 3:13-15.
358. *See, e.g.* Mark 16:15; Matthew 28:19.
359. Ephesians 2:8.

submitted to baptism. We only know that He did do it. A public confession of faith is a healthy thing. Being able to pinpoint a time and a place where we first confessed that faith is a helpful thing when facing life's trials and

To follow Christ means to do what He did.

tribulations. Baptism is one of the most special spiritual experiences we can have. Because Jesus did it, it somehow seems right to do it.

Shortly after my daughter Meredith's six birthday, she accepted Christ. A skeptic might argue that at six she was too young to know what she was doing. Regardless, it was an absolutely genuine experience. She prayed a simple prayer asking Jesus to come into her heart. After she accepted Christ, she decided that she wanted to be baptized. If you have ever had the joy of witnessing a small child's baptism, you know that this act can only be explained by God's intervention and the gentle guidance of the Holy Spirit. It's a God thing. There is no other reasonable explanation for why a small child would feel so led to act in this way. These sweet children aren't baptized because they are afraid of God. They are baptized because they are responding to God in love and obedience.

Share Your Faith

As Christians, one of our fundamental duties is to share our faith with others.[360] Certainly, sharing in this way can edify other Christians. And yet, this critical duty is primarily for the purpose of helping to set non-Christians on the path to heaven.

We've covered the ideas of "walking the talk" and your "faith walk." Being able to quote scripture that supports your position

---

360. Matthew 28:19-20.

as a Christian is important and can be persuasive. However, most non-Christians will look primarily at your life, in order to evaluate the validity of your faith.

If they see you acting badly, they will quickly decide that your faith is meaningless. Many of these people do not understand that all Christians are at different stages of sanctification. They tend to hold all Christians to an extremely high standard. At the same time, as we have covered elsewhere in this book, faith without works isn't really faith. Your life is powerful evidence of your Christian faith.

For Christians, it's only natural to worry about the eternal destiny of our friends and family. I had always worried about my parents. At that time, my mom was still alive. I talked about it with her. A few years before she died, she told me that she had accepted Jesus.

I worried about my dad, who had died a number of years earlier. One day, while praying, I remembered that last family Thanksgiving. Dad had closed the Thanksgiving prayer in Jesus' name. I can't know for sure, but I believe that his story may have been a lot like mine. He accepted Jesus at an early age, but became consumed by this life. He bought the lie. His was a sad story and a less than optimal life. But I believe that Dad's afterlife was as assured as mine. That's the way God works in our lives. Without a lot of fanfare, He comforts and reassures us. No matter how difficult or impossible the situation may seem, He will deliver us from it.

CHAPTER THIRTEEN

A Moot Point

Austin was a big, beautiful black Labrador retriever whose ninety-pound bulk was one hundred-percent heart. He was my constant companion; a friend who was always there for me. I picked him up as a little puppy at a kennel and watched him grow into a strapping champion. He rode with me to law school every day and stayed in the back seat of my car while I was in class. When class was over, he was always excited to see me. As I buckled my seat belt, Austin usually jumped into the front seat and my lap, unashamedly licking my face. I drove us home and we talked about the day.

He never asked for much of anything, except for the occasional belly scratch. He absolutely loved pig's ears. Pig's ears are exactly what you might think—a pork by-product, the actual ears, glazed and cooked expressly for use as dog treats. To the human eye, they are simply disgusting. To the keen eye of and palate of a Labrador retriever, they are filet mignon. Austin was too laid back to do much in the way of tricks like many dogs. Rolling over or sitting up were beneath him. He would do back flips and cartwheels for pigs ears. He would tap dance for them.

His pedigree was impressive and he was one of the most regal and beautiful animals I had ever seen. His Lab head was huge, with large, incredibly white canine teeth that looked as if they could take your arm off. He intimidated every squirrel he encountered. And yet, his ferocity was a ruse. Austin just wanted to play. Most of the time, he acted like a big, silly kid. He was also one of the kindest and gentlest creatures that God ever created.

In the water, Austin was incredibly graceful. He could swim for hours without tiring, cruising along like an aquatic animal. In Monterey, I often took him swimming in the surf. One day, a large sea otter suddenly appeared about a hundred yards from shore, presumably in search of a long-lost cousin. Austin never met a stranger and eagerly swam toward the otter. He became an increasingly smaller dot on the surf's horizon. My stomach tensed with the sudden realization that he was swimming out to sea. I yelled and whistled loudly. I didn't think Austin could hear me. I took my shoes off and got ready to jump into the water.

Just at that moment, Austin turned and looked at me, then back at his otter cousin. For a second he was undecided. It was Dad or the otter. The otter, Austin's new friend, held the promise of all kinds of adventure. Dad, on the other hand, might come up with a pigs ear now and again. I held my breath. Austin began swimming back to shore. As he swam closer, I could see his big Austin grin as his head bobbed behind the waves. It was as if he was saying, "*Just kidding around, Dad.*" I was his dad and despite the potential for adventure, his family always came first.

I watched him one day as he sat out on our back deck, the king of all that he surveyed. His golden eyes squinted into the sun and he stared at a huge cloud, drifting across an incredibly blue Nashville sky on a perfect afternoon. It was the spring of

2001, about a year before I graduated from law school. I had finished my law studies for the day and it was the first time in a long time that I closed the books before dark. Feeling a sense of temporary freedom from my studies, I took Austin for a walk.

We walked through the neighborhood. Austin stopped for a minute, sat on his hindquarters and looked up at me in a pleading sort of way. This was his way of telling me he needed a bathroom break. Unfortunately, there were no doggie bathroom spots in sight; instead only neighbors' well-manicured lawns. I tugged at his leash, which was our tacit signal that this particular yard was not intended to be a place where he could relieve himself. The pained look on his face told me that we had but a few minutes to make it to the vacant field just outside our neighborhood. Otherwise, I would be reduced to using every dog walker's emergency kit — the plastic bag in my pocket. This was something that I certainly avoided whenever possible. So, we ran for it. Tearing down the hill, we made it to the field just in time. We looked at each other in genuine appreciation. Afterward, we walked along the path next to the field for a few minutes.

I wasn't paying much attention to anything other than the beautiful day. Suddenly I felt the leash go completely taut. All ninety pounds of Austin pulled against the leash. It was as if the end of the world was right there in front of us. I looked behind me and realized that Austin had "the look" on his big face. The look was one of abject and utter terror. When Austin got the look, he froze completely. The look always meant one thing. A storm was coming. Something in his Lab psyche could sense it. Austin was completely and unabashedly terrorized by thunderstorms. He would begin to shudder and shake, long before the storm arrived.

Austin's fear meant that he had to deal with the storm twice. He was afraid not only of the storm, but also the anticipation of the approaching storm. Sometimes his fear of the coming storm was worse than the storm itself.

At that moment, there wasn't a cloud in the sky. I said to him, "Come on boy, everything's fine." Austin wasn't buying it. I tried to distract him. "Austin, look there's a squirrel!" I said, "Let's get him!" He still wasn't buying it. I pulled on his thick leather leash. I tried to drag his ninety pounds toward home. He wouldn't budge. He sat there, on his big hindquarters, looking at me with pleading hazel eyes.

So, I did what I had done many times before. I did what any dad would do. I put my arms around him, grunted and picked him up. Carrying him back up that hill was like moving a piano. I started to scold him as I struggled up the hill, but when I saw the look of terror remaining in his eyes, I kept it to myself.

Whether he realized it or not, Austin was always safe when he was with me.

Whatever it was, I had it under control. If a thunderstorm approached, I took Austin into the house where he was safe and cozy. There was no way that he could be harmed by that storm. I proved it to him, time and time again.

Each time a storm approached, Austin had a choice to make. He could either trust in me, or not. If he didn't trust in me, I would still take care of him. No matter how I would reason with him, comfort him or attempt to reassure him, Austin had the same abject terror any time he sensed a storm coming. Although he trusted me, no amount of trust could overcome his raw fear. I could never get through to Austin about his unjustified, irrational fear of storms. He died in 2002, at age thirteen; a ripe old age for a Labrador retriever.

One day, it occurred to me that in some ways, I'm just like Austin was.

The Fear Problem

Austin couldn't fully trust me because his fear got in the way. His fear outweighed his ability or willingness to trust. My childhood chaos caused me to have a great deal of fear. This fear prevented me from fully trusting in God. My inability to fully trust Him resulted in an ongoing vulnerability to fear. It was a vicious cycle.

As with any meaningful relationship, things generally work better when the parties are more interested in each other than themselves. A Christian who succumbs to fear cannot fully trust the Father. If you are consumed with fear, it will be difficult to think about much else. You won't be able to engage in a full relationship with God. Fear should be a *moot point*[361] to the Christian. With God on our side, there is no longer anything to fear.

Fear may very well be the single greatest impediment to a meaningful relationship with God.

Some psychologists believe that many of the root causes of fear are holdovers from mankind's days as hunter/gatherers. In those days, fear served the useful purpose of stimulating man's intellectual, emotional, and physiological systems, and thus provoking the "flight or fight" response. Man could respond to the threat, assisted by increased energy and strength-inducing adrenalin and enhanced neural, respiratory, and circulatory activity. A hunter confronted by an angry bear could run or choose to fight his way out of the situation. After a quick burst of the hunter's physical and intellectual systems that dispersed the various chemicals generated by the threat, the hunter's systems would return to normal.

Fear was a useful emotion and self-preservation mechanism. A person who knew no fear would most likely not last very long.

---

361. *"Moot"* means something that is of no importance.

Of course, things have changed. Today, most of the threats we are faced with are simply emotional rather than physical in nature. Fear no longer serves the purpose it used to.

Regardless, our response to fear still generates the same increased physical and emotional activity as it did for the hunter. Today there is typically no outlet for the increased physiological activity. For most of the dangers we face in today's world, there is little direct action we can take to address the threat. When the boss threatens to fire you, you cannot run away or throw your spear at her. About the only thing you can do is worry about it. Fear produces worry. Worry produces increased blood pressure, gastrointestinal distress, cardiac damage, and numerous other ills.

Fear is anxiety caused by immediate danger; worry is anxiety over the prospect of danger, and a subset of fear. Fear is what Austin experienced during the storm; worry is what he experienced while waiting for it to arrive. People worry about the possibility that the things they fear will actually occur. We become afraid when things happen in our lives we didn't anticipate. We are afraid of things we cannot control. If we allow it, fear can consume us.

Fear is a response to the unknown and uncontrollable. Worry is a response to unresolved fear.

Fear and worry, if not dealt with, will ultimately lead us to doubt God. Whatever the source, worry and fear can prevent us from trusting in Him.

Worry means that you are attempting to control life yourself. It creates a wedge between you and God.

Satan Is the Author of Fear and Worry

Worry is the opposite of trust. Jesus told us not worry.[362] It is therefore sin. It is an insidious sin because he desire to defend one's self is basic to the human psyche. We are taught that *God helps those who help themselves.* We glorify people who bring themselves up by their bootstraps. Further, we do have God-given skills and tools. He wouldn't have given them to us unless He intended for us to use them. He doesn't want us to sit passively by, waiting for Him to take action. On the other hand, we are told trust Him in all things.[363]

Conventional wisdom says that we are emotional products of our upbringing. Many psychotherapy dollars are spent each year in an attempt to resolve issues with our parents. Certainly, our upbringing has something to do with our emotional makeup.

Still, there is a more sinister, insidious source of fear in our lives.

Fear, as evidenced time and time again, is the single most devastating weapon in Satan's arsenal. Fear becomes so ingrained in our psyches that we aren't aware that it's there.

Satan will lie to you.

It might go something like this:

"Surely you don't think that God, the Supreme Creator of the universe, is going to concern Himself with something as trivial as your little issue, do you?"

This technique is one of the key weapons in Satan's arsenal. Just as he has done throughout man's history, Satan subtly plants ideas in our heads that on the surface don't seem so harmful. Perhaps there is

We convince ourselves that we are simply worriers or high-strung and that these feelings are simply part of our personality.

---

362. Matthew 6:25-34 (AMP).
363. Proverbs 3:5–6.

even a grain of truth in them. It makes them more believable. After all, God gave us our personalities; therefore, they must be good, right? We decide that we don't need to do anything to deal with this issue.

Moreover, Satan is usually the greatest beneficiary whenever we are afraid. Fear left unchecked will create a wedge of doubt between the believer and God. Satan uses fear and its companion worry with tactical precision to interfere with our daily communion with God.

You know what happened in the Garden of Eden. Adam and Eve lived there with everything they needed, but they decided that they needed more. The only rule God gave them was to not touch or eat fruit from the middle of the garden.[364] Satan convinced Adam and Eve that there was no real harm in eating the fruit.[365] *"After all, it is in your best interests to understand where God is coming from, right? He doesn't need all the pressure of taking care of you. You should take care of yourselves."*

Satan sowed a seed of doubt that germinated quickly. He caused Adam and Eve to doubt God. Then he nurtured the seed and cultivated the crop. His whisper caused them to doubt God, which led to fear, which led to the original sin. Satan convinced Adam and Eve that God could not be trusted. He told Eve that she wouldn't die if she ate the forbidden fruit.[366] Satan argued, *"Why would God create something that humans could eat that would kill them? His real motive is to keep you from becoming like Him."*[367]

Satan, with a few simple words, convinced Adam and Eve that God had not spoken truthfully to them and that God could not be trusted. He persuaded them that God did not love them but instead was jealous of them. They became convinced that if they took matters into their own hands, they could become like God.

---

364. Genesis 2:17.
365. Genesis 3:4–5.
366. Id.
367. Id.

Rather than believing that God's law was for their own good, Satan had convinced them that God had ulterior motives for not wanting them to eat from the tree. The wedge was complete.

They ate the fruit.[368]

Later, God walked in the garden and called to Adam.[369] Now, Adam knew fear.[370]

So began thousands of years of man's separation from God.

This is how fear begins. Satan, somewhere in our deepest psychic recesses, convinces us that God cannot be fully trusted. He whispers to us, *"You must take matters into your own hands. The way to deal with this issue is to deal with it. If you worry about it long and often enough, you will solve this issue."* Rather than turning where we should, to God, we turn to ourselves. Rather than trusting Him, we trust in our own abilities.

Using the ultimate in flawed logic, Satan plants assumptions in our psyche that become so integrated into the background of our thinking that we do not challenge them. Slowly, they become so integrated into our thinking that we aren't aware of them. They take over our thoughts. Eventually, they kill us spiritually.

Like a skin cancer that looks like a harmless blemish, these assumptions remain benignly in the background. But if allowed to ripen untreated, they are just as deadly.

Faith: the Antidote

Faith in God is the only real antidote to fear and worry. Through faith, we give all of it to Him. Unless we recognize the problem,

---

368. Id.
369. Genesis 3:8.
370. Genesis 3:10.

it is impossible to solve it. We are afraid when we are separated from the Father. We are fearless when we are connected to Him.

Fear is the opposite of faith. Faith defeats fear; a lack of faith allows it.

Worry unchecked interrupts our faith and is the single biggest impediment to a meaningful relationship with God. It's interesting to note that Jesus was unable to perform miracles in his hometown, where there was little faith.[371]

Fear is also the biggest reason new Christians fall away from their faith. Fear is a lack of faith. Fear means that you are not fully trusting God with your life. This makes it sin. Continuing to sin will interrupt the power of the Holy Spirit to work in your life. You can overcome any kind of sin in your

Fear sneaks up on us. Much of the everyday variety of fear lurks quietly in the background.

life simply by trusting in God to fix it. If you doubt God, then your relationship with Him is jeopardized.

The line between exercising prudent caution and fear arising from a lack of faith is difficult to discern. If you believe that God loves you and will take care of you, then you can deal with much of what life throws at you. If you are still handicapped by fear, worry, and doubt, then you will have a limited and unfulfilling relationship with God.

Perhaps you struggle with fear. It has become such a permanent part of your psyche that you don't know how to deal with it. You need to remember one thing. In the grand scheme of eternity, our lives here on earth are the blink of an eye. Anything that happens here to us is, by definition, pretty insignificant.

God will take care of you here on earth, if you allow it. God has solved the problem of our eternal destiny, thanks to His work

---

371. Mark 6:5 (AMP).

at the cross. God wants us to surrender our lives to him. As Jesus taught time and time again, God will take care of everything. Jesus' death on the cross paid for our sins, thus assuring us of eternal life in heaven. His death also means that our lives, if we allow it, will be infinitely better. Through faith, we have accepted this free gift. We have continuing in faith in Jesus, despite the obstacles we face in life.

It's our faith walk. It means the ongoing daily relationship we have with God is based upon our faith in Jesus. It has all been paid for, dealt with, and resolved. Until we fully surrender these details to Him, fear and worry will continue to control us. Jesus' work on the cross made fear a moot point. He solved the problem of sin by paying the price for it, once and for all. Our eternal destiny is assured. There is nothing to worry about anymore.

A common theme in movies today, typically in science fiction or horror genres, is how futile faith in God is when we face fear. The astronauts have no options left. Their spaceship has crashed on a hostile alien planet and there is no way home. They must hike into some unfamiliar dark recess, in order to find water or food. As they approach a ridge, they are confronted by a flesh-eating nine-foot-tall extraterrestrial whose jaws are razor sharp. There is no hope. And so, they begin to recite the familiar prayer contained in the Twenty-Third Psalm. They face their fear. Typically, right after this the alien kills and eats them.

We have pity on these fools who have relied on faith in God to deliver them from evil. We think, *"What idiots. Instead of praying, they should have made a run for it."* Nonetheless, Hollywood, as it often does, has missed the point. Its use of the device betrays its fundamental misinterpretation of the meaning of faith. Faith is a way of life, not simply a response to a threatening situation. Faith is a mindset that we adopt, a suit of armor that we put on consciously and deliberately every day of our lives.

The psalmist says that he will not be afraid because God is with him.[372] The eternal Creator of the universe is with me, at this very moment, and is aware of everything that is happening to me.

*God is with me. **The simplicity of the statement and yet the power that it represents is remarkable.***

Christians believe not only that God is with us at all times, but that He loves us and has a plan for our lives. We believe these things through our faith in God. Our faith is founded in God's Word,

Our faith is the antidote to our fear.

and our faith, like David's, is strengthened based upon the results of our faithfulness. Faith in God produces a certain result, and that result produces more faith. Faith begets faith.

That said, then why are Christians afraid? Why are there Christian counselors with thriving practices who help their clients deal with unresolved fears and other issues? The simple answer is that there is an inverse relationship between faith and fear. The more faith one has, the less susceptible to fear they are. Christians who don't understand this seek outside help

Faith is something that we must invest time in, in order to fully develop it.

when the answer, in the form of the Holy Spirit, rests within them.

Once you accept Christ, you are saved from your sins and you are forgiven completely by God for all of your sins, past, present, and future. This means that you've been released from the imprisonment of your sins. You become filled with the Holy Spirit, who helps you to live a better life now, here on earth. In one way, once you accept Jesus as your savior, all of your

---

372. Psalm 23:4.

problems are solved. The Creator of the universe is on your side. If God is on your side, you will win. And yet, as with all things God, you have to allow it to happen. You rely on God for everything in your life. You know that as long as you remain in faith, He will cause everything to work together for the good.[373] No matter what happens, you know and act as if He will make it work. If you do this, your Christian walk will be infinitely better. You will fear less, worry less, sin less and grow closer to Him.

Before they fell, Adam and Eve were in perfect communion with God. And still, they let the seeds of doubt affect their trust in Him. You don't have to doubt. God can be trusted. When faced with adversity, continue to place your trust in Him. If you have bought into the lie, then give your fears and worries to God today, right now. Don't let nagging fear and worry interrupt your ongoing communion with Him.

Heroes of the Bible: Not So Much

We think of many of the people described in the Bible as fearless and full of faith. After all, that's why they are in the Bible, right? They are bastions of the faith. And yet, as you study these people, you may be surprised that many, if not all of them, dealt poorly with fear. They aren't different from you and me. They were afraid. They doubted. In some cases, they failed. However, all of them ultimately were delivered and restored through faith in God.

The following are their stories of faith.

---

373. Romans 8:28.

Wrestling with God

Jacob was the son of Isaac, grandson of Abraham, and twin brother of Esau. Although he was Esau's twin, he was delivered second and therefore Esau had the birthright of being the firstborn and the corresponding rights of inheritance and the right to rule the family. Jacob was so named because as he and Esau were being born, Jacob grasped at Esau's heel, presumably in an attempt to be firstborn. Being the firstborn son brought with it substantial privileges and blessings.

The differences between Jacob and Esau are stark. Esau was a hunter, and Jacob, his mother's son, appears to have been a quieter, domestic type. Esau was a macho outdoorsman. Jacob preferred to cook. And yet, Jacob was a clever fellow who thought strategically. Esau's focus was on his next meal.

One day after hunting, Esau came home famished. Jacob convinced Esau to give him his birthright, as the firstborn male, for a bowl of stew that Jacob had prepared.[374] The birthright meant that Jacob would be the first to inherit from Isaac. In those days, being first in the line of succession was a very big deal. Esau traded it for stew. In today's terms, it would be like trading a Picasso for a plate fried chicken.

After Esau ate, he realized the full extent of what he had done, and he hated Jacob for setting him up. Later, Isaac, on his deathbed, summoned Esau so that he could bless him, presumably to mitigate the effect of the lost birthright. A blessing was the next best thing to a birthright. Again, Jacob outsmarted him. He tricked Isaac into blessing him instead of Esau. Esau was enraged. He tried to kill Jacob. Jacob fled.

Jacob had his own problems. His life was characterized by struggles. He continually tried to improve the hand he had been

---

374. Genesis 27:14 (AMP).

dealt. He manipulated his own father and brother. Even so, his efforts seemed only to result in greater problems.

Something happened. Jacob eventually found immense favor with God, who renamed him Israel. He became the patriarch of the twelve tribes of Israel. Somehow Jacob's very character was changed. What could possibly explain this radical change?

The answer lies with a dream. Jacob had a dream about God.[375] In the dream, God told Jacob that He was with him and that Jacob's descendants would be widespread all over the earth[376] God also told Jacob that He would watch over him and be with him wherever he went.[377] God's point was that if Jacob would put his faith in Him, He would take care of everything. Jacob knew that this was no ordinary dream but continued to struggle with life. At first, he missed the point. Even so, God continued to reach out to Jacob.

Jacob's life improved substantially nonetheless. It was almost as if the mere exposure to God had blessed him. He had a large family, a fruitful flock, and productive crops. God told Jacob to return home.[378]

His unresolved issue with Esau remained. Jacob learned that Esau was coming for him with four hundred men.[379] He was terrified.[380] He prayed for deliverance. Jacob's prayer appeared to be a final attempt to negotiate with God. He reminded God of His promises of prosperity.[381] Jacob tried to navigate his own way out of the situation. He sent a peace offering in the form of a herd of animals to Esau.[382] But he knew that he was in trouble.

---

375. Genesis 28:12 (AMP).
376. Genesis 28:14 (AMP).
377. Genesis 28:15 (AMP).
378. Genesis 31:13 (AMP)
379. Genesis 32:6 (AMP).
380. Genesis 32:7 (AMP).
381. Genesis 32:11 (AMP).
382. Genesis 32:13 (AMP).

That night, something miraculous happened. Jacob woke up and sent his family and all of his possessions across the river where they had camped.[383] Now, he was all alone. In a dream-like story, Jacob spent the rest of the night wrestling with a man, who was actually God.[384] God had abundantly blessed Jacob with family and material possessions. Jacob largely relied on his own resources to successfully deal with threats. Jacob knew that Esau had pledged to kill him. This time, he was terrified, frozen with fear. He wouldn't budge; nor would God.

In the midst of this apparent impasse, God asked him who he was.[385] This simple question required Jacob to think deeply about his relationship with God.

Jacob told God he wouldn't let go without a blessing.[386] In this sense, "to bless" means to make holy or to sanctify. This request speaks volumes and teaches us to-day about our relationship with God. First, Jacob realized that he needed to be sanctified. Second, he admitted that only God could sanctify him. Jacob was finally ready to end the struggle.

In that instant, Jacob surrendered all to God. His request revealed someone who was determined, above everything else, to cling to God for his very life.

God did bless Jacob. He did it in a fundamental and life-changing way. Jacob's very being was transformed. He was no longer the maneuvering, fearful man that he was before this encounter with God. As the sun came up, Jacob spied Esau. Instead of being terrified, Jacob was calm. Rather than murder in his heart, Esau had nothing but

---

383. Genesis 32:22 (AMP).

384. Genesis 32:24 (AMP).

385. The scripture tells us that God asked him, "What is your name?" (Genesis 32:27 AMP). Obviously, the Creator of the universe knew Jacob's name. This was a much more soul-searching question.

386. Genesis 32:26 (AMP).

love for his long-lost brother. Esau kissed Jacob and they wept together.[387] This simple passage describes the consequences of Jacob's surrender. His brother's hardened heart melted with God-provided love for Jacob. Jacob was delivered from his fear.

A Reluctant Leader

We've talked about Moses. Imagine yourself in ancient times, tending to your father-in-law's flock in the mountains. You were formerly a child of privilege, the son of Egypt's Pharaoh himself. You have committed murder and are now living in exile as a nomadic herder. One day, you are in the field with your flock and you see something curious.

You observe a bush that is burning, yet the flames do not consume it. As you cautiously walk toward it, you hear the voice of God coming from within the bush and calling you by name. God tells you that He has seen the oppression and misery of your people in Egypt and He is sending you to the Pharaoh on His behalf to inform him that you are taking them out of Egypt. You are incredulous.

In the first chapters of Exodus, this is exactly what happened to Moses. He was raised as royalty by the Pharaoh's daughter, but was now living as a fugitive. Moses was in his eighties and tending sheep. Suddenly, he found himself speaking to the Creator of the universe and the God of Israel.

The scripture tells us that Moses had two immediate reactions. His first reaction was fairly understandable. Moses hid his face, because he was afraid to look at God.[388] Moses' second reaction is not as understandable. Moses argued with God about the

---

387. Genesis 33:4 (AMP).
388. Exodus 3:6.

His instructions. God told Moses that He had seen the suffering of His people in Egypt and that He was concerned about them.[389]

God instructed Moses to go to the Pharaoh and tell him that he would bring the Jews out of Egypt. Moses responded by arguing with God about his choice of Moses for the mission.

We simply need to trust God, no matter what. No matter how difficult the task at hand is, or how frightened we are, we simply need to trust Him.

Consider that Moses was talking face-to-face with God. He had given Moses very specific instructions. Moses argued with God. He tried to persuade God that he was not suited for the task. He was afraid.

The Young Shepherd

Every school child knows the story of David and Goliath. We've already discussed David's character flaws. After he became the King of Israel, David lost his way with Bathsheba.[390] He paid dearly for it and I won't rehash it here. David was fearless, at least in the beginning. His fearlessness is a model of how we should rely on God, in faith, to face our fears.

The story of a young shepherd taking on a gigantic Philistine that the entire Israelite army feared is simply inspiring. It is the underdog story to end all underdog stories. More than that, the story of David is a model of how perfect faith in and obedience to God can work in our lives. If you read it carefully, I'm betting it will captivate you, in the same way that it has captivated millions before you. The story is a compelling narrative of the power of the love of God by a man, and the effect of absolute faith in dealing with adversity.

---

389. Exodus 3:7.
390. *See* Chapter Four.

You are probably already familiar with the story. In fact, the phrase "a David and Goliath story" has become synonymous for any story involving someone who is smaller and less powerful taking on a stronger and almost sure-to-win adversary. The remarkable thing about David is his absolute lack of fear when facing the most fearsome enemy the Israelite army had ever encountered.

David was the youngest son of Jesse.[391] Samuel, who was the last of the Hebrew judges and one of Israel's first prophets, was called by God as a boy while serving the judge Eli.[392] Unlike the judges of today, judges in Old Testament times were also military leaders of the nation of Israel in times of war. The people of Israel complained that they needed kings,[393] because the judges had become corrupt. The succession of kings over Israel ultimately took over the function of the judges as leaders. David served Saul, who was appointed as the first king of Israel.[394] If you read through the first book of Samuel, you will learn that Saul was a troubled king, at best. He was insecure, jealous, and fearful. Saul was the perfect antihero to David.

David was just a boy. In those days, shepherds were one of the lowest rungs on the socio-economic ladder. His father instructed the young shepherd to deliver food to his brother and others on the front lines, where the Philistines had pitched camp.[395] David obeyed and the story unfolded. The army of Israel had set up battle lines on one hill, and the Philistines had set up its forces on another.

At almost ten feet tall, Goliath must have been an awesome man to behold.[396] He was a "champion," meaning that he was the

---

391. 1 Samuel 17:14.
392. 1 Samuel 3:4.
393. 1 Samuel 8:5.
394. 1 Samuel 10:23.
395. 1 Samuel 17:17.
396. 1 Samuel 17:4.

fiercest warrior among the Philistines. His armor alone weighed five thousand shekels, or about 156 pounds, the weight of an average-sized man.[397] The tip of his javelin weighed six hundred shekels, or almost twenty pounds.[398] For forty days, Goliath had regularly stepped out into the battle lines and thundered derogatory comments toward the Israelites.[399]

David was deeply offended when he heard one of Goliath's diatribes insulting God's army.[400] To him, it was the same thing as insulting God. He went to Saul and volunteered to fight. Goliath was twice David's size and an experienced warrior. Nonetheless, David was determined to battle the Philistine. Saul expressed only hopelessness and fear. David was full of courage. It came from his love for God.

Despite the obvious disparity in size, skill, and experience between David and Goliath, Saul agreed to send him into battle. It's hard to say why Saul would send this young, loyal boy to certain death. We know that Saul worried about Saul and not much else. Sending David into battle against Goliath would cost Saul nothing. Although in the unlikely event he won, it would mean a complete victory for God's army. Further, he was the only one willing to fight Goliath. Saul sent the young shepherd into battle against the giant.

The imagery in the story is so vivid, that the encounter between David and Goliath practically leaps from the pages. Saul, likely feeling guilty, dressed David in Saul's own kingly armor for battle, including a large bronze helmet.[401] He had never worn armor in his life. He must have looked like a little boy dressed up

---

397. 1 Samuel 17:5.

398. 1 Samuel 17:7.

399. 1 Samuel 17:17.

400. 1 Samuel 17:26.

401. Id.

in his father's clothes. The armor was unwieldy.[402] It just got in the way. So David turned it down.

Under Mosaic Law, Goliath's insults amounted to a capital offense. Curiously, in those days, capital offenses were punishable by stoning. David loaded his pouch with stones and decided to do something about it.[403] The young shepherd fought the huge giant armed only with a sling, some stones, and his faith in God.

This is one of the first lessons we learn from David.

With God on your side, you don't need a lot of apparatus. All you need is simple faith.

As David moved toward the battle line, Goliath saw him. He didn't think having a boy challenger was funny. Goliath was insulted.[404] He cursed David. Most of us in this situation would approach a man like Goliath very carefully. Bobbing and weaving, we would move toward him, every sense heightened and muscles tensed, prepared to dodge his horrific weapons. David ran quickly toward the battle line to attack Goliath.[405] He showed absolutely no fear. Rather than darting nimbly around Goliath, the young shepherd David charged full steam at Goliath, gaining speed as he approached the giant Philistine. He knew that he could not fail.

There is something incredibly brave, and yet at the same time touching, about David's actions. He never thought about the risks. He never thought about the possibility of failure. He didn't think about himself. All he could think about was this Goliath, who had insulted God.

---

402. Id.
403. 1 Samuel 17:40.
404. 1 Samuel 17:43.
405. 1 Samuel 17:48.

What happened next was miraculous. David reached into his shepherd's bag and pulled out one of the five smooth stones. He launched the stone and it hit Goliath, embedding into his forehead. Goliath fell facedown to the ground. Perhaps Goliath was just dazed or temporarily unconscious.

Again, David showed no fear. He approached the fallen giant, took Goliath's sword, killed him and cut his head off. The Philistine army seeing the defeat of its champion turned and ran. In the span of a few minutes, Israel's future is determined by a shepherd boy and a pebble.

Why wasn't David afraid? Why would he submit to an almost assured death? He was not afraid was because he placed God above all else. Simply, he loved God with all of his heart and placed his entire faith in Him. His bravery is impressive. More impressive is the motivation behind his bravery. It was due to his love of God.

David had forged his faith in similarly dangerous situations and relied on God to protect him. He had a habit of relying completely on God. David had previously trusted God to save him in perilous situations. As a result, he lost himself in this cause for God. The young boy was not afraid, or concerned at any time before or during his encounter with Goliath. Fear simply never entered into his equation.

We must ask ourselves, *"What would God want me to do?"* We will avoid the fear that rushes to fill the spiritual vacuum. If our dedicated passion for God and doing His will are our priority, we will become oblivious to the insecurity and doubts that plague us. In addition, we learn to trust God by doing. The more we trust Him, the more we become able to trust Him.

If we place God squarely at the center of our thinking, then our fears will dissolve.

I Will Not Sink

Jesus was fully God and yet fully human. He faced the same fears and temptations that we all face. The story of Jesus is a story of absolute faith in God. He said that we are to seek God above all else and everything else will take care of itself.[406] No one could have faced what he did, without being completely filled with the Holy Spirit. Jesus knew what was going to happen to him on Calvary, and probably for more than a short while. And yet, he continued his ministry, performing miracles, healing people and teaching God's love until the very end.

Peter's faith, on the other hand, was inconsistent at best. He was the boldest of Jesus disciples in declaring that Jesus was the Christ. And yet, he abandoned Jesus in his hour of need. An example of his boldness occurs during the miracle of Jesus walking on water, as described in Matthew. After Jesus fed the five thousand with five loaves of bread and two fish, he dismissed the crowd and retreated to the hillside to pray.[407] Jesus had already sent his disciples out on the Sea of Galilee.

Later that evening, the boat is buffeted by high winds and presumably the disciples could not return the boat to pick up Jesus. Instead, Jesus walked over the water of the Galilean sea to the boat. The simple and matter-of-fact description of Jesus walking on the water is in stark contrast to the description of his disciple's reaction. They were terrified. Believing that they were seeing a ghost, they cried out in fear.

Jesus reassured them.

Peter was still apparently unsure that this was in fact Jesus. Jesus told him to come. Peter stepped out of the boat and onto the water. At that moment, Peter's faith enabled him to overcome his fear. For a moment, Peter walked on the water! Despite

---

406. Matthew 10:28 (AMP).
407. Matthew 14:13-32 (AMP).

this fact, the howling winds and enormity of his decision got the best of Peter. Peter had good reason to fear. At its deepest depth, the Sea of Galilee is about 150 feet.

Imagine yourself in this situation, suddenly coming to your senses and realizing what you had just done. Thanks to your impulsive exuberance, you find yourself standing in the middle of the Sea of Galilee during a violent storm. The feeling beneath your feet is almost surreal, not exactly like standing on solid ground but more of a mushy feeling, sort of like foam rubber. It is like nothing like you have ever felt before. *"Maybe,"* you think *"I am dreaming."* You are buffeted by waves and soaked to the skin. Perhaps a lightning bolt flashes, followed by the loud rumble of thunder.

The boat is now far behind you.

There is no way that you can reach it to save yourself.

"What have I done," you think, *"I am going to drown. What a stupid way for it to end."* Suddenly, the weird feeling of firmament beneath your feet gives way. Water is now up to your knees and you are sinking quickly. Satan whispers something like, *"Have you lost your mind? How well do you know this Jesus fellow anyway? Why would you risk everything for this Galilean? If you want to live, you had better start swimming, now!"* As you sink deeper, the panic begins to grip you.

Peter cried out to Jesus.

Jesus calmly reached out and saved him. He then asked Peter why he doubted him. Jesus did not ask him, "What were you afraid of?" He didn't ask "Peter, why were you so scared?" Instead, he simply asked Peter why he had doubted him. To Jesus, this was a simple matter of a lack of faith. The source of Peter's fear was irrelevant. Peter was afraid because he lacked faith in Jesus. With faith Peter would have had no fear.

Jesus' simple question reveals volumes about how God looks at fear.

Think of the pointlessness of Peter's fear. After all, he had placed his faith in someone who was, at that minute, defying at least a couple of laws of nature. This was someone who had just walked across the Sea of Galilee to Peter's boat. This was someone who had asked Peter to get out of the boat and defy those same laws of nature. Peter had defied the laws of nature. Regardless, Peter did not fully trust Jesus.

Peter had known Jesus for a while and witnessed some major miracles. He saw the miraculous loaves and fishes that fed five thousand people. He was with Jesus when he healed seriously sick people and driven out demons. Peter allowed his fear of the perceived immediate threat to control him. He believed Satan's lie. He began to sink.

This is exactly how many Christians respond to fear and worry. We allow Satan to whisper his lies to us. *"Perhaps God didn't hear your prayer."* Or, *"Perhaps He thought your prayer was self-interested and unimportant."* Or, *"Perhaps God's will is for you to suffer."*

We are so close to this threatening forest that we cannot see the trees. Rather than simply placing our trust in God and leaving it there, we allow ourselves to continue to be afraid and worry.

Initially, we trust God with the issue. We give the problem to Him. When the problem is not solved according to our schedule or plan, we begin to doubt.

Rather than giving the fear to God unconditionally, we give it to Him with strings attached. At the first sign of a howling wind, we tug at those strings, mistakenly believing that God may need some help from us in dealing with the threat.

To God, fear is fear. Fear is the absence of faith. To God, the magnitude and source of the fear are irrelevant. The only thing that matters is our response to the threat. We can either respond by faith in God, or we can respond to Satan's lies.

Instead, anytime we are faced with a fear that threatens to compromise our faith, we should declare: "I will not sink." We should think of Peter, exuberant and faithful, stepping out of the boat towards Jesus. Had he continued to his destination in faith, unwavering and unafraid, there is no doubt that he would not have begun to sink.

We need to develop a spiritual alarm that sounds whenever we begin to feel afraid. As soon as it happens, we remind ourselves that through faith anything is possible, including resolution of the threat at hand. Certainly, as with anything in the Christian's daily faith walk, the resolution may not occur in the timeframe that we would like. But it will occur. God has promised it. Therefore, we need only to remind ourselves that God is with us, and as believers, so long as we remain faithful in His perfect will, all things will work together for His good.

He has heard your prayer. He will deal with the issue, often in ways that we could never have imagined. Don't allow Satan to fool you into believing that the issue is not important enough for God or that God expects you to do something else. Continue to pray and listen for God's response.

Once you give a fear or worry to God, don't take it back.

Above all else, let it go and quit worrying about it.

You will not sink.

Paul's Advice

If there was anyone who had a lot to worry about, it was Paul. Before his conversion on the road to Damascus, Paul had largely dedicated his life to the eradication of Christians. Presumably, his actions would have not endeared him to the new Christian movement. If that weren't trouble enough, he switched sides and dedicated his life to Christ. This meant that he would incur the wrath of numerous other factions, including the Jewish establishment and the Roman authorities.

Paul was frequently challenged to debate his Christian beliefs by the Jewish authorities. They were experts on the scripture and the law. The outcome of these debates was not good, regardless of whether he won or lost. If he won the debate, these experts would deem him as insolent or heretical, a guaranteed recipe for a beating or worse punishment. If he lost the debate, they might punish him anyway. Paul had an incredible amount of faith. He describes it eloquently in his epistles. This faith made him one of the most fearless and impactful Christians in history. As he was nearing the end of his life, he was imprisoned and likely knew that he would die soon. He never gave up hope.[408]

I pray that at the end of my life, I can say the same thing. My struggle to remain in a state of faith is a constant one. The fears, worries and problems of this life are a constant distraction from my relationship with God. But I know that every day, I am moving closer to the goal. I know that God will take care of it. He always has and He always will. That knowledge gives me the courage to press on.

Christian Steps to Conquer Fear

Are you wrestling with God? Are you trying to run your own life? Are you depending upon your own resources to deal with fears and worries, rather than God's infinite resources?

God can handle it. Regardless, Satan may continue to seek an

If you are still wrestling with God, then end the match now. Surrender all of it to God.

---

408. 2 Timothy 4:7.

opportunity to plant seeds of doubt and fear. We may begin to second-guess ourselves. We may wonder whether God will involve Himself in our trivial issue. We may worry that our sins will prevent God from hearing us.

He has provided the way to a restored relationship with Him. If you have already surrendered your life to Jesus, then rededicate yourself to him. Recall all of the times in your life in which God delivered you. Rest in the assurance that He loves you and will take care of you. He knows how many hairs are on your head.[409] Give to Jesus in prayer every worry and fear that you have. If Satan has planted seeds of doubt regarding God's love for you, then allow the Holy Spirit to weed them out of your spiritual garden. God has also has provided us with His final Word on any situation that may confront us. Reading and integrating the Word into our thinking will enable us to draw on it immediately during times of fear and worry.

The following are additional suggestions to help you deal with fear and worry:

Resist the Devil

Jesus provided us with a model of behavior when Satan attacks. We are to arm ourselves in God's Word. We are to resist Satan. When you are confronted by the enemy, remember that Jesus is stronger than he is. Don't buy the lies. Don't allow yourself to be tempted. Resist.

---

409. Luke 12:7.

Arm Yourself for the Battle

Dealing with fear head-on requires you to be armed for battle when it presents itself. The best way to be armed is to learn God's Word. The Bible tells us how God's chosen people deal with fear. Learn those stories, learn the scriptures, and learn from their mistakes. Regular Bible study is a key weapon in your arsenal against fear. Dedicate or rededicate yourself to immersing yourself in God's Word. Reading the Bible on a regular basis will help you to remain in God's will for your life. The lessons it contains will instruct you. The influence of the Holy Spirit prompting your heart as you read will help you to apply the lessons to your life.

The first step in dealing with fear is to be prepared for it by reading God's Word on a regular basis. The second is to confront your fear, by giving it to Him and letting go of it completely.

When we face our fear, two things happen. First of all, the fear turns out to be not nearly as bad as the anticipation. More importantly, when we give the fear to God and say, *"Father, I cannot handle it. I give it to you,"* something happens within. We feel less stressed and worried.

Consult Your Father Regularly

One of the greatest gifts that God has given us is the ability to pray and the privilege of communing with Him. Imagine having the ability to consult with the Creator of the universe and not taking advantage of it. Many Christians neglect to take full advantage of this incredible benefit. Another key weapon in your fear arsenal is to avoid fear before it begins. Prayer is your direct pipeline to

God. Praying regularly will enable Him to influence you and to work within your heart. It will stop the downward spiral of fear.

Many of us tend to think of prayer as a ritual rather than what it really is — a conversation with your Maker. Because prayer is typically such a visible part of the worship service, we think prayer requires eloquent verbiage and a logical order of petition. In worship service, it is likely that you have never witnessed prayer in anything other than a composed and well-organized presentation.

Certainly, reverence should be a key aspect of our prayer. Still, the Bible indicates a different, more passionate attitude toward prayer. For example, the psalmist's prayer is often accompanied with passionate pleas to God to hear his cries.[410] Shortly before he was crucified, Jesus prayed passionately and fervently.[411] Reverence and passion in prayer are not mutually exclusive.

When You Pray, Listen More Than You Speak

An old etiquette axiom is that, during a conversation, people should listen about three-quarters of the time, and speak about one-quarter of the time. This will show genuine interest in your conversation partner. You can learn a lot more from listening than you can from talking.

When we pray, we should spend less time worrying about what we will say to God, and more time quietly listening to Him.

This principle should also apply in our Christian dialogue with God. We should listen more than we talk to God. Among other things, we should try to focus on the things He places on our heart during prayer.

410. Psalm 6:9; 17:1; 39:12; 86:6; 88:2; 142:1 (AMP).
411. Luke 22:44.

Jesus teaches us about prayer. He tells us that if we want to pray to God, we shouldn't worry about the words. When we pray, we shouldn't worry about the eloquence of our words. We shouldn't think about how it will come across to others. Instead, Jesus says we should pray alone.[412] It means that the important part of praying is listening. God already knows what we need before we

Eloquent prayer may impress our friends and make us feel better, but we won't learn anything from it.

need it. Instead, we should pray in such a way that we are willing to receive God's instruction through the quiet influence of the Holy Spirit.

God wants us to be absolutely real and honest with Him. He wants us to open our hearts to Him through prayer. He is less concerned with what we say, than the sheer act of complete submission to Him. When we give a problem to God and absolutely let go of it, He answers the prayer in ways that we could never imagine. His response is always better than our requests. He blesses Christians, and He does so abundantly. When you are faced with a difficult situation, think about prior similar situations and their outcomes. How did you deal with these situations? What were your prayers? How did God answer these prayers?

Continue to Develop Your Faith

Faith is a very simple notion. On the one hand, it is the faith of a child, reaching out to his Father. On the other hand, it is the faith of a man climbing out of a boat in the middle of the sea, believing that he can walk on water. Jesus himself taught us that there are degrees of faith. His disciples had unsuccessfully attempted

---

412. Mathew 6:6 (AMP).

to drive out a demon that had possessed a young boy.[413] After Jesus drove the demon out from the boy, the disciples asked Jesus why they were unable to do it.[414] Jesus responded that it was because they had such little faith. It is reasonable to infer from this passage that Jesus was also exhorting his followers to increase their faith in God.

In a parable, Jesus described the kingdom of heaven, which is one of the goals of our faith, as a mustard seed.[415] Jesus taught us that faith is something we can develop. Jesus use of the mustard seed as a metaphor for faith also gives us insight into how we can nurture our faith. God plants the seed of faith on our hearts.[416] Faith does not have to be blind. Instead, faith is something that increases as we exercise it. The more frequently we rely on our faith in various life situations, the more our faith will increase.

The more we exercise our faith in God, the more it will grow.

Keep a Prayer Journal

In Chapter Twelve, I suggested that you keep a journal as part of your Bible study. It will enable you to record the lessons you have learned, and provide you with a foundation to increase your knowledge and faith. As part of my journaling, I also record answered prayers. It's simply so easy to quickly move past these small (and sometimes large) miracles that occur on a regular basis in our lives. Over time, we tend to explain things away. It is so easy to rationalize things away. It's human nature. Like the

---

413. Matthew 17:14–15 (AMP).
414. Matthew 17:19 (AMP).
415. Matthew 13:31 (AMP).
416. Matthew 6:28 (AMP).

ungrateful Israelites, we can quickly get tired of manna, while overlooking the fact that a short time earlier, we were starving.

Journaling about it will help you to think about it. Review your journal periodically. Reading about your own answered prayers will help you to put them into the holy perspective that they deserve.

When something good happens in our lives, especially when it is counter to what should happen, it deserves some scrutiny.

Use your prayer journal to help you keep track of situations where your faith has been rewarded. You will begin to see that God has a remarkable way of rewarding faith. You will also see that for those who live in complete faith upon God, He takes care of us in ways beyond our imagination.

Confess Sin Regularly

One of the more subtle sources of fear in our lives is unconfessed sin. Either deliberately or unintentionally, we fail to admit our sin and claim the forgiveness provided by the cross. As a result, we find ourselves laden with guilt, which creates fertile ground for Satan. This is why it is so important to confess to God sins in our lives. The Holy Spirit, if we allow it, will convict us of our sin. As soon as He does, we should confess it. We should repent of it. We should turn away from it.

Perhaps the hardest thing that any human can do is to admit that we are wrong. It's difficult to be truly objective about our own actions. We rationalize things: *"It's not my fault. It's her fault"*. We justify our actions: *"They did it to me first."* We make excuses: *"I had a rough childhood."* Sadly, many people never come face to face with their own issues. We get so caught up in justifying ourselves that we cannot let down the armor for a minute and admit that we've made mistakes. Admitting we are wrong and *repenting* is fundamental to a relationship with God. It doesn't mean justifying one's actions. It doesn't mean arguing with Him. It means telling Him that you are sorry. Being sorry means you are willing to change. For most of us, repentance should be a daily occurrence.

Becoming a Christian is not a license to sin. If a person is truly a Christian, truly born again, the manifestation of this change is in their changed lives.[417] You can't have it both ways. You can't believe that Jesus died for your sins without repenting of those sins. If you accept the forgiveness of sins, you repent of them and do everything that you can to live the way that Jesus did. In other words, a Jesus follower cannot selectively follow him. You can't be forgiven and then go on sinning and claim that you follow him. However, we all do, and this is why regular repentance is important.

> *A repentant heart is more important to God than is the punishment for the sinful deeds themselves.*[418]

Jesus was criticized for associating with sinners.[419] And yet, he focused his energy exactly where it would yield the greatest result. Jesus' parable of the prodigal son shows us that to God, repentance is much more important than punishing the sin that let to that repentance.[420] Christians believe it is the repentance and turning back to God, who consistently receives them, that is what is important. Jesus paid the price for our sins, but we need to repent of them as soon as we become aware of them.

---

417. Romans 6:17.
418. Leviticus 26:40; Deuteronomy 4:29.
419. Matthew 9:11 (AMP).
420. Luke 15:7 (AMP).

Human nature being what it is, many of us take a while to realize that what we thought was decent behavior was actually sinful behavior.

There are big sins, and there are little sins. There are sins that are relatively easy to deal with and others that can become a life-long struggle. If we are faithful to confess them and give them to God, He will help us to deal with them. Know that God will not allow you to be tempted beyond what you are capable of handling.[421] Continue to give it all to Him, and He will deal with it.

Stay in Your Faith Walk

The best way to deal with fear and worry in your life is to stay in God's will. This is easier said than done. It requires work and discipline. The truth is that all of it is designed to increase your faith in and dependence on God. It turns out that the Christian life isn't all that difficult, after all. If we allow Him, God will handle it. I invite you to let Him handle it today; right now at this minute. He loves you. He can be trusted. He will take care of you.

He just will.

---

421. 1 Corinthians 10:13.

CHAPTER FOURTEEN

In Conclusion

We've reached the end of this segment of the journey. Thank you for accompanying me.

The thing about God is that He will continually surprise and delight you. About the time that I think I've figured out His plan, something happens that completely surprises me. The consistent thread throughout all of it has been that He has shown me, and proven to me, how much He loves me. I've strayed, I've wandered; I've doubted and I've worried. Sooner or later, He grabs me by my proverbial lapels and shows me that there is only one thing in this life that matters.

What matters is to live in complete trust and obedience to Him.

The great myth of Christianity is that it is a religion of emotion, rather than intellect. But as I grow intellectually, I realize that Christianity makes incredibly logical sense. That, more than anything else, is the message contained within this book. God's plan for mankind and for you in particular, was decided many, many years ago. He has continually reached out to mankind and did something absolutely amazing when we did not respond. He died for us.

When I decided to go to law school, I had no idea that it would lead me closer to Him. In fact, I worried that it might have the opposite effect. I surely had no idea that it would ultimately lead me to write this book. Nonetheless, it did. In hindsight, I can see God's purpose for all of it. Who knows what God has in mind for you? Whatever it is, I can assure you that if you trust Him and obey Him, it will be better than anything you could have dreamed.

God is there for you. Since the very beginning, He has reached out to mankind. He is here, right now, in this place. He is waiting for you to reach back to Him. He won't force it. He will wait for you. He loves you and cares more about you than you can possibly imagine. He proved it on the cross at Calvary. Stay in your faith walk.

If you have reached out to God as a result of reading this book, I would love to hear about it. If you haven't, I would love to talk about it further with you, if you are so inclined. Or, if you have questions or want to continue your search, I'll do my best to help you find answers. You can connect with me through the website at www.reasonable-person.com.

Made in the USA
Lexington, KY
03 July 2012